# The
# Velvet
# SKY

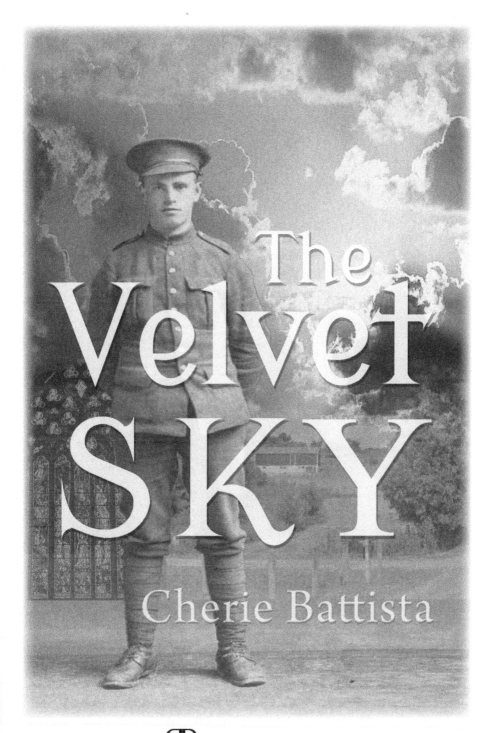

# The Velvet SKY

Cherie Battista

**CIR** *Dusty Rose Books*
Bedazzled Ink Publishing Company • Fairfield, California

978-1-949290-57-8 paperback

Cover Design
by

Dusty Rose Books
a division of
Bedazzled Ink Publishing, LLC
Fairfield, California
http://www.bedazzledink.com

*To the family of Edgar and Ada Alde McPhail,*
*especially their great granddaughter Margaret Bonham McPhail.*

# Acknowledgements

I would like to thank my supervisor Dr. Ursula Hurley for her support and guidance during the work for my PhD thesis and for sharing this journey with me. Also, thanks and appreciation to my co-supervisor Dr. Jane Kilby for her valuable time.

I also want to thank Ian Johnston, the University of Salford Archives & Special Collections Co-ordinator who helped me trace my family in the USA. I am grateful for the time he gave and the wonderful discoveries that came from it.

I am deeply grateful to my family in England and the USA, and the McPhail family in Canada for their love and support, and giving me their precious time so freely, to share family stories. Also, for the warm welcome I received during my field trips to Canada and the USA. Thank you.

And to everyone at Bedazzled Ink Publishing Company who believed in this book--thank you.

# Preface

The life story of my great uncle, Stephen Duckhouse is a combination of archive and field research, family history, and fiction. It has been my intention to stay as close to documented evidence as my research journey has allowed. However, a certain amount of Stephen's experiences are undocumented, so I have used gentle fiction to fill the gaps in research, and bring Stephen back into memory. With respect to those voices who can no longer speak for themselves, I feel it is important to acknowledge that Stephen and Albert and their close family are real people, but I have woven a tapestry of characters within the story, some authentic and some inventive. Stephen's story has developed from darkness to light and evolved into a gently fictionalised biography—I have honoured the facts where they are known but used imagination and intuition where they have become lost in the realms of time.

# 1
# The Beginning

*"Out of your vulnerabilities will come your strength."* — *Sigmund Freud*

THE DISTANT ECHO of a silent voice cried out in pain, as blood gushed from a splintered groin, soaked through the cloth of a torn, mud-riddled, brown-green uniform. It was the uniform of the 87th Battalion, Canadian Grenadier Guards, CEF. He wore it with pride. His eyes lingered on the tortured faces of his comrades. He waited beside them, in the cool smoke-sealed air, where ice-breath reflected a dismal light from their stunned eyes.

The blade of the knife ripped open the first in line . . .

He could only watch, reflecting the agonised terror of knowing the sharp-edged blade was getting closer. His heart sank into a void of surrender, where there was no escape, no mercy, no freedom . . . until . . .

A dancing light shone from a glistening shadow in the darkness, as he looked up from the pool of blood mingled with clustered mud, past the dust and smoke of gunfire. He blinked and with his right eye could see the velvet sky stretched out above—waiting for him. He choked on the last, rattled breath leaving his defeated body, and whispered . . .

*47 Little Green Lane, Small Heath, Birmingham*

A DEEP SILENCE reigned over resting shadows, waiting in anticipation of a new dawn. The second hand of time continued to dance its way forward, without knowing how to return to the last movement. But memory can travel through generations, decades, light and darkness.

Stephen lived with his family in a back-to-back terrace with bricks that came from the local clay pits. The bay window reflected the early morning winter sunlight. Heavy white nets draped down to the inside ledge. Outside near the doorway lay a tin bath, face down on the cobbled pavement. The bath was used as a table at night, for candles embracing their wax inside empty jam jars, to light the front courtyard. The house looked peaceful set within the tranquil lane.

The quiet remained until a horse drawn milk cart trundled by and disturbed the silence.

Behind the door of number *47* the peace of the lane was reflected inside. The children were sleeping, unaware of their father preparing to leave. Stephen's ragged blonde hair mingled with his younger brother's darker shades on the grey pillow. He shared a bed with Albert, in the back room, with peeled wallpaper riddled with damp, from the unattended leaking roof. Stephen's older brothers, Fred Junior, John, and George snored in synchronicity in the next room. The clock on the mantelpiece in the front parlour struck five am.

Ellen stroked the top of her youngest son's head, Walter, as he lay asleep on the double bed, heedless of the tension seeping through the cool, spring morning. Ellen's fair hair was tied back from her face, her blue eyes clouded with sadness, as she wiped her brow with her apron. She reached for her husband's hand and whispered, 'I don't understand Fred. How can you leave us?'

Fred stood before her. He trembled in the cool frosty air, from the icicles inside the window. He slid his chapped hands through the strands of hair on his polished head and put on his black woollen coat.

'I can't support you or the boys. You'll be better off without me,' he said as he shuffled his feet in the empty space on the cold wooden floor.

'Is there someone else?'

'No . . .' he mumbled with his head bowed.

'Why, Fred? I know we've had a hard time lately, but I thought that business with the stolen cycles was behind us?'

'Yes, but I still agreed to store the cycles for Jim, even though I didn't know they were stolen,' said Fred, staring into an empty space.

'But you were acquitted over seventeen months ago,' said Ellen, desperately.

'And I haven't worked since. I can't provide for my family, I've tried . . . I've really tried to make it work, Ellen. I can't even feed my own boys. Have you any idea what that feels like?'

'We've been married all these years. Do you remember our wedding day, Fred? It was one of the happiest days of my life,' said Ellen, smiling into a distant memory.

'You always did have a good memory, Ellen. But time has moved on. I'm not that young dreamer anymore. Real life is just too hard,' replied Fred.

'But the children, what do I say to them? How do I explain their father has just walked out?'

Fred bowed his head and stared at his darned socks.

'I'm sorry, Ellen.'

He stepped heavily towards the door, which hung from the top, rusted hinge.

'Fred! Please don't leave us . . . the children . . . think of the children,' whispered Ellen.

Fred turned away and stepped into the back bedrooms to look for the last time at the closed eyes of his sons. *Fred Junior, kind and gentle—you'll do well for yourself. John, always been the lazy one, haven't you? George, try your hand at anything. Stevie, you live in your own little world, and Albie, always asking questions.* Fred's clear blue eyes glazed over. His dark brown Brylcreemed hair and his white gaunt face reflected in the dressing table mirror, like a troubled ghost searching for his lost soul.

He dragged his feet to retrieve his packed case with the broken handle from the front bedroom. And the silent dawn suddenly crashed into the sobbing sounds of heartache.

'What will I do without you, Fred?' Ellen choked on her stifled screams. 'Where are you going?'

'It's over, Ellen. It's time for me to go,' said Fred, with a distant chill in his voice.

'But the children . . .'

'I'll send some money when I'm settled,' said Fred, staring at the grey, chipped wall behind her.

And that was all that was left of their relationship.

His footsteps echoed on the stairs until the front door closed behind him for the last time. He glanced back at number 47 and reflected on the life he was leaving behind . . .


IT WAS THE chilling month of January 1909, the year of change in the form of the *People's Budget* about to be introduced into the British Parliament by David Lloyd George. Speckles of white flakes slid down the outside of the square single-glazed window to meet the ice, building a bridge below the split wooden frame. Stephen sat with his elder brother, Fred Junior, by their mother's bedside, with yesterday's crunched up local newspaper. Stephen mirrored the squint in Fred Junior's crystal blue eyes, as he read with a sense of hope, whilst Ellen lay exhausted with despair.

'Listen, Ma . . . Lloyd George is trying to help us. Change is coming.'

Fred Junior's voice only drifted from Ellen's consciousness, as she fell into a deep and lonely sleep, with the light from their silhouettes fading in the distance. The *People's Budget* felt as far away as a clouded aura from a faceless moon on a dark and starless night. But Fred Junior remained determined to continue reading from the printed newspaper in his hand.

'Ma, wake up, please wake up,' pleaded Stephen, as he gently shook her arm.

'This is a war budget. It is for raising money to wage implacable warfare against poverty and squalidness. I cannot help hoping and believing that before this generation has passed away . . .'

Stephen's eyes widened as he choked from the back of his dry throat, leaving a sense of relief trembling through his body. Fred Junior smiled at Stephen and continued reading.

' . . . we shall have advanced a great step towards that good time, when poverty, and the wretchedness of human degradation which always follows in its camp, will be as remote to the people of this country as the wolves once infested its forests.'

Ellen stirred from the discomfort of her motionless body, long enough to notice Stephen leaving with Fred, moving slowly away from her bedside.

'Thank you, boys,' she whispered.

'Get some rest now, Ma. What is it you always say? It will all look different in the morning.' Fred Junior smiled into the lost gaze of his mother, and Stephen closed the bedroom door behind them, wiping his tear-stained cheek with his free hand.

When Stephen opened the door leading to his own bed, he noticed his four-year-old brother, Walter, had climbed in next to Albert, snuggled up close, and snoring out of sync with each other. He walked slowly down stairs to find Fred Junior building a log fire in the back room and lowered voices. He stared at his three older brothers as if he were watching them for the last time.

'Wasn't there something about an Old Age Pension Act, last year?' John asked, as he stretched out his feet, with socks in need of darning, to the warmth from the crackling flames.

'Ma's not yet thirty-eight, how could she possibly be eligible for any benefits? It's a shame though, I've heard it's around five shillings a week,' Fred said, as he threw the last of the logs onto the fire.

'I'm due to leave school this year. I'll get a job,' said George, trying to come up with a solution.

Stephen trembled as he stood in the shadows of the room, trying desperately to go unnoticed.

'What are you doing in here? Go and play,' John said.

'Can't I just stay, I'm not doing anything?' Stephen asked.

'Go and play,' George repeated, not wanting Stephen to hear how desperate the situation was.

Stephen quietly left the chilled room and wandered into the small hall way. He opened the front door and stepped out into the flurry of snowflakes that seemed to welcome his feelings of difference and loneliness. As he looked up at the glass-like mosaic covering the hidden sky, he silently asked, *what's an old age pension?*

Later that night, when the house was silent with sleep, and the moon was his only light through the window, Stephen lifted the corner floorboard in his bedroom where he hid his secret journal. He transferred his thoughts to paper. Writing was like a friend in the dark, holding his hand with the pen that he wrote with, and bringing him comfort. He never once felt alone . . .

The sun rose on another day. Ellen's eyes flickered open, only to stare aimlessly at the yellow stained ceiling above. *Fred promised to decorate this spring—who will do that now? I don't know what to do. How will I feed the children? There's no money* . . . Ellen knew she wouldn't be eligible for anything like an old age pension, as she wasn't yet over the age of seventy.

The external political conflict reflected Ellen's inner turmoil. She lay in bed, drifting in and out of sleep; unable to raise herself to explain why her sons' father had left. Hungry faces gathered round her bedside. Her chest tightened as she murmured to her fourteen-year-old son.

'George, take Stevie and Albie to school for me, and where's John?'

'I don't think he's up yet. I've called him three times,' said Stephen, pushing back his round shoulders.

The three boys fell into their usual routine and quietly left the house. There was something different about the second day of their father's desertion. They didn't quite understand what that difference might be but felt it all the same. The light disappeared from their eyes, as their busy minds took over with unanswered questions, which contrasted with the empty pavement on the road to school.

Ellen reflected as her mind wandered into the darkness of the past years she had shared with Fred. She realised, somewhere in a secret corner of her heart, that she had always known something she couldn't bear to think about. Convincing herself that the fantasy in her imagination was so much easier than facing the darkest truth, she played her part, determined to keep her family together. But now it was time to wake up to a reality that she had buried somewhere out of sight.

Ellen dragged her sore and heavy feet towards the kitchen. She reached for the tea tin on the top shelf where the grocery money was kept. *This won't last the week, I must get another cleaning job.* She took out sixpence, enough for milk and bread, and made her way to the hallway. But just as she reached for her hat on the coat stand she noticed Fred's overcoat that he always wore for work. Ellen touched the sleeve and buried her face in the woollen texture. The smell of oil and coal tar soap tinged her nostrils until she could hardly breathe. Tears welled in her eyes. Then she felt something in the coat pocket. She reached inside and pulled out two address labels. She blinked as she read Fred's writing. *Moor Green Mills, Selly Park*. Ellen's eyebrows knitted together as she stared at her reflection in the cracked mirror almost hanging off its hook on the wall.

Within seconds she had closed the door behind her and stepped out into the light drizzle falling from the dark cloudy sky. She walked as fast as her tired feet would allow until she found herself standing outside Moor Green Mills. She knew the address. It was familiar. She knocked on the brown door and waited. A frail woman appeared, her grey hair tied back from her pale face, and wearing an apron covered in flour.

'Good morning, Mrs Johnson. I'm Ellen Duckhouse. I believe Nellie lives here. She used to work with my husband,' said Ellen.

'Oh yes, you'd better come in,' said Mrs Johnson, as she glanced nervously down the street, to make sure neighbours were out of sight.

Ellen was invited to take a seat in the front parlour. Mrs Johnson removed her apron and sat down, with her eyes lowered to the ground.

'Would you like some tea?'

'No, thank you, I'll get straight to the point. My husband's left and I have no idea where he's gone. I found your address in his coat pocket. I know he used to work with your daughter, Nellie,' said Ellen, struggling to remain composed.

'Yes, it's a sad business,' mumbled Mrs Johnson.

'I need to know . . . if you can help me contact him?'

'The truth is, Nellie left home this morning to go to Sheffield. Mr Doughty, who owns the corner shop, saw her in the company of your husband. I'm afraid that's the only information I know,' said Mrs Johnson, wiping her brow.

Ellen put her hand to her mouth and gasped. Then a calming serenity took hold of her. 'I've suspected for some time that my husband was having an affair with your daughter. It's been something that I've not wanted to come to terms with.'

'I'm so sorry, Mrs Duckhouse. We knew Nellie had some kind of infatuation with your husband when she worked with him in the cycle business, but we had no idea.' She gazed off into an empty space.

'I don't suppose Nellie left any forwarding address?'

'I'm afraid not. But if I do hear from her, I will of course let you know,' said Mrs Johnson.

'Well, thank you for your time. I shall bid you good day,' said Ellen, as she stood up and made her way to the front door.

Mrs Johnson bowed her head respectfully.

Ellen walked back down the unfamiliar street, with watchful eyes from neighbours with grim faces, tight lips, and folded arms. She wiped her eyes with her handkerchief and tried to make sense of the jumbled thoughts spinning round her head. But all she wanted to do was scream out . . . *Fred, why? After all we've been through.*


TIME MOVED SLOWLY through the essence of hunger and struggle. Ellen was unable to recover from symptoms of fatigue and tightness in her chest as she struggled to breathe. The pain of her husband leaving was too much to bear and so she collapsed under the patchwork blanket that was her only source of comfort. But she could not hide from the reality of her situation, knowing that her eldest son's weekly wage would not stretch to feed the mouths of all her children.

Stephen sat at the edge of his mother's bed with Fred Junior and Albert. Stephen followed Fred Junior everywhere, as he aspired to be just like his eldest brother. Albert followed Stephen, watching and waiting. It meant that the three brothers became almost inseparable.

'My dearest boys, I'm so glad you're here. I love you all the same, but John and George are so like their Pa. I think you're the ones who inherited my qualities, but don't tell John and George,' whispered Ellen, forcing a weak smile.

'We'll always be here, Ma. I just wish we could send for the doctor,' said Fred Junior.

'No money for doctors, and without your Pa's wage we're missing around twenty shillings a week. I don't know how we're going to make ends meet,' said Ellen.

'But Pa hasn't worked for nearly two years, and we've managed so far,' said Stephen.

'I'll get a job as a rag and bone man, and me and Stevie can do it together,' said Albert, with an excited glint in his eye.

'You're too young to work, Albie, and you and Stevie need to keep going to school,' said Ellen.

'We could do something early morning and after school,' said Stephen, as he leant his face in his hand, whilst his mind raced in deep thought.


THE HOURS OF the days passed, showing time on the wall-mounted walnut clock in the kitchen. But this was the most activity in this particular part of the house. Ellen's health deteriorated, and her meagre savings from her cleaning job quickly dried up. She was too ill to continue to work. As her fragile body collapsed with exhaustion, Stephen pushed his ear against his mother's bedroom door. He was determined to hear the voices inside, above the sound of the rain thrashing against the small square window. Stephen was about to give up the struggle, when he felt the sensation of touch between his eyes, transporting his vision into the room . . .

Ellen's gaze drifted from the shadows and into the clear blue eyes of her eldest son. She noticed how he had started to use Brylcreem on his hair. *You look so much like your Pa.* Fred Junior pulled the chair closer to his mother's bedside and held her hand gently. He then wiped a grey cloth across the top of her brow, seeped in ice water from the cracked bowl on the bedside table. She tried to speak but a bout of persistent coughing compelled her to silence. Until she was able to clear her throat and force the words from her mouth.

'You're so good to me, Fred. So different . . .' she whispered.

'I've got something to tell you, Ma. Grandpa has asked me to move in with them. It means I can work longer hours at the shop, and give you more money to help out,' he said.

'Fred . . . that's such a relief . . . No matter what happens, we need to all stay together, as a family.'

'We will, I'm sure of it. I always thought I'd like to be a butcher one day, and this way, we might have a chance.'

Ellen smiled weakly, then her eyes glazed over. 'What about John? I worry about him. He doesn't seem to want to do anything.'

'I'll look after John. Grandpa said he can run some errands for him until he sorts himself out with something more permanent.'

'Thank you, Fred.'

'Don't worry, Ma,' said Fred Junior.

But the words were lost to her as Ellen drifted off into a deep, but restless sleep.

Stephen stepped back and leaned against the wall, as he watched his eldest brother close their mother's bedroom door quietly and turn to reflect tearful eyes. Stephen's right arm fell around Albert's shoulders. Three years separated them, but they were more like twins with their sparkling blue eyes, dimpled chins, and arched eyebrows defining their pale complexions. Only the colours of their hair distinguished them.

'What's wrong with Ma?' Stephen asked.

'She's just resting. There's nothing to worry about,' said Fred Junior.

'Grandpa thinks Ma's got consumption,' whispered George, as he climbed the stairs.

'I've heard you can die of that. And it's her . . . hereditary. Does that mean we'll get it?' said Stephen.

'You need to stop listening to the neighbours, Stevie. It doesn't help your vivid imagination,' said Fred Junior.

Are you leaving as well?' Albert's bottom lip trembled.

'Listen . . . I'm only going to stay with Grandpa and Grandma for a while, to earn some more money. I'll come and visit, I promise,' said Fred Junior.

He reached out for his younger brothers and they hung on to him, clinging without knowing how to let go.

Stephen felt a gentle, peaceful energy leave the house, with his elder brother's departure. And although he could see Fred Junior trying to support their mother as much as he could, Stephen watched from a distance her continual struggle to pay the rent and feed her remaining five children. So, he cared for his mother in the only way he knew how.

'That's nice and soothing, Stevie,' whispered Ellen.

Stephen's hand rested gently on the soft layer of skin above her brow. And soon his palm tingled from the heat transferred to his mother. Ellen sighed with relief, as time lapsed for longer periods between bouts of a dry cough that cut into her sore and tired throat, like pieces of fine glass.

'Read to me, Stevie. Tell me a story . . .'

Stephen reached for one of his favourite books, Anna Sewell's *Black Beauty*, on his mother's bedside table. He began reading from where he had left off, with a voice as soft as velvet. Although he struggled with some of the words, he remembered his mother telling the story, and held it in memory.

> One day, when there was a good deal of kicking, my mother whinnied to me to come over to her, and then she said: "I wish you to pay attention to what I am going to say to you. The colts who live here are very good colts, but they are carthorses, and of course they have not learned manners. You have been well-bred and well-born; your father has a great name in these parts, and your grandfather won the cup two years at the Newmarket races; your grandmother had the sweetest temper of any horse I ever knew, and I think you have never seen me kick or bite. I hope you will grow up gentle and good, and never learn bad ways; do your work with a good will, lift your feet up well when you trot, and never bite or kick even in play."
>
> I have never forgotten my mother's advice; I knew she was a wise old horse, and our master thought a great deal of her. Her name was Duchess, but he often called her Pet.

Stephen looked up from the page to notice his mother's breathing had become quieter as she fell into a deep and peaceful sleep. He climbed up on the bed and lay beside her and closed his eyes.

With Stephen's forbearance and determination not to leave his mother's side, and Ellen's strong will to fight back, she slowly recovered from an illness that she once believed would result in permanent separation from her children . . .

Then one day, when streams of light danced their way through the square window, she found herself able to leave her bed, and slowly make her way downstairs, with Stephen at her side. He watched and waited patiently whilst Albert played with Walter. Ellen sat motionless in the oak wood rocking chair near the log fire in the front parlour. She stared into the withering flames, as she continued to turn the gold wedding ring on her finger, until it somehow slipped into her right hand.

Ellen's mind suddenly drifted back to the present moment, and as her tempered rage surfaced she went to throw the ring in the fire until . . . she heard Walter whimpering in the corner of the room. He was clutching his stomach at the emptiness that synchronised with her heart.

'Walter, come over here to me,' she croaked.

Her youngest son, barely four years old, stumbled in his ragged clothes before collapsing in his mother's open arms.

'There, there . . . don't you cry now. It's all going to be all right, you'll see,' she whispered.

Ellen held him close to her and rocked gently until he drifted back to sleep. And as she continued to watch the choking, spitting, crackling of the dying fire, she knew what she had to do. A sudden strength filled her with some element of hope from the darkness of despair.

'Stevie, look after Albie and Walter for me. And ask George to put some more logs on the fire,' she said.

'George has gone out looking for work, and that's the last of the logs Ma,' said Stephen.

'Where are you going? Are you coming back?' Albert asked.

'Now don't you fret. I won't be long,' she said, as she put on her long coat with holes in the pockets and wrapped her hand-knitted shawl around her shoulders.

The front door closed behind her, and Stephen wiped Albert's wet cheek with his sleeve.

'Don't you cry. Ma will be back soon,' said Stephen.

'You promise?'

Stephen nodded; unable to say the words his brother was so desperate to hear.

And when Ellen returned home, there was an uncanny silence in the air. She listened at the front parlour door . . .

'Of course, in the end Wendy let them fly away together. Our last glimpse of her shows her at the window, watching them receding into the sky until they were as small as stars . . .'

The hinge on the door creaked, as she opened it.

'Look, Ma, Fred came around with some logs and lit the fire, and he left some ham in the kitchen,' said Stephen.

'Stevie's reading. I think I'd like to live in Neverland,' said Albert.

Ellen smiled as she watched her children huddled in front of the warm glow from the log fire. And a deep feeling of relief embraced her heart, even though she questioned how long it might last.

'Where's your wedding ring, Ma?' Stephen asked.

'We're having broth for supper tonight,' said Ellen.

The children echoed a 'thank you.'

'It's a shame they don't give out advice at school on how to go about getting a job,' said George, as he helped Fred Junior put more logs on the dying fire in the front room.

'I was reading in the local newspaper, the other day, about the new Labour Exchanges Act that the government have brought out. But unfortunately, it doesn't apply to anyone under the age of seventeen. I think that might change though, sometime in the future,' said Fred Junior.

'Nothing seems to change soon enough for us,' grumbled John, who sat in his father's armchair, and closest to the flames of the fire.

'Well, you don't seem to be helping, John. When did you last go out looking for work?' Fred Junior asked.

But John only closed his eyes and sighed heavily.

Time moved on, until the only thing they had left to share, as a family, was Stephen's stories. And the cold and the damp, and the hunger were sometimes forgotten when their imaginations took them to a different place . . . to Neverland.

Following a long and hopeless struggle, Ellen finally collapsed and gave in to the only option left to her. She closed the door of number 47 behind her for the last time, with her four youngest children beside her.

'What do we do now, Ma?' Stephen asked, shivering.

'I'm hungry,' said Albert, with his hands on his stomach.

'If only I could find a job,' muttered George, folding his arms.

Walter coughed from the back of his dry throat and snuggled closer to Ellen's chest as she held him tightly. Together, they turned to face the empty space in front of them, but could only stare at the falling snowflakes, from the hollow, grey sky.

*Selly Oak Workhouse*

ELLEN COULD BARELY stand upright outside Selly Oak Workhouse. George and Stephen held her close, their arms linked with her own, whilst they held onto Albert and Walter, who straggled beside them.

'What's a workhouse? I don't want to go in there,' cried Albert.

His wide, tearful eyes made him look determined to turn and run. He pulled away from Stephen's hand.

'Come on Albie, it won't be for long. I'll look after you,' said Stephen.

The dark distress in Albert's expression subsided as he snuggled close into his brother's shivering body, whilst Ellen squinted at the dark red brick building that towered above. The roof was covered with bright red Broseley tiles that shone in the early spring sunlight, a stark contrast to the drab, grey rags that had worn to shreds and hung from the children's undernourished ghostly figures. Ellen noticed the date, 1897, engraved into the wall at the top of the building. *Just seven years after we were married.* She was unable to take another step before falling to her knees. *At least my children will be safe here.* Her eyes blinked away the last strands of light until she fell into a deep and lonely darkness.

Ellen was immediately admitted into the infirmary—a separate building from the workhouse. It was light, bright, clean and practical—a stark contrast to the dark shadows Ellen had left behind. But it wasn't home, and her heart cried out for the familiar that was now lost in a past time that she could no longer reach out for. She woke up from a restless night's sleep, crying out in despair, 'Children! Where's my children?'

The light from the full moon shone brightly through the square window and followed the steps of one of the resident nurses. She moved closer towards Ellen's bed and reassured her that her children were safe in the workhouse, and a high dividing wall only separated them.

'Can I see them?' Ellen asked.

'You need to rest, it's late. Most patients are sleeping. We'll talk again, in the morning,' said the nurse.

Ellen was touched by her kindness as she felt the warmth from an unknown hand. And as she began to feel a little easier, she looked around at the painted white brick walls and stared hard as if trying to penetrate them to catch sight of George, Stephen, Albert, and Walter. She continued with her quest until sleep took over.

A few days later, Ellen noticed dark clouds across a vast grey sky, spilling pellets of rain against the small windows. She called out to a nurse.

'Excuse me, can you tell me what month it is?' Ellen asked.

'It's late September,' said a nurse, with spectacles resting on the edge of her nose, as she rushed towards the other side of the ward.

'Can I see . . . my children?'

But Ellen's question remained unanswered, as the nurse disappeared. When Ellen had fully recovered she transferred from the infirmary to the workhouse. She was allocated to the appropriate ward for her category: able-bodied women between fourteen and sixty. Ellen was handed a blue and white striped dress, which she wore underneath a smock and was given tasks that included cleaning and assisting with care for the sick on the Nightingale wards.

'How many wards are there?' Ellen asked.

'We have about two hundred and fifty patients in eight of the Nightingale wards,' said a burly matron with a wart on her cheek.

'I miss my children,' said Ellen, as she stared at the floor.

'You can have Walter with you, as he's only four years old. But only children under the age of seven are allowed in the female section of the workhouse. He can share your bed. You can have an interview with your other children once a day. This is at the discretion of the Guardians, so you're very lucky,' said the matron.

Ellen choked in silence at the thought of holding Walter again. When he stumbled towards her, holding the matron's hand, Ellen wrapped her arms around her youngest child, and cried with joy as his blue eyes sparkled at the sight of his mother. But she had no conception of circumstances surrounding her other three children in the boys' section of the workhouse.


A TALL BOY, with short ginger hair and pointed ears, known as Carrots, pushed Albert into a dark corner.

'Hey, you, with no fingers. What happened to you then, got caught thieving did ya?'

Loud laughter chilled the air, whilst an interested crowd gathered around him.

'No . . .' murmured Albert, as he tried to hide his hand under his worn-out jumper with loose stitching.

'Leave him alone. A horse crushed his fingers. It was an accident,' said Stephen, rushing to his defence.

'And who are you?' The tall boy sneered.

'I'm his brother!'

'Well I think he's a thief! So, what are you going to do about it?'

Stephen pushed through the crowd, put his arm around Albert, and remained defiant in his silent protection.

'So now we have a thief and a coward,' he taunted and stepped towards Stephen.

'I wouldn't do that if I were you,' echoed a voice from behind him.

'Who are you, to tell me what to do?'

'I'm their brother!'

George came from behind the crowd and stood in front of the tall boy. And what George lacked in height, he made up with wide round shoulders.

'Hit him Carrots, he's smaller than you,' came a heckler from the crowd.

Carrots' fist cracked George's cheekbone, which led to scuffling on the floor. Stephen grabbed Carrots' foot and pulled him away from his elder brother. Within seconds one of the guardians intervened and stopped the fight. No one teased Albert again.

Later that day, the three boys were reunited with their mother, for their daily twenty-minute interview.

'Tell me how you are, and I want the truth,' Ellen ordered.

'We have to attend class,' said Stephen.

'And we get food three times a day,' said Albert.

'Breakfast at six thirty, dinner at twelve, and supper at six. Don't worry about us, Ma, we're just glad to see you,' said George.

'What's that bruise on your left eye?' Ellen asked.

George scuffled his feet on the stone floor.

'I fell and hit my face on the corner of the table,' he said unconvincingly.

'What really happened, George?'

'One of the boys punched him . . . he was bigger than George. But he backed off when Stevie . . .'

Both Stephen and George turned to glare at Albert.

'Listen to me, all of you. I need you to stay out of trouble. Promise me, you will,' she said.

'We promise,' they chimed together.

The first daily interview was over.

Later that evening, Ellen lay awake, listening to the birds outside. An elderly woman in a bed next to her remained still, as if frozen. Ellen accepted her silence, as the frail woman continued to stare at the ceiling. But then Ellen's eyes widened, as she heard her speak for the first time.

'They're leaving for warmer shores,' whispered the elderly woman.

'I wish we could go with them,' said Ellen, as she shivered beneath her woollen blanket.

'At least you have your children. I'll most likely die in this place,' said the elderly woman, her eyes not moving from the empty space above her.

'But I no longer have responsibility for them. I feel like I've lost all control,' said Ellen, as tears burnt the inside of her eyes.

'You think you know what losing control feels like,' said the elderly woman.

'What's your name?' Ellen asked politely.

'I forget,' said the elderly woman.

Ellen silently cried out her children's names through the stillness of the dark, empty night. But she had Walter to comfort her, as he slept soundly next to her.

And the day would begin again. Rising at six to be ready for bread and gruel for breakfast, sitting on a wooden bench amongst rows of other women, crammed into a tight space. Then a ten-hour work shift with dinner in between, consisting of cooked meats, pickled pork or bacon with potatoes, and vegetables, yeast dumpling, soup and suet or rice pudding. The working day ended with a supper of bread, cheese, and broth. And the night came around again, with Ellen lying awake listening to the groans of women missing their loved ones, as she fought to suppress her own grief that was too painful to pass through her dry, choked throat.

*10 Dolphin Road, Greet, Birmingham*

AFTER A MONTH in the workhouse, Ellen found respite when she was granted out-relief allowance by the Guardians, of 3 shillings a week. She left the workhouse to share a house with her paternal step-aunt, Mrs Minnie Bates and her husband. Minnie, a slim, grey haired woman with spectacles perched on the edge of her long nose, walked with a limp, because of chronic pain in her hip. Her husband, Thomas, sat in the arm chair nearest the log fire most of the time, sucking his empty pipe, as unemployment forced him to only imagine the tobacco smoke, swirling down into his lungs.

'The rent's six shillings and eight pence a week, and your three shillings out-relief allowance a week won't cover it. I don't know how we're going to make ends meet,' Minnie stated, staring at the tortoiseshell carriage clock on the mantelpiece.

'I'll go out looking for work again tomorrow. There doesn't seem to be a need for carriage-lamp makers these days, as there used to be, but I'm sure we'll manage somehow,' said Thomas, coughing from the back of his throat.

'How about I do all the washing and charing in the house, and it covers some of the rent? And in my free time, I'll go knocking on doors offering my services to try and make up the rest?' Ellen suggested.

'Well . . . it's a start, as long as the rent's paid every week. My Tom does try, but he's not as young as he used to be,' said Minnie, wiping her hands with her apron, which hung from her hidden waist.

Stephen shared a dim attic room with George and Albert and slept on a lumpy mattress on top of a small rug on ice-cold floorboards that creaked in certain places. Ellen slept in one of the two bedrooms on the first floor, with Walter.

The season of Autumn, where leaves let go of their branches, was the start of an even deeper transformation that could not have been foreseen. There were no spare blankets, so the children slept with their coats over them for warmth. They were cramped, but it was their silence that disturbed Ellen most of all.

'Stevie, you look white as a ghost. Are you having one of those funny turns?' Ellen asked.

'The room's so small, it feels like the walls are caving in,' gasped Stephen.

'Breathe deeply . . . what are you looking at?' Ellen asked.

'I'm waiting for the sun to come around,' he said.

And her eyes followed Stephen's, as he continued to squint through the small skylight at the clouded grey sky, waiting for a brighter day.

Ellen was determined to keep her family together, rising at five in the morning to start the day before the rest of the household awoke. The kitchen became her sanctuary where she spent time alone doing the chores and planning the rest of the day. She rubbed pearls of sweat from her brow with the back of her chapped hand, before adding soap to the washtub, scrubbing dirty clothes clean with the washboard. Then she hauled the clothes into the rinse tub.

Stephen had always struggled with sleep and heard his mother in the kitchen during the early morning, as he lay awake in the attic room. The air in the small room was stifling and Stephen suddenly felt unable to breathe. He choked as his dry throat closed.

'Are you having one of them funny turns?' Albert whispered, only half awake.

Stephen fought to breathe deeply, and slowly calmed down.

'It's okay, go back to sleep,' said Stephen.

Albert turned over and returned to sleeping soundly beside him, whilst George was still and silent in the corner of the room. Stephen got up and ventured downstairs quietly, so as not to wake anyone else. He stopped on the landing of the first floor and heard a duet of loud nasal snoring, out of rhythm with each other, coming from his aunt and uncle's bedroom. He put his hand over his mouth to suppress the giggles that wanted to fly out, before venturing further down towards the kitchen, where he opened the latch door.

'Can I help, Ma?' Stephen asked, as he looked into her tired eyes.

'Ahh Stevie, you can help me put these clothes through the ringer, then we can hang them on the line,' said Ellen, breathing a sigh of relief.

Stephen enjoyed spending time with his mother, it felt precious and he knew he wanted to make the most of it but wasn't quite sure why.

Whilst Stephen and Albert went to the local school, George tried to find work in the nearby factories. Ellen walked the streets offering to wash, char, do anything needed in the household to try and make her money stretch to pay the rent.

Stephen and Albert ran towards home after a school day, determined to have fun after the confinement of the classroom. Ellen was on her knees scrubbing the outside step with a small bucket of water full of carbolic soap and a stiff bristle brush in her hand.

'Can we play out on the street, Ma?' Stephen asked, as he rushed through the small gate, in the overgrown hedge.

'As long as you don't wander too far away,' said Ellen, continuing with her task and not looking up from the concrete step.

Stephen and Albert hurried into the street and just managed to dodge a horse and cart before resting near a lamppost, trying to settle their breathing.

'Let's play hide and seek,' Albert suggested with a spark in his eyes.

'Oh, alright then, I suppose you want to be the one to run and hide?' Stephen said.

'Can I? Can I?' Albert asked, jumping on the spot, unable to contain his excitement.

'Yes, go on then, but watch you don't step in the horse muck, you know what happened last time,' Stephen said.

'Okay, but close your eyes and don't cheat,' said Albert.

Stephen covered his face with his hands and counted to ten very slowly.

'Coming, ready or not,' yelled Stephen.

This was an easy game for Stephen, because Albert usually hid in a neighbour's front garden, and he could hear his brother's stifled breathing, which always gave him away. And when it came to Albert's turn he would give up half way through looking for Stephen, and yell it was teatime.

But one late afternoon, when they entered the house after playtime, Stephen heard raised voices in the back room.

'But I'm doing everything I can, some people want me to do washing and charing for next to nothing, they can't afford to pay me,' said Ellen.

'Your earnings are working out on average six shillings a week, but you know the rent is six shillings and eight pence a week,' said Minnie.

'Just give me a little more time, I know I can pay you back,' said Ellen.

'It's too late, you're in rent arrears, you'll have to leave tomorrow, we can't manage,' said Thomas, who returned to the empty dark veil over his eyes, where hope had long left the space within.

'But tomorrow is the fifteenth November, it's just a few weeks away from Christmas. Please have mercy,' pleaded Ellen.

'I'm sorry, Ellen, but there's no money to feed the children. You'll have to go,' said Minnie, folding her arms even tighter around her chest.

'You can always go back to the workhouse, at least they feed you in there,' said Thomas, oblivious to Ellen's tears.

*181 Coventry Road, Small Heath, Birmingham*

TRAPPED WITHIN A whirlwind of turmoil, Ellen sold most of her household effects. She was given shelter by her parents and moved to the back of 181 Coventry Road, Small Heath, Birmingham—the home of William and Elizabeth Pardoe who were both sixty.

'There's not much space here, Ellen. I don't know where the boys will sleep,' said William, his hand on his lower back, as he bent forward to put more logs on the fire.

'At least you're not walking the streets,' said Elizabeth, as her rocking chair squeaked slightly in time with the sound of her knitting needles.

'Boys, sit and lean against the wall for now. We can all sleep on the floor near the fire tonight. Then I'll try and think of something tomorrow,' said Ellen.

Her eldest son Fred Junior, continued to work as an assistant to her brother James, in his butcher's shop at the front of the house, where he slept on the premises and earned twenty-one shillings a week. John was temporarily employed to run errands but remained uninterested in gaining full-time permanent employment.

'John, we can't go on like this. You need to find work,' pleaded Ellen.

But John only stared into the flames of the log fire, unable to meet his mother's gaze. *Just like your father.* Ellen worried that John seemed to live inside his own imagination, where nothing else mattered except himself.

George, who had just turned fourteen, found work as a factory hand and brought home four shillings and nine pence a week. Ellen continued to encourage the effort he was making but knew the money wouldn't stretch that far.

The cottage at the back of the butcher's shop was small with only specks of light seeping through the Georgian square window overlooking a walled yard. The Guardians obtained a warrant for Thomas Frederick's arrest, but he had not been traced.

Ellen lay on the stone floor in the back room with Stephen, Albert, and Walter beside her. The threadbare blankets gave them little warmth, as the log fire from the night before had long burnt its last embers. Walter murmured in his sleep. How pale and sad her three youngest children were. Icicles looked like splinters on the inside of the small square window overlooking the yard. The snow had fallen heavily over the last few days bringing temperatures below zero. Ellen was exhausted from looking for work. Constant rejections for offering her services to wash and char were taking their toll. She had managed to save some money from a few hours' work, for food over the next couple of days. She kept it in a green tea tin above the fireplace. But she knew it wasn't enough. Something had to change. *Maybe John will get a job soon. It's been six months.* But her second eldest son's behaviour only deteriorated as he stumbled through the front door, shaking the foundations of the small cottage. Whilst John had similar features to Stephen, with the same fair hair, his temperament was quite different.

'John, where've you been? It's four in the morning,' whispered Ellen.

'I've been out!' he slurred, as his body slithered towards the rocking chair.

'You're drunk! Where did you get the money?'

His dark eyes flickered from the empty void within. Ellen dragged herself up and stumbled towards the fireplace. She reached for the tea tin.

'The money's gone. This was the last for food. Have you spent it on beer?' John smirked.

'I'll win it back. It was just a game of cards,' he mumbled.

'You've been gambling?'

'Well someone has to do something. We can't go on living like this, can we? All cramped together with nowhere to go.'

'How could you? How could you be so stupid?' Ellen screamed.

She launched for her son and shook his shoulders to try and bring him round to some kind of sense.

'You've taken the last of the food money!'

'Get off me! It's not my fault Pa left. Why is everyone blaming me just because I haven't got a job? Pa was out of work for nearly two years,' yelled John vehemently.

In contrast to the screaming between them, Stephen, Albert, and Walter cowered in the corner of the dark room, with tears burning from swollen eyes and staining their sallow skin.

Trapped and riddled with guilt, John grabbed his mother by the arms and pushed her away from him. Ellen fell and hit her head on the hearth of the log fire. Stephen ran to her side.

'Leave her alone, you've hurt her,' he cried.

John stood over his mother and glared from his own hands, to her twisted figure collapsed on the floor beneath him. He hadn't realised his own strength, and now he could only fall to his knees in remorse.

Stephen put his woollen, threadbare blanket underneath her neck and ran to the kitchen to pour cold water on a tea towel. He returned to wipe her head. He was relieved to see no blood.

John swayed until he collapsed in a drunken heap on the floor.

'It's okay Ma, everything will be all right, we'll look after you,' said Stephen.

Albert helped Walter as he crawled towards their mother. They snuggled close to her breast, and held her chapped hands, with splintered nails from hours, days of cleaning work.

'My boys . . . I love you,' she murmured.

The three of them kept their mother's body warm, surrounded in a haven of silent tears until the sun began to rise, and in contrast, John snored, oblivious to the chaos and pain he had caused.

A new day dawned. It was time to make decisions—but at what cost? Ellen watched Stephen as he sat near the hearth, staring into the empty space before him. She had always noticed, since he was born, how his expression changed as his mind drifted and his eyes reflected a familiar light. Ellen had long accepted he was listening to someone she held very close to her own heart.

*Stevie . . . listen to me. Hey, are you listening?*

*Annie, is that you?*

*Who else would it be? The Queen of Sheba? Have you suddenly become hard of hearing?*

*I'm listening.*

*I should think so too. My time is very precious, you know? I have a busy schedule and I haven't got all day to hang around here.*

*What's so important, you need my attention right now?*

*Well, there's no need to ask so many questions!*

*I'm still listening.*

*There's going to be a big change within the family. You must try and be strong . . . stronger than you've ever been before. There's a long journey ahead of you.*

*(Fair curls twisted their way over blue crystal eyes. And a distant light glided closer like the gentle ripples beneath the flow of a waterfall.)*

*What kind of journey?*

*There you go again, asking questions. What am I, the Encyclopaedia Britannica?*

*Okay, I'm here and silent.*

*You will know soon enough. I need you to prepare. Keep writing in your journal . . . it brings you comfort. I am coming with you on this journey, I promise.*

*Really? I mean, that's nice, but what if I get scared and I don't know what to do?*

*Questions . . . questions . . . Don't be afraid. I'm always here.*

*I never doubt that.*

*Just look up towards the sky when you need me, and I'll be right by your side.*

*Do you promise not to sing?*

*No!*

*Is Albie coming with us?*

*Yes.*

# 2
# A Mother's Love

*"One word frees us all of the weight and pain of life: That word is love."*
— *Sophocles*

CHRISTMAS 1909 MOVED closer, with the echo of sweet carols beneath the chimney tops in the bustling city of Birmingham. It was a time for families to gather around the warmth of the crackling log fire and hold out a hand full of love, if there was nothing more to give. The pointed arrow of bird formations had long left for warmer shores, miles away from the bitter ice-cold air of England. And the trees remained naked in their isolation, waiting for the change of season.

*181 Coventry Road, Small Heath, Birmingham*
STEPHEN SAT IN the corner of the back room of his grandparents' small, dark cottage, with his ragged coat wrapped around his shoulders. His brothers continued to snore next to him, out of rhythm with each other, but consistent with sleeping through the night. Insomnia was a condition Stephen was used to, and he learnt to use the time writing in his secret journal, shifting his mind into a trance like state. It was the only way he found comfort, away from the real world outside his imagination. As he drifted into thoughts like shooting stars inside his head, trying to make sense of his changing world, the words took on a life of their own.

Today, I saw Ma wipe a tear from her face, whilst she was making jam with raspberries again. She told me she had just chopped up an onion to make soup. I didn't know onions could make you cry. Something doesn't feel right. It hasn't felt the same since Pa left. I wish he would come back. I miss him. Ma won't tell me what's going on. But something is. No one seems to talk anymore. Everyone whispers, or voices change to silence. I want to do something to help but I don't know what to do. If only things would go back to the way they used to be, when Pa came home from work and told us stories. I wonder where he is now? I'm scared that Pa's not the only one to leave. I don't like raspberries.

Stephen's eyes moved from the inked paper, to reflect the light in his brother's sleepy gaze.

'What are you doing, Stevie?' Albert whispered.

'I'm just writing something. Go back to sleep, Albie,' said Stephen.

The charcoal sky began its transformation, as sunrise remained hidden behind a blank canvas of grey cloud. Ellen sat in the front parlour, staring at the white paper in front of her, placed neatly on top of the walnut table.

*What about the old log shed . . . could it be converted? If only John would find permanent work . . . Surely Fred will send some money for the boys . . . it's Christmas after all . . .*

Her eyes flickered as her mind spun like a spinning wheel out of control. She sighed deeply and reached out with a trembling hand. The ink from her pen found its way across the paper, as if her entire body was far removed from the reality of the words she so diligently wrote.

When the letter was finally sealed, she collapsed in the mahogany-framed wing chair, near the Georgian side window and prayed. She stared at the desolate yard reflecting her empty heart.

*There's still time for a miracle . . . I won't give up . . . I can't . . .*

But all seemed lost to her, as day and night circulated into one.

It was in the silence of her despair, that she heard the whimpering cries of Walter in the back room. She dragged her weary feet to the door, pressed down the latch, and opened it. Ellen leant against the wall as she watched George, Stephen, Albert, and Walter huddled together watching the last sparks of the log fire disappear. Their bare feet poked through the end of their thin ragged coats as they lay on a patchwork woollen blanket against the cold stone floor.

'I'm hungry,' groaned Albert.

Stephen's right eye twitched as he stared into his mother's eyes. He felt her sadness touch him more deeply than ever before. There was something different about her.

'Walter's been sick. I cleaned it up,' said Stephen.

'Thank you, Stevie . . . what would I do without you?'

Ellen lay beside Walter and cuddled him into her breast. She stretched out her arm across the worn blanket, and Stephen and Albert reached for her hand. She sang their favourite bedtime lullaby, in a soft, whispered tone.

Hush, little baby, don't say a word,
Mama's gonna buy you a mockingbird.
And if that mockingbird won't sing . . .

George snored, oblivious and weary from his long day at the factory. Stephen and Albert joined in the verse, whilst Walter hummed over his sucked thumb.

Mama's gonna buy you a diamond ring.
And if that diamond ring turns brass,
Mama's gonna buy you a looking glass . . .

Stephen continued to stare deeply into his mother's eyes, almost afraid to look away. But his eyelids became heavy, and he could no longer resist the temptation of sleep.

And if that looking glass gets broke . . .

Ellen's voice trembled into silence, the words of the lullaby reflecting her broken heart. She lifted her head from the floor and noticed her children were sleeping. And she could only close her eyes and pray for sleep to take her darkest nightmare away and relieve her of a decision that haunted the depths of her tortured soul.

It was during sleep that a young girl came to her on the wings of a dream that brought her comfort and peace, amidst the chaos and heartbreak.

*Don't worry . . . I will look after Stevie and Albie for you.*
*Do you promise?*
*I promise.*

Fair curls glowed in the aura of transparent light around her, and her blue crystal eyes glistened like pools of deep water reflecting her quiet tranquil spirit, captured forever. Ellen held out her hand and felt only the deepest love transpire through her frail and weak body. It was always during these moments of reconnection that Ellen felt stronger than she had ever done before, with the power of love and understanding she could only make sense of when she had fallen into the deepest sleep.

THE HUNGRY DAYS stretched out to meet the cold, bitter nights whilst Ellen paced the floors of the small stone cottage. Her father, William left early each morning to earn eighteen shillings a week as a gardener. He enjoyed being out in the fresh air, but he suffered in the winter season with the frost. His wife, Elizabeth who he fondly called Beth, was bedridden, still weak from a fall on the stairs, but determined to knit with the little wool she had.

Time passed slowly with Ellen trying to make the scraps of food she had last and feed four hungry boys. She spent hours staring into empty space, cutting mould out of dry bread and serving watered down broth in cups. She carried on until she could no longer bear to hear the painful cries of hunger echo her own despair.

It was the frosty morning of Christmas Eve, with the cool midwinter air circling the children's chapped lips, when Ellen heard the distinctive sound of a hand bell and the familiar deep penetrating bellow of 'any old iron' . . . She rushed outside to greet Jack, who she had known from childhood, growing up on the same street. As he climbed down from his cart, Ellen noticed how his long black coat flapped around the thighs of his bow legs, his battered hat tilted to one side, and his fingerless gloves, in need of a good darn. *Just like your father.*

Stephen followed his mother out of the front door.

'Albie! Iron man's here,' he shouted to his brother.

They both scrambled through the yard, with their tattered coats flapping in the light breeze, and Stephen's eyes sparkled at the sight of Jack's old carthorse. Albert hesitated.

'You watch your fingers now, Albie, you know what happened last time you got too close,' said Jack.

'Hello, Daisy,' whispered Stephen, as he patted her long grey mane. And he snuggled close to her as if they were somehow connected.

Jack's eyes lingered in the reflection of Ellen's, as he felt a deep and unspoken sadness. 'No sign of Fred, then?'

Ellen shook her head.

'Don't you worry, girl. Things have a way of working out.'

'Jack, I need you to do something for me,' said Ellen.

He listened attentively.

'Will you take me and the two boys to the Bullring at the end of your morning rounds?'

'I'm going that way now. It's quiet today. The boys can climb in the back and help out if I need them.'

'Thank you, Jack. I just need to make sure Ma can listen out for Walter. He's sleeping now,' said Ellen.

Stephen and Albert clambered into the back of the cart, until you couldn't distinguish between the rags on their bodies and the rags surrounding them. Only the light shining from their eyes and the smiles on their faces were different. Jack held out his hand and helped Ellen up to the seat next to him. And Daisy trotted in her slow and diligent way the couple of miles towards the centre of Birmingham. Stephen cried out 'any old iron' intermittently until his voice became dry, and Albert rang the bell until his hand got tired and he gave up. But the excitement of riding in the back of a horse and cart with the rag and bone man remained with them, lighting the way towards a new adventure.

*Bullring, Birmingham*

JACK STEERED HIS old faithful horse, until they arrived at the Bullring.

'I'll be coming back this way later today, if you need a ride back?' Jack grinned, showing a gap in his teeth.

Ellen rested the palm of her hand over his and smiled at his kindness. Stephen helped his mother down from the cart, and she put her arm around both her boys.

'Come on now, let's have a walk around the market,' she said.

Stephen and Albert held her hand as they leaned in beside her. They pushed through the small gatherings of unknown faces shrouded with hats and turned up collars of coats, negotiating the price of fruit and vegetables, and all good things for sale. One stall mingled into the next.

'Hey, Ellie . . .' yelled a voice from the crowd.

Ellen turned to notice Bess, who she remembered sitting on the front step with, when she was a young girl, and playing together.

'Not seen you down these parts for a while,' said Bess, as she exchanged coins for a bag of apples to a happy customer, with her big hands and wide shoulders.

Ellen's eyes became lost in their own distance.

'Why are her cheeks so red?' Albert whispered.

'Shh . . . I think it's the cold air,' said Stephen.

'I heard about Fred. Sad business,' she said, scratching her head under her headscarf.

'Yes . . . but it's nice to see you, Bess. How's your Bert?'

'Well . . . he's been out of work these last six months, but he sometimes comes down and helps out on the stall. He's not the same man he was, my Bert. He needs a job, that's what he needs,' said Bess, reflecting her sadness on the shiny cox apples on sale in front of her.

'I hope something turns up for him soon, Bess. Maybe the New Year will bring some good news,' said Ellen.

The two women shared a smile.

'Look at you two boys, how you're growing up. I don't know where time goes . . . here, take these Ellie, and have a Merry Christmas,' she said, handing her three tangerines in a brown paper bag.

'But, Bess, I've no . . .'

'Don't you worry about that. It's a gift from me. If we can't give at this time of the year, then when can we?'

'That's so kind of you, Bess, but . . .'

'Just take them, for me . . . please.'

'Thank you,' said Ellen, as tears shone in her tired eyes.

They hugged the way they did as children, and Ellen's heart felt like it might break as it was held by one of her oldest and closest friends.

'Come on now, boys, thank Bess,' said Ellen, bringing her emotions back into control.

They both repeated the words, but their eyes never once left the brown paper bag in their mother's hand. They slowly moved away, to continue their steps down the elongated path of market stalls.

'Why do they call it the Bullring?' Albert asked.

'Because a very long time ago, they used to have bulls here,' said Ellen.

Ellen squeezed Stephen and Albert's hands tightly as they reached the last of the market stalls and looked up at the church steeple reaching for the unsettled clouds in the over cast sky.

'I thought we'd go to the service, as it's a special day,' said Ellen.

'Will we have to sing?' Albert asked.

'Only if you want to, Albie,' said Ellen softly.

'I like singing,' said Stephen.

Ellen smiled at both her boys, led them to the entrance of the church, and stepped inside. Overhead wooden arches towered down the sides of rows of pews. They sat a distance from the pulpit, where stained glass images of an unforgotten past reflected back a stillness of unspoken peace captured in the surrounding cool air.

Stephen looked at the empty space beside him and smiled at the warm familiar glow that filled his heart. A thousand voices echoed from a place of ancient souls in their protective home of worship. The sermon continued from a voice that mumbled and became lost in the midst of the congregation, until the time came to sing.

Away in a manger, no crib for a bed,
the little Lord Jesus laid down his sweet head;
the stars in the bright sky looked down where he lay . . .

Stephen knew the words from memory, and Albert's lips moved seconds behind his brother. But there were long pauses, when Stephen shivered from the cold. Whilst Albert stared at the brown paper bag in Ellen's hand, hiding the tangerines from sight.

> Be near me, Lord Jesus, I ask you to stay
> close by me forever, and love me, I pray.
> Bless all the dear children in your tender care;
> prepare us for heaven, to live with you there.

'Don't cry, Ma. It's Christmas,' said Stephen.

Ellen wiped her tear-stained cheeks with her handkerchief and pulled both Stephen and Albert closer to her side.

'It's just some dust in my eyes, Stevie,' she said.

The service came to a close and they slowly made their way towards the exit, leaving behind the soft glow of candlelight, and strangers moving in the same direction. The church rooftop changed to a sheet of grey matted sky. Albert stopped suddenly and looked back.

'Who's St Martin?' Albert asked, with his eyebrows twisting into each other, as he stared at a figure from one of the stained-glass windows.

'One day, Albie, you'll find a way to answer all your questions, but sometimes you have to accept that there isn't always the answer you're hoping for,' said Ellen, as she put her cold hands in the pockets of her long coat, with her fingers slipping through the holes.

A stranger—an elderly gentleman, who had been in the pew in front of them, followed them outside. He smiled with serenity glowing from his light blue eyes, and lines of time left their mark across a face that lived beyond his years. When he spoke, a velvety tone rippled through his mouth, but from a deeper place inside his heart.

'St Martin was a soldier. He was born in Hungary in 316 and never wanted to join the army but was obliged to by law. At the age of eighteen, he was posted to Amiens in France. One bitterly cold winter's night he was riding through the city when he saw a half-naked beggar huddled against a wall. Martin was so moved by the sight that he cut his cloak with his sword and gave one half to the beggar. That night he had a dream in which Christ appeared to him as a beggar and thanked Martin for clothing him. In response, the young soldier got baptised. Later he was to leave the army to become a soldier of Christ, eventually becoming the Bishop of Tours in France. St Martin is remembered today for his service to the poor.'

'Thank you, sir . . . It was very kind of you to explain in such detail. Can I ask how you know so much about St Martin?' Ellen asked.

'Excuse me, I should have said, my name's Martin Brightman, recently retired vicar of the parish,' said the stranger.

'I'm very pleased to meet you, sir. These are my boys, Stephen and Albert,' said Ellen.

'Ah yes, young soldiers shining towards their destiny,' he said.

Ellen's eyes reflected ripples of sadness, but she managed to exchange a smile before they all moved away and went their separate ways. Stephen noticed how tightly his mother was holding his hand as she led him and his brother just a few steps away from the entrance of the church.

'Now then . . . let's sit here for a while. There's something I want to show you. Do you know who that is?' Ellen asked, as she pointed her finger to the nearby statue watching over them.

Stephen and Albert snuggled close to her on the small bench and looked up with wide, bright eyes, and a confused expression on their ghostly-white faces.

'That's Admiral Horatio Nelson, and he joined the Navy when he was just twelve years old,' said Ellen.

'That's just one year older than me,' said Stephen.

The boys had their mother's full attention.

'He was a strong and mighty Admiral, and saved our country from invasion by France,' said Ellen.

'How did he die?' Albert asked.

'Well . . . during his last battle he lost the sight in his right eye, and later lost his right arm . . . can you see?'

Ellen's eyes lingered on the right side of Horatio Nelson, whilst she handed the boys their tangerines. They sat and peeled the skin slowly, wanting to savour the moment, knowing that the juice would quench their thirst. And their curiosity about the stone-cold statue continued, as they licked their dry lips, soothed from the juice of the tangerines.

'I lost my fingers, but I've still got my whole arm,' said Albert.

'Yes, Albie . . . so can you see, you're not the only one who has lost some part of you,' said Ellen.

'My right eye aches sometimes, but I can still see through it,' said Stephen.

'Sometimes, Stevie, it's not what we see, but what we sense that makes all the difference,' she said.

Both boys looked at their mother with wonder in their faces, and Ellen continued with her story.

'In 1805, during the Battle of Trafalgar, Nelson said to his fleet, England expects that every man will do his duty. He was killed just a few hours later.'

'What's duty mean?' Albert asked.

'It means you fight for King and Country to keep us free.'

Stephen stared into the distance of his mother's eyes and felt his heart beat faster than he had known before. Then he choked on a piece of tangerine.

Ellen patted his back gently.

'There now, Stevie, take a deep breath,' she said.

Stephen's throat began to clear.

Trickles of dark shades started to shift and dance their way over the hidden clouds, as the early stages of dusk prepared to meet twilight.

'It's time for us to get back . . . Jack will be waiting,' said Ellen.

Stephen stretched out his arms towards the distant sky.

'I wish we could stay here for a bit longer,' he said.

'It's getting late Stevie, and Albie's falling asleep . . . it's been a special day . . . promise me you will never forget this time we've spent together,' she said.

The boys heard their mother's words, but had no idea of their true meaning, as they travelled in disguise from her veiled heart. Ellen hid the trapped tears in her glazed eyes, as she squeezed their hands gently, and led them slowly back down the path, lined with market stalls—where canopies were being pulled down, flowers wrapped in paper, and fruit and vegetables put back in boxes . . . everything hidden away, before the last tiers of light disappeared into the canvas of darkness.


*Christmas Day*

THE DAWN OF Christmas rested in the majestic rays of white glistening snowflakes finding a home over naked trees, rooftops, and deserted pavements. Circles of grey-tinged smoke whirled their way from the crackling log fires below the chimney pots, to meet the iced air, and escape into oblivion, towards the smooth chalk sky.

Stephen leaned against the kitchen door and watched his mother bustle around the small square kitchen. Beads of sweat glistened on Ellen's forehead, and with her apron twisted around her hips, she settled with knife in hand, peeling potatoes over the sink. He noticed his uncle James, battling with the goose in the meat tin, and pushing it back into the heat of the oven. He was slim and taller than Ellen, but with the same blue eyes and similar amount of hidden sadness.

Stephen continued to stare into the kitchen, as if he was watching a silent film, from a distance. Then Albert rushed in.

'Can I go outside and play . . . it's snowing?'

'It's freezing outside, Albie, and we'll be having dinner soon,' said Ellen.

'What are you doing, Uncle James?' Albert asked.

'I'm checking on the goose,' he said.

'Are we having meat today?' Albert asked, with wonder in his eyes.

'Yes, it was left over from the shop, and it is a special day, Albie,' he said.

'I think I'd like to be a butcher when I grow up and eat meat every day. Can I come and work for you?'

Ellen's eyes welled with tears as she met the gaze of her younger brother. He lowered his head, and the moment was frozen in silence with an unanswered question lingering in the cool air.

Stephen's head leant to one side. *Why does Ma look so upset?*

'Stevie, take Albie outside to play for a while,' she said, struggling to find her voice.

'Yeah . . . let's have a snow fight,' said George, as he entered the kitchen.

'Put your coats on,' said Ellen, grazing her finger with the sharp-edged knife.

The three boys disappeared out of the back door and into the white haven that had become the back yard. Ellen stared at the red spots of blood oozing from her finger, as they mingled with the ice-cold water streaming into the grey cracked sink like twisted autumn leaves.

A frail woman with grey hair tied back in a loose bun, stumbled slowly into the kitchen, leaning on a stick.

'Do you need any help, Ellen?'

'No, Ma, it's all under control,' she said.

'I don't know where we are all going to sit.'

'Don't worry, Ma, the children can sit on the floor and have their dinner on their lap. They're used to it,' said Ellen.

'I just wish we had more room,' she said, gazing into the distance of her own reflective sadness.

'What are Fred and John doing?' Ellen asked.

'Fred was reading the newspaper to your Pa, but he's fallen asleep in his armchair. He's a good boy, is Fred. And John . . .'

'I'm here,' mumbled John, as he followed his brothers out of the back door.

The sound of raucous screams of laughter echoed from the yard, and a snowball fired at the window.

'I'll have to go and calm them down,' said Ellen.

'Don't worry, Ma . . . I'll sort them out. Walter's just woken up and wants to go out too,' said Fred Junior, holding the hand of his youngest brother, and steering him towards the white wonderland.

Ellen watched her children play from the small square window. Her hand tightened around the knife she was holding, and she wanted to scream, *Why?*

Elizabeth Pardoe slowly stepped closer, using her stick for support, put her arm around her daughter's shoulders and gently removed the knife from her trembling fingers.

'There now, listen to me. You need to remember this, like a picture postcard. It's a memory—a happy time, with the boys playing together. Hold it gently in your heart, because no one can ever take this moment away from you,' she said.

Ellen held on to her mother's strength, embalmed in the frailness of her aged body, determined not to avert her eyes from her children, for even one second.

'Don't throw snowballs at Walter, he's too small,' said Fred, as one skimmed the top of his head.

Stephen dived to avoid white pellets like bullets flying through the air and landed on his back. He stretched out his arms, sweeping the crushed snow in and out until the print of wings surrounded him. He gazed at the brilliant white sky before him, and a familiar light glistened its way closer.

'Look . . . I'm an angel,' he said.

But no one heard Stephen, or the voice that whispered back to him. And the sound of crackling laughter echoed in the distance.


*New Year 1910*

IT WAS EARLY one morning when there was a heavy knock at the door. Ellen was expecting a visitor. She had waited for this moment to come with every hope in her heart that it would never transpire. But it was here now. And she had to face it with a piece of courage she wasn't sure she had. A bit like the loaf of bread in the pantry, knowing it wouldn't last the week.

Ellen showed a tall man with pale skin and protruding eyes into the front parlour. He was dressed in a dark sack coat with matching single-breasted waistcoat, with black toecap, lace up boots. He introduced himself as Mr Davies. Ellen looked up and politely shook his hand. They sat facing each other, wondering who might speak first. Mr Davies cleared his throat with an authority that unnerved Ellen. *I wish Fred was here—he would know what to do.*

Ellen struggled to listen to the advice he gave—with overwhelming detail. Mr Davies spoke in a deep and daunting voice, whilst Ellen remained disorientated, with feelings of depression blocking her ability to think clearly. Her small frame trembled in the winged armchair, and still Mr Davies continued in his monotonous and detached manner.

'But most of all, Mrs Duckhouse—the children will be looked after in a most compassionate way,' he mumbled, as he shuffled uncomfortably in a chair that appeared too low for his gangling body.

'Compassionate. It has to be the right decision then,' she whispered from the depths of her anguished heart, desperate to convince herself she was doing the right thing.

Her eyes glazed over as she became lost, somewhere beyond the sound of his distant voice. *All I have to do is sign . . .*

Later that day, whilst thunderclouds lashed pellets of raindrops at the small window, Ellen sat the boys down at the oak table in the corner of the dining room. The chime clock ticked on the mantelpiece to the rhythm of Ellen's heart. Her breathing was heavy, and a tunnel of darkness engulfed her. The boys watched her, sitting in the silent room, as she had asked them to, waiting.

'I just want you all to listen to what I have to say.' She cleared her throat. 'Sometimes we have to make choices that aren't always easy to make. We've been struggling for a long time now, since your Pa left. We can't go on like this.' She choked, fighting to find a strength that was lost to her.

Fred sat next to his mother and held her hand, trying to bring some kind of comfort that was only shrouded in his own heartbreak.

'I'm trying to get more shifts at the factory,' said George.

'But George, the money won't stretch to feed us all, and we can't stay here permanently, there just isn't enough room. I have had to make some very difficult decisions and I want you all to be brave.'

Their eyes widened with fear of the unknown. Ellen coughed, trying to hide the choked ball of fire in the back of her throat.

'I've decided that two of you have to go away. It will only be until I feel well enough to go back to work. You will be cared for there. It's for the best. We can't manage, you know we've been struggling for too long now.'

The silence deepened, stifling the air until all breathing ceased.

John's eyes returned to the log fire, where he knew he could remain detached from his mother's voice. He shuffled forward and leant against the mantelpiece, close enough to almost touch the flames. *It's my fault.*

George covered his face with his hands, to hide from her words. Stephen lowered his head, averting his aching eye. Albert's bottom lip trembled. And Walter slept soundly in the corner of the room, oblivious of his surroundings. Only the sound of the chime clock could be heard, chipping away at their last minutes together.

'I don't want it to be me! I don't want to go away,' cried Albert.

'I'm sorry, Albie . . . I don't have any choice. Stevie will look after you, won't you Stevie?'

Stephen froze, almost lost beside his own shadow, until his body crumbled and he fell to his knees. His right eye flickered as he struggled to find his voice. Within seconds an unfamiliar sound propelled from his stomach, but stuck somewhere in the dry brittleness of his throat.

*No* . . . he silently screamed, as he tried to find solace in the cold, concrete floor beneath him.

Ellen reached out and Albert ran and clung to his mother, determined never to let go. His body trembled in rhythm with uncontrollable sobbing, in the ice-cold air. And all she could do was collapse to the floor and pull both Stephen and Albert close to her, knowing that any day they would be wrenched from her heart and the chord between them would be broken.

The sound of the ticking clock died beneath the heavy rhythm of cries, echoing their different monotones from an untold song. But Stephen continued to remain lost in his own silence. And Ellen's energy seeped away from her, like the blood leaving her veins, to await death.

'We all need to be brave, and everything will work out . . . you'll see,' she whispered softly in their ears.

Ellen kissed them on the top of their heads as she held their trembling bodies and listened to the choked sobs that Fred, John, and George tried so hard to hide. Walter woke from his sleep in the corner, next to the crackling log fire, and cried, clutching the hunger pains in his stomach—oblivious of the stirred emotion swirling around the darkness from the storm clouds outside, seeping through the window of the back room.

The dust continued to gather over the *Intermediate Monarch Gramophone,* which sat silently on top of the satinwood cross-banded music cabinet—signifying a lost time when joy had once filled the house. As the hour passed, Fred and George helped their mother back to bed, where she lay and wept in synchronicity with the lashing storm throughout the night.


*Birmingham New Street*

THE DAY ARRIVED for Stephen and Albert to leave. It was all arranged. There was no going back. Ellen had ensured two rooms around the corner from her parents' cottage, for her, George, and Walter. But there wasn't enough space for all her sons. The reality of Stephen and Albert finally being taken into care immobilised her completely, and only she could hear the screams that tore her inside out.

This was to be the last time they would spend together as a family. Lightning struck the rooftops in the empty street, as thunder crashed from the dark, angry sky, stifling tormented grief into silence. Ellen had tried to prepare Stephen and Albert for the worst possible outcome, but had continued praying for a miracle, with the hope that divine intervention would show her another way. But no answer came. Only continued poverty and the pains of hunger prevailed in every minute of the long torturous hours as time ran out.

Now, they faced this unwanted moment together. The boys hugged each other and their grandparents for the last time. Stephen was determined not to cry—he had already decided he wanted to be strong for Albert. But his eyes still glazed over the lost sparkle that had always been there. Albert was unable to hold back the tears.

'Why can't I stay with Walter? I won't be any trouble, I promise,' Albert cried as he pointed at his youngest brother sitting on his grandmother's lap, on the still rocking chair.

'This is a dark day, Ellen. Is there no other way?' Beth asked desperately, as she held Walter closer.

Ellen collapsed her face into her hands and prayed for the strength to go on. She finally found some segment of courage from the depths of her torn and shattered heart.

'Listen to me,' she said, as she reached out for both Stephen and Albert. 'Sometimes we have to do things because we have no other choice. Believe me, if there was another way . . . I want you both to have a chance of life. At least this way you will be fed and clothed and educated . . . all the things I can't give you. I want you to remember that the one thing you will always have is my love, right here in my heart.'

Ellen gently pulled their trembling hands towards her chest and felt that it might explode with the weight of grief. The boys snuggled in to her neck and rested their weary heads on her shoulders as she fell to her knees and held her sons so tightly, she thought she could never let them go.

The mahogany carriage clock chimed the passing of the hour from the mantelpiece. It was time. Ellen's arms felt like glue stuck to her children as she desperately tried to wrench herself from an energy that was stronger than any she had ever felt before.

'Fred, can you help me?' Ellen whispered.

Her eldest son softly guided his younger brothers towards him. Fred took hold of Albert's hand and gently led him out of the front door. Stephen followed his mother. Together the four of them waited for the bus. The journey was short, with the sound of muffled cries and stained tears leaving their white chiselled faces, like ghosts in the night.

Finally, they entered Birmingham New Street Station, where separation was inevitable. Ellen stepped slowly and painfully along the freezing cold platform and shuddered when she noticed Mr Davies waiting for them. His awkward stance seemed detached, as if he was living in another dimension, unaffected by the raw emotion that was revealed in Ellen's eyes. She wondered . . . *Maybe that's just how he copes.*

Both Stephen and Albert clung to their mother for the last time.

'Now listen to me . . . both of you. I have written something for you, and when you read it, I want you to try and understand this has been the hardest thing I have ever had to do. I need you to promise me that you will look after each other. Be good, always say please and thank you and don't forget to say your prayers every night . . . promise me.'

'I promise,' choked Stephen and Albert at the same time as they reached for the small envelopes.

'And this is a little something for the journey,' said Ellen, as she handed them a small parcel wrapped in brown paper.

'Will you come and visit?' Albert cried.

Ellen fell to her knees and held them both in her arms, tightly until she could hardly breathe.

'Remember . . . I will visit you every night in my prayers, and I will always love you,' she said as her voice choked on the word *love*.

Albert sobbed in her arms. Stephen wept silent, torturous tears that twisted and stung the side of his pale cheeks but remained invisible. And her arms released her children . . .

Ellen reached for her cotton handkerchief in her coat pocket and wiped her wet face. She had not stopped crying since her husband had left. Now she had to face the deepest most painful reality of saying goodbye to her younger sons, who were only eight and eleven years old. *How will I ever bear it?*

Fred took his mother's arm to stop her from collapsing. Within seconds she had let them go, after weeks of tortuous thinking, planning, rethinking. Fred looked into the eyes of his brothers and smiled bravely. He stroked the tops of their heads, hugged them close to his chest for the last time, and reminded Stephen, 'Look after yourself, Stevie, and take care of Albie.'

Then he turned and held onto his mother, who shivered in his arms.

The London train had arrived on time. Layers of steam clogged the early January air. Mr Davies guided the boys towards the second-class carriage. Stephen and Albert's swollen eyes never for a second left their mother's. But it was when

Albert's bottom lip trembled that he pulled away from Mr Davies, a stranger in a black coat, and ran back to his mother's familiar arms.

'Please don't make me go . . . you don't have to feed me. I will never say I'm hungry ever again . . . I promise,' he cried.

Ellen's heart felt like broken glass as she clung to the rags falling from his body. Her eyes flickered whilst tears drowned her face. She stared into the distant gaze of Stephen, who seemed frozen in motion, and silently pleaded for his forgiveness.

The second hand of time continued with relentless strokes departing from each roman number on the ivory face of the station clock, suspended from an iron cast bar, fixed to the wall of the platform. Stephen stumbled back towards his mother and whined with pain, tearing a muscle in his shin as he tripped over the pavement. He extended his arms to embrace her, with Albert retching in her chest. Ellen held on to them both, like tidal waves in her arms, and raised her pierced eyes to the tangled sky, above the reflective light of the glass roof.

'God help me to let them go,' she cried, with a voice she did not recognise.

'Don't make us go . . . please let us stay,' Albert choked on his dry mangled throat.

The sound of multiple cries fell into a chorus of no return. But Stephen remained dazed, trapped in his own silence, as if he was watching from a distance.

Ellen took the deepest breath.

'Listen to me. I love you with all my heart, but you won't survive if you stay with me. I can't look after you, and God knows I have tried. I want you to be safe and well and have a good life . . . and stay together. I promise I will write to you often. But you have to be strong now and go with Mr Davies.'

It took the remains of whatever strength she had left to unclench their fingers from the palms of her hands and let go.

'The train's about to leave,' said Mr Davies, clearing his throat.

Stephen put his arm around his brother as they slowly moved in a trance-like state into an unfamiliar distance between them and their mother.

'I will look after you, Albie, I promise,' he whispered.

They climbed the step into the carriage and sat close to the window. The final whistle was blown. They reached out their hands to touch the stone-cold glass that separated them for the first time in their young lives from the arms of their loving mother. Albert cried tears that welled from the back of his throat and stung like nothing he had ever known before. Stephen remained silent, unable to move, as if his body was locked away in a different time and place.

The train chugged slowly out of the station, leaving Ellen and Fred behind. The steam started to swirl around them, until Stephen and Albert could only see what seemed like shadows of ghosts in the distance between them.

Ellen felt her heart split into two as she fell to the ground, on her knees, her body trembling on the stone platform. Blood seeped from her mouth where she had cut her lip. She looked up at the vast, velvet sky through the glass roof.

'God forgive me,' she whispered as Fred wiped the blood mingled with tears from her swollen lips.

The distance between Ellen and her two young boys continued as the train left the city of Birmingham behind. Time moved slowly through the initial stages of separation. Stephen heard a muffled snore from Mr Davies, as he snoozed with his head leaning on one side. He suddenly realised he was clutching the envelope his mother had given to him at the station. He opened it carefully. His right eye ached as he read the words slowly.

A Mother's Love

Is always there
Sometimes invisible
In the distance of time
But still there
A voice to listen

Words unspoken
And wisdom
To light the darkness
When life's challenge
Comes around

Trust your destiny
Speaks its truth
Rise to the rhythm
Of your silent awakening
And you will find

A Mother's love

Stephen folded the paper and removed his journal from his coat pocket. He placed the envelope inside the secret pages and closed it, returning it to an unseen place. He stared at his own reflection from the train window as Albert whimpered in his sleep beside him. Dry tears stained Albert's face and stuck to his sallow skin. And out of the darkness, a familiar light shone from Stephen's eyes.

*Stevie . . . I'm here.*

*I can't speak right now. Did you know this was going to happen?*

*Don't you know by now, I know everything, Stevie.*

*You could have warned me. I don't know what to think.*

*You're going to have to be strong to face what lies ahead. But you can do it. Try to be brave. Know that I will never leave you. You're stuck with me forever, like it or not.*

*Why? Why have we had to leave?*

*There you go again . . . asking questions.*

*I don't know what to do.*

*Over the next few days your journal will bring you comfort. Continue to write about your experiences and feelings. It will help you. Trust that whatever comes, you will be safe, and never alone. But you need to pull yourself together and stop closing down.*

*And what if I don't know how to do that?*

*Try.*

# 3
# Voyage To Canada

*"We are the children of our landscape; it dictates behaviour and even thought in the measure to which we are responsive to it."* — *Lawrence Durrell*

STEPHEN AND ALBERT walked the narrow street by Stepney Station, hand in hand. They were inseparable. Mr Davies guided them towards a building that towered above them. Stephen read the words across the top of the double doors of number 18: *No Destitute Child Ever Refused Admission.* He counted four floors as he looked up at the small square windows. He gasped, as the deepest breath shot from his trembling body, like a seamless mist in the ice-cold air. Albert's eyes froze inside Stephen's, like a lost signal from a broken transmitter, as he squeezed his brother's hand even tighter, for fear of letting go of his only connection with home.

They climbed the five stone steps together, to enter the double doors taking them into an unknown world. Albert's eyes flickered at the brightness of the hallway. Stephen bit his bottom lip but remained silent as he noticed the high ceiling above him and a flight of wide stairs to the right.

A small man with a silver-streaked beard and light blue eyes sat behind a semi-circular mahogany desk. He greeted them with a kind voice.

'We've been expecting you. I'm Mr Nobbles. Welcome to Stepney Causeway. Come in, come in,' he repeated enthusiastically.

Mr Davies nodded respectfully towards Mr Nobbles and handed him the papers that Ellen had signed—the boys' last connection with their mother. Albert moved closer to his brother. Stephen put his protective arm around him. *I have to be strong for Albie.* But his legs shook, as he found himself unable to lift his feet to take another step.

'I don't like it here, Stevie, I want to go home,' choked Albert.

'We'll be all right, Albie, I'll always look after you, I promise,' whispered Stephen, fearful that his brother's words might offend Mr Nobbles.

It was late. The boys were shown downstairs to the kitchen. A round-faced woman with bright red cheeks and ginger curls smiled at them with relief that they had at last arrived.

'This is Mrs Darlington, she's been waiting to serve your supper,' said Mr Nobbles.

'Thank you, Mrs Darlington,' said Stephen politely.

'Well now, when was the last time you had something to eat?' She asked kindly.

'We had a jam sandwich on the train,' said Stephen.

Albert's lip quivered at the memory of their mother handing them a small parcel each before they left, the jam spread with her own hand.

'Come and sit down here, you must be tired after such a long day,' said Mrs Darlington.

She placed two dishes of vegetable soup, two slices of white bread, and two glasses of milk on the oak table. They ate quickly, filling the grief-stricken moments with the temporary distraction of satisfying their empty stomachs.

'There's a lot of tables and chairs here, Stevie, how many boys do you think live here?' Albert whispered to his brother.

'Don't worry about that, Albie . . . drink your milk,' said Stephen, trying to reassure him from the surface of his own distress.

'Are they all in bed . . . this isn't what time we usually go to sleep?' Albert persisted.

'They must do things differently here . . . We have to trust that whatever comes, we will be safe,' said Stephen.

Supper was soon over and Mr Nobbles appeared from behind the open door in the faded light from a distant oil lamp.

'Come now, boys, it's time for your baths,' he said, scratching the silver line on his beard.

'How come we have to have a bath? It's not Saturday night,' Albert whispered.

'Shh . . . he might hear you,' murmured Stephen.

Mr Nobbles walked slowly with a slight limp and led them up the wide staircase towards one of the dormitories on the top floor. The boys breathed heavily, tired from their long journey, and paused on the landing.

'Follow me to the bathroom. We need to get you out of these ragged clothes. I have some clean nightwear for you,' said Mr Nobbles.

Stephen and Albert entered the boys' bathroom and noticed two tin baths full of water.

'There's soap here and your night shirts are hanging up behind the door,' said Mr Nobbles, as he left the bathroom.

Stephen helped his brother undo the buttons from his thread-worn, torn shirt. Together, they diligently released the stained rags from their naked bodies.

They stepped into the baths side by side to meet the sensation of crystal pellets tingling over the layers of grey matted skin.

'The water's not cold,' whispered Albert, surprised.

Stephen sank deeper into the warm water with ripples of splashes dancing between his toes. The soap slipped though Albert's fingers.

'Ah . . . can we go for a swim in the river tomorrow?' Albert asked.

Stephen wondered if his brother had forgotten where they were, but Albert seemed comforted by his own fantasy.

'Do you think we might have a bath every day, Stevie?'

Stephen smiled at his brother and a sparkle of light reflected in their eyes. The water soothed the lingering uncertainty that filled the unspoken grief in the space between them.

As they each climbed out of their bath, they wrapped themselves in the cotton towels and shivered slightly. The smell of Wright's coal tar soap replaced the ingrained dirt that had travelled with them—something else had been lost and replaced.

'Stevie, I can't get this over my head,' said Albie.

Stephen quickly pulled his night shirt into place and helped his brother.

Mr Nobbles returned to pick up what was left of the rags they had peeled away from them.

'Where are you taking my shirt?' Albert cried.

'You'll be supplied with new clothes and boots tomorrow morning before breakfast,' said Mr Nobbles.

'No . . . no please don't take it,' Albert grasped the shredded grey cotton and held it to his face, breathing deeply.

'Now come on, Albert, let it go,' said Mr Nobbles.

'Please, sir, he can smell our mother's talcum powder. Can he keep it just for tonight? It might help him sleep,' Stephen asked politely.

'Well . . . well . . . just for tonight,' said Mr Nobbles.

They stepped quietly across the hallway in their white cotton nightshirts and entered a shaded room. The darkness was heavy with the breathing and snoring from other boys, asleep in their small cots, positioned side by side on the creaky wooden floor.

Mr Nobbles pointed to the end of the room, with two empty cots waiting for them. They were exhausted from their long train journey, the overwhelming grief of separation from their beloved mother, and their first experience of London. They climbed into the cots, ready for sleep to take over.

'There, there . . . we'll see you in the morning, yes, we'll see you in the morning,' whispered Mr Nobbles.

The door closed quietly, and the fog swirled across the window from the darkness outside. Stephen and Albert stared into the shadows above them, suddenly confronted with the reality of sharing a room with what felt like a hundred other boys—strangers in a place of uncertainty.

Time moved through the cold essence of the night.

'Ma . . . Ma . . . Help me . . .' Albert screamed out of the nightmare and into the darkness of the dormitory.

'Shh . . . it's okay Albie, I'm here,' whispered Stephen.

A number of boys stirred, and their snoring eased, until seconds later they drifted back into the rhythm of their heavy breathing. Stephen climbed into Albert's cot and held his brother in his arms, terrified of what might happen if someone heard. The last remnants of their mother's talcum powder lingered from Albert's shirt, cradled between them, as Stephen's mind drifted to the many miles that separated them from their mother. His resolve began to weaken, in the chamber of his fragile heart.

*Why . . . ? Why . . . ? Why . . . ?*

They cried together in silence, with only the familiarity of the full moon looking back at them.

The following early morning, a bell rang out in the hallway. Trickles of light seeped through the clouded sky and into the small square window. Stephen blinked himself awake as he noticed a boy about his own height sitting at the edge of his cot. He had dark brown hair and hazel eyes that shone with curiosity, from a hidden darkness.

'I'm John,' he said. 'What's your name?'

'Stephen, and this is my younger brother, Albert. We have a brother called John,' said Stephen, politely.

'Where have you come from?' John asked.

'Birmingham,' Stephen answered, without the inclination or the energy to continue the conversation.

It didn't matter to John, whose eyes remained transfixed on Stephen.

'Did you know, that way back in 1871, a young boy called John was turned away here, because there was no room? They called him Carrots because he had ginger hair. Two days later he was found dead in the street,' he said, in a low-pitched voice.

Stephen's eyes widened, as he remembered the boy called Carrots in the workhouse. Albert's bottom lip dropped. But all they wanted to do was think about how to get back home, to the familiarity of Birmingham.

They returned to the bathroom to wash with the other boys, where they were given a change of clothes, and Albert planned their escape.

'I don't like London. There are too many big buildings. Let's run away, Stevie,' he whispered as he pulled his polo neck woollen jumper over his head.

'We can't Albie. Where would we go? We have no money. Remember what happened to the boy they called Carrots,' said Stephen, as he buttoned up his cardigan over a round-neck cotton shirt.

So instead of running, which in their hearts felt like the only thing they wanted to do, Stephen persuaded Albert to stay.

'Just for now.'

Stephen and Albert followed the other boys downstairs as they headed towards the kitchen—and walked into a very different atmosphere from the night before. At the long tables, the buzz of chatter hovered over the heads of boys scraping their dishes with spoons and savouring each mouthful of porridge as the day stretched before them.

They joined the queue behind John, who continued to stare at Stephen.

Although Stephen wanted to reach out to a new friend, something held him back. There was a nervous feeling inside his stomach that he didn't quite understand. Moments later, they reached the front of the counter where they collected their bowls of porridge and went to sit at the end of one of the long tables. No one spoke to them, the boys too engrossed in their breakfasts. Stephen prayed for an invisible cloak to shroud them, so they could just get through the shock of their first day. It seemed to be working, because they went unnoticed. Only John continued to watch Stephen from the next table, with his lingering cold stare.

Breakfast was soon over, and Stephen heard some of the boys talk about where they were heading next as they left the kitchen in an orderly way.

'What's a drill yard?' Albert asked.

'I'm not sure, Albie,' said Stephen.

Mr Nobbles appeared as Stephen and Albert were frozen to their seats, unable to move in the swirl of disorientation that surrounded them.

'Follow me,' said Mr Nobbles.

He guided the boys upstairs to the first floor and into a bright light room, where Mr Davies was waiting, behind a stand covered in a black cloak.

'Come in,' said Mr Davies.

Stephen noticed a charcoal black-seated box with a silver plate screwed into the front, with his name S. Duckhouse, and the date below: 6.1.10. There was a number at the bottom of the plate.

'What does 67215 mean, sir?' Stephen asked.

'It's just your reference number, nothing to worry about. Every child has one when they enter Barnardo's.'

The boys stood holding hands, staring at a number that meant nothing to them. They trembled, as the reality of their situation registered, amongst the fear and confusion surrounding the stand covered in a black cloak.

*What is that?*

'Are they going to shoot us, Stevie?' Albert whispered.

But before Stephen could think of an answer to reassure his brother, Mr Nobbles summoned him.

'Now, Stephen, let's have you first. Just sit here and dangle your legs over the side . . . there . . . that's perfect, perfect,' he said. 'Look into the camera . . .'

Stephen's tired eyes stung from the flash, and the image was captured. The plate was unscrewed and replaced with Albert's name. The procedure was repeated. The boys were then asked to sit on the seated box together, side by side. Stephen put his arm around his brother's waist, and they both stared into the empty space before them—every feeling numbed by the automatic, mechanical routine. Unspoken grief spilled from the deepest sadness in their eyes, and into the flash of the camera.

There was no time to reflect on what had just happened. The boys were ushered into the hospital wing next door, where they met Mr O'Brian, the Medical Officer—a sturdy, rounded man with a dark beard covering a pointed chin. The boys allowed themselves to go through the motions of being examined, but remained silent in his presence, still trying to come to terms with how they had ended up so far away from home.

Stephen was reported to have a slight problem with his right eye. He was given spectacles to wear. Stephen's life was changing, but it was only when he caught sight of himself in the mirror, wearing spectacles for the first time, that he realised he was looking back at a reflection he barely recognised. He was suddenly distracted as he noticed his brother behind him, looking lost and disconnected from his surroundings. His sense of duty and responsibility brought back his mother's words: *promise me that you will look after Albie*. Stephen somehow found the strength to focus on helping his younger brother and mask his own breaking heart. He reached out and pulled Albert closer.

'It's okay, Albie. We're safe here,' whispered Steven, putting his arm around him.

'Can we go home now, Stevie? I miss Ma.'

Following the medical examination, the boys were taken to the outside drill yard at the back of the building. Their pale faces tingled with the cool air as they watched lines of boys stretch their bodies to the left and to the right.

'This is Mr Smug, our drillmaster,' said Mr Nobbles.

Mr Smug was slim with high cheekbones and smelt of light sweat.

'Join in boys, we've nearly finished, but you'll know where to come tomorrow morning straight after breakfast,' said Mr Smug with a smile.

Stephen and Albert joined in at the end of the last line of boys and tried to follow the drillmaster's instructions. But their bodies were weary from so much change, and exercise was the last thing they wanted to do. Albert lost his balance and fell. Stephen just caught his brother in time, before he hit the floor. They lagged behind the others during a short run around the yard. It was soon over. Then lines of boys re-entered the four-storey building, with circles of air like candy floss leaving their dry lips and evaporating into the cool breeze. They seemed to know exactly where they were going. To Stephen's relief, Mr Nobbles re-appeared.

'Come now, boys, I shall show you our workshops, yes, our workshops,' he said.

'Do you have many, sir?' Stephen asked, wanting to sound interested.

'Oh yes, we have the carpenter's shop, the boot maker's, the wheelwright, the tinsmith, the blacksmith's, and the bakery. This is a chance for the boys here to learn a trade,' said Mr Nobbles.

'What's a workshop?' Albert whispered.

'I think we're going to find out, Albie.'

Mr Nobbles proudly led Stephen and Albert into different rooms on the ground floor. Each space was filled with the focus of young boys learning a trade that prepared them to leave the home and to fend for themselves.

'Is there anything that interests you, Stephen?' Mr Nobbles asked.

'I like making things, sir. I thought the carpenter's workshop looked interesting,' said Stephen.

'What about you, young Albert?'

'Eh . . . I think the carpenter's workshop too,' said Albert, wanting to say the bakery, but fearful it would mean being away from his brother.

'Well, well. We are now going to meet the schoolmaster. Come along,' said Mr Nobbles enthusiastically.

They entered another room with a huge window overlooking the back yard. A grey-haired man with a long moustache was leaning over a pile of books, sitting at a wooden desk.

'Mr Bains, these are the two who arrived late last night, Stephen and Albert,' said Mr Nobbles.

'Ah yes, I see,' said Mr Bains, peering over his round spectacles.

'Well, now . . . when was the last time you went to school?' Mr Bains asked curiously.

'It was a while ago now, sir,' said Stephen, having forgotten.

'What's that big round ball?' Albert asked.

'It's a globe ball with a map of the world on it, can you see?' Mr Bains spun it around slowly for the boys.

'I didn't know the world was so big,' said Albert.

'This is where we are, England,' said Mr Bains.

'We look so small, compared to the rest,' said Stephen.

'Yes, and this vast country here, is what we call Canada,' said Mr Bains, as his eyes drifted into the empty space beyond the globe.

'I don't think I'd like to go to Canada, I think I might get lost,' said Albert, peering up at the globe on Mr Bain's desk.

'But you'd have your brother to look after you, wherever you go,' said Mr Bains.

Albert smiled, feeling slightly reassured.

The door suddenly opened, and a group of children rushed in.

'Walk, don't run. Sit down quietly,' said Mr Bains.

The rows of desks soon filled as Mr Bains directed Stephen and Albert to sit near the front of the schoolroom behind two spare desks. Here, they waited to continue their geography lesson and find out more about the unknown country they had been introduced to. Stephen's right eye ached as he noticed John continue his icy stare across the schoolroom. Stephen tried to hide his discomfort by concentrating on Mr Bain's globe. But his mind wandered back to their grandparents' cottage, and he would have traded the stone floor with the shredded woollen blanket, his rags for clothes, and his mother's arms for everything that was clean and warm in this unfamiliar building with high ceilings and unknown faces.

As the first touch of twilight filled the early evening, the lesson came to a close. Stephen and Albert followed the others towards the kitchen for supper. Everything seemed orderly, even the way the boys walked from one area to another. It was as if there was a routine in every moment. Time could not be lost; there was always something in it.

Later that evening, the boys queued for their usual bath and prepared for lights out. Stephen climbed into the cot next to his brother, near the small window, and felt relieved that Albert's mind had been occupied throughout the day. He watched his brother sleep, with his tear-stained cheeks hidden beneath the cotton sheet and woollen blanket. Stephen's eyes caught the light from the changing full moon on a mission towards its next cycle. And the more he tossed and turned, wanting sleep to take over, to take away the memory of their reality, he remained wide awake. During the early hours of the morning, he could no longer put off the inevitable, and made his way quietly to the nearest lavatory. He tried to avoid the creaking floorboard near the door but stepped on the edge of it anyway. He froze in fear of waking the other boys, until he felt able to continue out of the dormitory and into the hall.

He entered the boys' lavatory and blinked in the darkness. Only a flicker of light came in at the window from the full moon. As he relieved himself he took a deep breath. Then he felt his way back to a wide shelf where he poured some water from a jug into a small basin to wash his hands. Looking for a towel, he turned to notice a shadow near the door.

'Who's there?' Stephen asked.

Out of the shadows, stepped John. His eyes flashed with contempt, as his right hand clenched into the shape of a fist.

'Who's there?' mimicked John, with distaste in the tone of his voice.

'I need to go back to the dormitory now,' said Stephen quietly.

'Look at you, sucking up to Mr Nobbles all day. Getting the grand tour of the premises,' snarled John.

'I don't know what you mean. I'm tired. I need to leave . . . now.'

But John's fist swung into action and bounced off Stephen's nose. Blood squirted all over his face and dripped onto the white cotton of his nightshirt, changing it to a deep red purple. Stephen gasped in agony as he felt the next punch almost perforate the insides of his stomach. But it was the kick to the groin that left him falling to the floor, with his mind racing towards a deep painful unconsciousness.

The door suddenly swung open, and Mr Nobbles grabbed John as he was about to swing his right foot into Stephen's head. But by this time John was hysterical, screaming that Stephen had attacked him first. Mr Nobbles dragged him into a nearby store cupboard and locked the door.

A small group of boys had heard the screams and hovered on the landing in the hallway.

'Go and tell Mr Hope to fetch the doctor from the hospital. He's downstairs clearing up the Carpenter's Shop. Make haste,' said Mr Nobbles to a boy who was standing near the wide staircase.

And he quickly returned to the bathroom, where he soaked a towel with cool water and tried to stop the flow of blood from Stephen's nose.

'There, there now . . . Stephen . . . Stephen, can you hear me?'

Stephen drifted in and out of consciousness. But he could clearly see the velvet sky before him and could almost touch it. He lifted his arm to reach out for a hand shrouded in dancing light that glistened in the darkness and moved gently towards him. He smiled out from the pain attacking his weary body, as he felt the sensations of comfort and healing from a source known only to him.

The doctor arrived with Mr Hope, and together they helped Stephen to his feet. He was taken downstairs and moved to the hospital wing in the building next door. There, he was told that his nose had not been broken, but they were going to keep him in overnight for observation. As soon as he was cleaned up, and the blood had stopped spurting from his nose, Stephen drifted into a deep sleep. Mr Nobbles asked the few boys who had woken from the noise to go back to bed, and he called the police.

The next day, Albert woke to an empty cot beside him. He rubbed his eyes and looked around for his brother. A feeling of panic struck his heart as he jumped up and ran out into the hallway.

'Stevie . . . Stevie . . . Stevie . . .' he cried, as he ran into the bathroom.

Mr Nobbles appeared in front of him.

'There, there now . . . don't you fret, Albert. Your brother is next door in the hospital. He's had a bit of an accident. Come with me, I will take you to him.'

'What's happened to him, sir . . . is he hurt?' Albert's voice quivered.

Mr Nobbles put his arm around Albert's shoulder as he led him downstairs, towards the hospital wing.

Stephen woke from a restless sleep to a kindly nurse, with clear blue eyes, like pools of water, leaning over him in a white apron.

'How are you feeling this morning, Stephen?' she asked softly.

'I don't know what happened,' croaked Stephen.

'Don't you remember anything?'

Stephen shook his head, and as he turned he noticed Albert running towards him.

'Stevie, I woke up and you weren't there,' cried Albert.

'I'm here, Albie. I promised to look after you, didn't I?'

Albert's whole body shuddered as he threw his arms around Stephen's neck.

'What happened to your nose?' Albert asked, as he peered at the white tape across it.

'I had a fall, in the bathroom,' said Stephen, glancing at Mr Nobbles.

Dr Cartwright appeared on the ward, ready for his early morning rounds. He stepped gently towards Stephen's bed.

'Well now, Albert, you can see that your brother is just fine. He's recovering well. You can stay with him for a short while,' said Dr Cartwright.

'Thank you, sir,' said Albert.

'Can I ask where John is, sir?' Stephen asked.

'He's in a safe place, where he can't do any harm. We will talk about it later in the day, when you're up and dressed,' said Mr Nobbles.

Stephen held his brother's hand to comfort him, determined to protect Albert from any further upset. Mr Nobbles spoke quietly to Dr Cartwright, in the far corner of the ward. Stephen noticed how they both seemed to nod gravely, as if they were agreeing some kind of plan, but he couldn't quite hear what they were saying.

'Excuse me, sir, I would like to get up now, and go with my brother,' said Stephen, concerned that Albert would be asked to leave the ward, and he wouldn't know where his brother was.

'I just need to put a clean dressing on your nose, and you can both go down to breakfast. Albert can wait for you in my office with Mr Nobbles,' said Dr Cartwright.

Stephen smiled with relief. And a reluctant Albert was led out of the ward, his gaze not leaving his brother for one second.

'Now then, Stephen . . . why don't you tell me what really happened last night, because you don't get injuries like this from a fall,' Dr Cartwright said gently.

'I went to the bathroom, and a boy called John followed me in. He wouldn't let me pass and just started punching me. I don't know why, sir,' said Stephen.

'You've done nothing wrong, so please don't blame yourself,' said Dr Cartwright kindly.

'I don't want my brother to know the truth. It will only upset him,' said Stephen.

Dr Cartwright smiled and agreed.

Later that morning, both Stephen and Albert were taken down to the kitchen for a late breakfast. It seemed even quieter than when they had first arrived, maybe because they had become accustomed to the clanking dishes and busy chatter. Now the space belonged only to them, until the time came when they were both summonsed to Mr Davies's office.

Mr Davies shuffled some papers around his desk and cleared his throat before speaking.

'I am sorry to hear about what happened to you last night, Stephen,' he said.

'Stephen fell and broke his nose,' said Albert.

Mr Davies raised his left eyebrow, and Stephen shook his head, in the hope that he wasn't given away.

'Yes, well I have asked to see you both because I have some news for you. We have decided to move you to Sheppard House. It's one of our smaller homes, and you will be leaving this afternoon. I would like you to go and gather your things and meet me in the hallway in thirty minutes,' said Mr Davies.

'Have we done something wrong, sir?' Albert's lips quivered.

'No of course not, Albert. Why don't you go ahead? I just need to ask Stephen to sign some papers,' said Mr Davies.

'It'll be okay, Albie, I'll follow you up,' said Stephen.

Albert closed the door slowly behind him.

'We need you to read and sign this statement. The police have taken John into custody, but I believe they are more worried about his mental state', said Mr Davies.

'Yes, sir,' said Stephen.

'We're sorry about this unfortunate incident, but we hope you and your brother will feel more settled at Sheppard House,' said Mr Davies.

'Thank you, sir,' said Stephen, as he signed his name and handed the statement back.

Then he left the office and found Albert sitting on the bottom step of the stairs.

'I thought they were taking you away, Stevie,' said Albert, as he ran towards his brother.

'No, Albie. I'm here,' said Stephen, holding Albert close to him.

Their short time at Stepney Causeway had come to an end. They were on the move again. It had only been two days, and they were staring once more into the face of change.

John was later admitted to a mental institution and would only answer to the name of Stephen . . .

*Sheppard House 182 Grove Road, East London*

STEPHEN LOOKED UP at the four-storey building, feeling disorientated. He noticed the bay windows on either side of the stone steps that led to the front door. They reminded him of Little Green Lane. The building seemed smaller than Stepney Causeway. He hesitated, as his mind flashed back to John in the bathroom.

'I want to go home,' Albert whispered, as he tugged at Stephen's arm.

'Maybe we will, Albie, soon,' Stephen said softly.

They entered the building, accompanied by Mr Davies. Stephen noticed the high ceiling in the hallway and a wide staircase to the right. There was a small man with no hair, peering over his spectacles from behind a counter on the left-hand side of the hallway. He smiled widely at Mr Davies, who cleared his throat.

'This is Stephen and Albert Edward Duckhouse. They've been transferred here for the time being.'

Mr Davies turned to Stephen and Albert. 'Mr Young will take care of you from here.'

'Good afternoon, sir,' said Stephen politely.

'You are very welcome . . . yes indeed,' said Mr Young, as the lines on his forehead folded into one.

Albert moved closer towards Stephen's shoulder.

'Why is he called Mr Young, when he looks so old?' Albert whispered.

But Stephen was too distracted as he watched Mr Davies leave the building, as he was his last link with home.

'Well . . . well, let me see now. We have up to a hundred and twenty boys here from the age of six to twelve,' he said proudly. 'I am sure you have noticed that the building isn't as big as Stepney Causeway, but we get along fine.'

A middle-aged woman with auburn hair, green eyes, and wearing an apron over her long blue dress, walked slowly towards them, smiling. Stephen felt a sense of relief when he looked directly into her eyes, but wasn't sure why.

'This is our Matron, Miss Ratcliff. I shall leave you in her kind hands,' said Mr Young, stroking the beads of sweat from his brow with his handkerchief.

'Good evening boys, it's Stephen and Albert, isn't it?' Miss Ratcliff asked.

They nodded.

'Follow me, and I shall show you to your dormitory. Then you can join us in the kitchen for supper,' said Miss Ratcliff, touching their cheeks softly.

They followed her up the steps to the third-floor dormitory, where they were shown two cots side by side, near the sash window.

'The bathroom is across the hall, first door on the left. It's usually quiet here. But if there's any sign of trouble, or if you want to talk to me about anything, you just come and find me. My sitting room is downstairs behind the staircase on the right-hand side. Look for the blue door with my name on,' said Miss Ratcliff.

'Thank you, Miss Ratcliff,' said Stephen, with Albert's echo not far behind.

'The other boys will be in their workshops for another half hour. I will leave you to settle in and will come back for you later to show you where the kitchen is downstairs,' she said.

Miss Ratcliff left the dormitory, with her kindness still lingering in the air.

'I can see the street from the window, Stevie,' said Albert, with his nose squashed against the glass.

'Look up, Albie . . . can you see the clouds? They've made a cross in the sky,' said Stephen.

Their eyes remained still in a moment that felt frozen in time, with their reflections looking back at them.

STEPHEN AND ALBERT found a way of settling into their new home. The atmosphere was quieter than Stepney Causeway, and less busy. The same routine continued with the drillmaster in the drill yard early morning after breakfast, workshops, and the schoolroom. Both Stephen and Albert attended the carpenter's shop and found the work a distraction from the sadness they continued to carry in their heavy hearts, like a hidden carving in the middle of a deep forest.

It was late one day, when Stephen overheard a small group of boys talking in the dormitory. He was only able to catch odd words from their muffled sounds, but enough to make him realise it was highly unlikely he and Albert would ever see home again:

*Canada . . . plans . . . huge ship . . .*

Stephen felt a shooting pain in the left side of his chest as he forced himself to stop retching. He checked on Albert and noticed he was asleep in the cot next to him. *I have to get out of here.* He lifted the sheet and woollen blanket away from his body where beads of sweat had stuck to his nightshirt. He wiped his wet forehead with his forearm and stepped onto the floorboards that creaked slightly out of rhythm with his racing heart. He closed the dormitory door quietly behind him as he made his way down the hallway until he found the wide staircase that led downstairs.

Mr Young was sitting at the front desk, his back upright but his head to one side with his eyes closed. Snuffled snores penetrated the air around him. Stephen crept slowly past him and continued until he found the blue door behind the staircase. He knocked gently. No answer came. He touched the door with both hands and his forehead, as if he wanted to become invisible and move through it unnoticed. His legs felt like they were about to give way beneath him, when he felt someone touch his shoulder from behind. He felt his whole body tremble out of control.

'Stephen, why aren't you in bed?' Miss Ratcliff asked, softly.

'I . . . I . . . just wanted to . . . talk to you,' choked Stephen.

He felt Miss Ratcliff put her arm around him, and she opened the door to her office. It was a small room with a desk and chair, a small oak bookcase and two armchairs.

'Sit down, Stephen, and tell me what's troubling you,' Miss Ratcliff said.

But Stephen was unable to move his body away from her and collapsed in her arms, sobbing until he retched and had to fight for his breath.

'It's okay, Stephen. You have a good cry, and when there are no more tears we'll sit down and talk this through,' said Miss Ratcliff, holding Stephen close to her.

But Stephen couldn't let go. This was the first female contact he'd had since leaving the arms of his mother, and the more he cried, the more his body collapsed, as he buried his head in her chest.

Stephen felt a long time had passed, as his sobs became less frequent, and his breathing slower. But his mind became empty as it shut down, feeling like he was trapped in a tunnel of dark oblivion.

'Come now, sit here, and I'm going to put this blanket 'round your shoulders. You're shivering. I'll just get another cup, you can share my cocoa,' said Miss Ratcliff.

'Thank y . . . you,' whispered Stephen, unable to find his voice.

Stephen drank the warm chocolate flavoured liquid and calmed down.

'Now then, does that feel better?' Miss Ratcliff asked.

Stephen nodded slowly and continued to drink from the china cup.

'I'm sorry . . .' murmured Stephen.

'You don't have to apologise to me, now tell me, has someone hurt you, Stephen?'

'No . . . nothing like that . . . I've just heard we might be going to Canada, and I thought we might be able to go home soon,' said Stephen, staring at the wall behind her.

'Oh . . . I see. Well, you know why your mother had to let you and your brother go, don't you?' Miss Ratcliff asked.

Stephen bit his lip and slowly nodded, not wanting to remember.

'Canada will be an opportunity to start a new life. When you come of age, you can always return to England if you want to,' said Miss Ratcliff.

'It seems so far away. I don't know what to say to Albie. I want to look after him, but sometimes I'm scared I won't be strong enough,' said Stephen.

'It is a time of uncertainty, but you will both be far better off, living with a family in Canada. You will have education, learn how to work a farm, have food and shelter,' said Miss Ratcliff.

'But I feel lost, and I miss my Ma . . . Can I see her to say goodbye?'

'I'm afraid it won't be possible to see your mother again . . . not until you reach the age of eighteen. It's understandable that you feel like you have no direction right now. But that will change, you'll see,' said Miss Ratcliff.

'I don't know how that can be possible,' said Stephen, his eyes flickering over the shelved books on the bookcase.

'Do you like to read, Stephen?' Miss Ratcliff asked.

'I like stories,' said Stephen.

'You can come to my sitting room and read one of my books, at any time if you want to. Don't ever feel you're alone, Stephen,' said Miss Ratcliff.

'Thank you,' said Stephen.

Miss Ratcliff reached for her Bible, from down the side of her armchair, and turned the pages slowly.

'Let's read something from the Book of Proverbs and see if it helps. Give me a number between one and thirty?' Miss Ratcliff asked.

'Three,' said Stephen.

Miss Ratcliff continued to turn the pages until she found proverb 3.6.

'Ahh . . . here we are. Listen carefully . . .'

*In all thy ways acknowledge God and He will direct thy ways.*

' . . . you see, there's no need to feel lost, Stephen. God has a plan for you. Trust in Him, and He will show you the way,' said Miss Ratcliff.

This was the first of many conversations with Miss Ratcliff, and her sitting room became a place where he felt comforted when he needed someone to listen, and he couldn't sleep, or if he just wanted to read quietly from one of the books from her bookcase.

But the time spent in care was one of uncertainty. Stephen and Albert had very little time to settle at Sheppard House before it was confirmed they were to join a party of 395 'Home Children' who were to be sent to Canada. Miss Ratcliff told the children, after supper one evening.

'I believe some of you have heard you will be leaving to go to Canada? Well, this is true. It will be an opportunity for you all to start a new life.'

'Canada? Is that the big country far away across the sea?' Albert asked, as he leant close to Stephen's ear.

'Yes, Albie, but we'll be all right. We have each other, don't we?' Stephen said.

'Will we ever see Ma again?' Albert whispered.

'I don't know, but don't worry, Albie . . . I said I would look after you. You'll be safe with me,' said Stephen, trying to reassure him.

At night, Stephen told Albert stories to comfort him. Albert's favourite was *Hansel and Gretel*, by the Brothers Grim.

> At the edge of a large forest lived a poor woodcutter with his two children and their stepmother. The children were called Hansel and Gretel. The family were very poor . . .

Stephen was certain that the reason why Albert loved this story so much was because in the face of adversity, the children find their way home through the woods, and all live happily ever after. He knew the stories from memory—and it was the only way he could be sure that Albert would sleep. He watched over his brother and sometimes mirrored the sadness in his eyes. But he knew he had to be strong.

*I am three years older than Albie.*

Stephen lay awake watching his younger brother sleeping—his short brown hair, pale skin, and blue eyes were a mirror to his own appearance. He continued to struggle to get to sleep, so he decided to get up and make his way downstairs. *I need to say goodbye to Miss Ratcliff.*

He crept towards her blue door and noticed it was open. He didn't need to knock.

'Come in, Stephen, I was expecting you. Are you having trouble sleeping?' Miss Ratcliff asked.

'Yes . . . I just wanted to say goodbye, as we're leaving early in the morning, and I might not get chance with everyone around,' said Stephen.

'I know, I shall miss you,' said Miss Ratcliff.

'Eh . . . thank you for letting me read some of your books,' said Stephen.

Miss Ratcliff smiled and opened the drawer to her desk. She pulled out a small package.

'I want you to have this, Stephen. It's just something I thought might help you on your journey. But I don't want you to open it until you are on the boat. Promise me now,' said Miss Ratcliff.

'I promise . . . thank you,' said Stephen, as he held the package covered in brown paper close to his chest.

'I've enjoyed our conversations. You have many gifts, Stephen, don't ever forget that,' said Miss Ratcliff.

Stephen removed his spectacles and wiped his eyes with his sleeve, unable to stop the tears any other way.

'There now, don't you cry. This is the start of a new life for you, and you take all my blessings with you,' said Miss Ratcliff.

Stephen felt her arms around him, as he buried his head into her chest. He couldn't bear to say goodbye. The words got stuck somewhere in the back of his dry throat. So, he remained silent whilst he stayed in the warmth of her closeness, praying she would never let him go.

Stephen returned to his dormitory and put the small package in his coat pocket. He looked to the end of his bed and noticed the dancing light of a silhouette that was always there at night, ever since he could remember.

*Stevie . . . don't be sad.*
*Annie, are you coming to Canada with us?'*
*Of course I'm coming, why wouldn't I?*
*I'm only asking.*

*Oh, but I'm not looking forward to that boat journey. It's not good for my balance. All those waves going up and down. I think I'll sleep through it, so don't talk to me on the way.*

*Okay, but what if I need to ask you something?*

*I shall consider how I'm feeling at the time. Really, Stevie! I can't always be available . . . I'm very busy you know?*

*Busy doing what?*

*Stuff . . . important stuff . . . oh never mind, you're just a boy, you wouldn't understand.*

*I'm going to sleep now. Goodnight, Annie.*

*(A distant voice echoed back to him. Eventually Stephen closed his eyes and allowed himself to drift into the restless night.)*

## SS Tunisian

THE DAY CAME to meet a new beginning, in the way Spring always came, with its inevitable appearance to change the season. Stephen and Albert left Sheppard House with a large group of other boys and girls, and were taken by train to Liverpool, their port of departure, supervised by Mr Price—a dark haired man with a moustache reaching for both ears and hazel eyes that squinted between a distant, but kindly stare.

Before leaving the port, the children enjoyed a tea party. Tea and cakes were served whilst a group of clowns demanded the children's attention from centre stage. Laughter filled the sunlit afternoon as the shadows from the canopies danced with the rhythm of the music. Finally, the mayor of London stood up to greet the children and wish them well on their new adventure. But Albert soon became bored and distracted.

'Look, Stevie, can you see the name of the ship?' he asked, straining his eyes to read it.

'It says *SS Tunisian*,' said Stephen.

'It looks so big,' whispered Albert as he slurped his tea.

The entertainment continued as the children were presented with a wooden trunk and a blue crayon to write their name and their allocated number inside. It was the number of their cot in the ship cabins. Stephen and Albert opened their trunks to discover new winter and summer clothes, boots, hats, handkerchiefs, a sewing kit, a tin of pins, thread and bobbin and writing materials. Their eyes widened, and wonder shone from their smiling faces as they touched each item with a mixture of fear and excitement.

'I've never seen so many clothes before,' said Stephen.

'Look, Stevie, we can write a letter to Ma . . . Maybe she's found enough money to take us home?' Albert waved his writing pad in the air.

Stephen smiled at his brother and choked on the silence that left him without words. He wrote the number seven above his name and helped Albert write his.

'Look Albie, you are number six. That means you're next to me.'

The trunks were closed, and each child had to carry their own onto the ship. Albert struggled to lift his, not realising just how heavy it was.

'Albie, there are wheels at each corner, see? You can slide it along beside you,' said Stephen.

Stephen held his brother's hand tightly as they walked slowly in line with hundreds of other children, holding on to their wooden trunks and each other, to take their last step on English soil together.

'I'm scared, Stevie,' whispered Albert, as his bottom lip quivered.

'Don't be scared . . . you're with me,' said Stephen, trying to sound reassuring, and trying to calm the ache in his right eye at the same time.

Stephen mirrored Albert's fear as they embarked on the biggest adventure of their young lives.

The two boys shared a cabin with ten other children. It was cramped, smelt of salt, and was full of noisy chatter.

'There's no air down here,' said Stephen, his right eye twitching.

His heart raced as he struggled to breathe. He clutched his chest as he felt himself losing his balance.

'Stevie . . . are you having one of them funny turns?' Albert asked.

'I'll be all right in a minute. I just need to sit down,' said Stephen, as he forced himself to breathe deeply.

Stephen sat on the bottom of one of the bunk beds as the room spun inside his head. He was relieved that the other boys were too distracted to notice. He closed his eyes and slowly felt calmer. *I wish Miss Ratcliff were here, she would know what to do.* He put his hand in his coat pocket and lifted out the small package that she had given to him, wrapped in gold paper. He opened it gently. It was a small blue book with orange flowers and yellow, brown, and green leaves on the sleeve. *Duchess Renee—An Episode In The History Of The Reformation by Sarson C.J. Ingham.* Stephen opened the sleeve of the book carefully, and his bottom lip trembled as he recognised Miss Ratcliff's handwriting inside . . .

With Love, From Miss Ratcliff, To Stephen Duckhouse, leaving England for Canada March 10th 1910. In all thy ways acknowledge God and He will direct thy ways. Prov-3.6. God Bless You.

Stephen removed his spectacles and wiped the tears falling from his face with his sleeve. He suddenly noticed Albert looking out of the small porthole as the ship started to pull out of port. Stephen's heart felt heavy and hollow, like it was missing something. He placed the book inside his coat pocket and stepped closer to Albert. He put his hands on his brother's shoulders and looked past him, determined not to continue to feel sad, or feel anything.

'Will you help me write a letter to Ma? She'll need to know where we are,' said Albert, turning around and looking directly into Stephen's eyes.

'Of course, I will. Let's go up on deck and find somewhere a bit quieter, where we can be on our own,' whispered Stephen.

He wasn't convinced any letter would ever reach their mother, but he went along with it anyway. It was an opportunity to leave the enclosed cabin below deck for a while. Stephen would have done anything to comfort and distract his brother from the painful truth of leaving behind the only home they had ever known. The boys climbed the steps to the top deck where it seemed even more crowded, with children huddled together in groups, and the ship's supervisors trying to keep order and control the level of vomit with tin buckets.


THE *SS TUNISIAN* sailed for eight days and nights through stormy, early spring weather. And when Albert was sea sick from the constant swaying of the ship, Stephen would reassure him that he would get used to the movement, only to run and throw up himself. But the journey became easier after the first three days and they felt a bit more settled as their destination drew closer.

It was during the fourth night when whispered fairy stories didn't help Albert to get to sleep, that Stephen suggested they creep up on deck. It was past midnight. The boys quietly tiptoed out of their cabin for fear of waking anyone and climbed the steps to the top.

'You're squeezing my hand,' moaned Albert.

'Shh . . . someone's coming.'

They ran back down the steps and hid in a dark corner. One of the crew whistled past them without noticing they were there. When Stephen knew it was safe, they began their climb again. Further and further they climbed until they reached the top of the deck.

'Take a deep breath and smell the sea air,' said Stephen.

Albert mirrored his brother by putting his hands on his stomach and breathing deeply through his nose. Then Stephen led Albert quietly to the edge of the deck where they watched the reflection of the full moon dance with the waves of the dark blue ocean.

'I've never seen the moon look so big,' said Albert in wonder.

Stephen pointed even higher to the surrounding vast purple skies.

'Look, Albie, we're following the stars,' he whispered softly.

Albert snuggled closer to his brother. 'I wish Ma was here, she always said she wanted to see the colour of the ocean,' he murmured.

Stephen held his brother tightly, so he couldn't see the tears he fought so hard to hide.

'Don't worry, Albie, Ma will find out where they've taken us and maybe we can come back for a visit, you'll see.'

'You promise?'

'I promise.'

Albert became convinced, but Stephen continued to feel secretly betrayed by his mother. *Does Ma know they are sending us to Canada?*

Suddenly, they heard low voices on deck, and a huge splash in the water, like a tidal wave.

'What's that noise?' Albert whispered.

Stephen squinted to try and make out the shadows in the surrounding darkness.

'I'm not sure, Albie. It looks like they're throwing something overboard . . . I can't make it out . . .'

*It's children . . . they're throwing children overboard.*

Stephen covered Albert's eyes.

'Don't look, Albie. We need to go back to the cabin,' said Stephen, fearfully.

'Hey, you two! What are you doing out of bed?'

The boys trembled at the bellowing sound of the assistant supervisor, as Mr Grunge's voice switched their emotion to fear. He scared most of the children, but he was also the subject of ridicule when he wasn't around. His gruff manner was cold and harsh. Stephen had heard he believed in tough discipline and demanded attention by yelling louder than anyone else. Children whispered in corners about the smell of whiskey on his breath. His black greasy hair was receding whilst his pointed beard always looked out of shape and in need of a trim. He was clearly overweight as he shuffled towards them.

'Get below deck, where you are supposed to be . . . and don't let me catch you up here again when past midnight! Do I make myself clear?'

'Yes, Mr Grunge,' echoed Stephen and Albert.

The boys ran past him and headed for the safety of their cabin where they collided with Mrs Potter.

'Come now, you two, it's way past your bedtime,' she said with a kind and gentle manner. 'You'll catch your death running around on this chilly night . . . hop into bed and let me have no more of your mischief.'

Mrs Potter's slim figure mingled with the shadows entwined within the cabin from the seeping light of the moon through the porthole. Her red cheeks glistened in the darkness as she tucked them both into their bunk beds, then she wiped her hands on her apron as she always did after every completed task.

'Goodnight children,' she whispered.

Stephen and Albert snuggled under their grey woollen blankets and welcomed the safety of sleep, with dreams of their passage back to England.

*St John, Canada*

THE *SS TUNISIAN* arrived at St John, Canada on 19th March 1910. Liverpool had been the biggest port they had ever seen, but this was on a completely different scale. They were instructed to form two lines and were slowly guided off the ship and onto land. Three-hundred-and-ninety- five Home Children had left England's shore. Those who survived the boat trip struggled to take in their new surroundings as their feet touched Canada's soil for the first time. Stephen held his brother's hand.

'It's like stepping out of Noah's Ark and discovering a new world,' said Stephen.

'But where are the animals?' Albert asked.

'Maybe we'll find some.' Stephen smiled.

All children were transported by steam train to either Hazelbrae for girls in Peterborough, or the Toronto home for boys—large homes that served as major distribution centres for Barnardo Home Children.

They waited patiently for their names to be called out. Stephen and Albert heard *Duckhouse* twice and boarded the first carriage. The steam lingered in the air of the station like a cloud of angel dust as children boarded for the closing part of their long and tiring journey into the unknown. Their vision was partly blurred until the steam of the train settled down, and they felt the rumbling of the oiled engine drive them forward towards their final destination.

*50-52 Peter Street Boy's Home, Toronto*

STEPHEN AND ALBERT were sent to the Toronto home for boys—an imposing building. They cast their wide eyes upwards at the surrounding tall buildings that loomed down on them as they walked along unfamiliar streets. It felt ten times bigger than England—wide and vast. Albert shuddered and wanted to cry, but the shock of seeing this huge city for the first time slightly distracted him.

'I don't like it here, Stevie. I want to go home,' said Albert.

'I know, Albie, but we're here now. Let's see it as an adventure,' said Stephen, trying desperately to be brave.

The children soon arrived at Peter Street, feeling tired and hungry. They walked slowly into a wide entrance hall with a high ceiling stretching above them. A tall, slim man with a curled moustache and pointed beard, and a wide, rosy-cheeked woman with frizzy red hair appeared through a doorway, from the side parlour. Their position allowed them the comfort and seclusion of their own private, well-furnished room.

'We're Mr and Mrs Griff, and we will be looking after you during your stay here. If you have anything important you want to talk about then Mr Owen is the superintendent in charge of this home. We have a household of ten staff, and we expect everything to run like clockwork. We do not tolerate any mischief . . . is that quite clear?'

Mr Griff's serious expression accompanied piercing, dark eyes that had a tendency to glare over the top of his spectacles.

'Yes, Mr Griff,' the children echoed together.

They proceeded to mumble and whisper together as they tried to make sense of his strange accent and take in their new surroundings. Mrs Griff clapped her big hands and demanded *quiet.* The children instantly became silent. Stephen kept his arm around Albert and held him close. He felt afraid of losing sight of his brother—but wasn't sure why.

They were escorted in an orderly manner, through a door to the right of the wide staircase and hallway, which led to a well-lit playroom that had been the former drawing room of the residence. The tall Georgian windows stretched from floor to ceiling and overlooked the colourful garden. The space was full of toys to capture the imagination of children of all ages—wooden hoops with sticks, marbles, skipping ropes, crock dolls, and a rocking horse majestically commanding the corner, tempting them to take a magical ride.

The kitchen downstairs had been converted into a dining hall, which led off to an annex, fitted as a lavatory. All staff slept on the second floor, whilst the children were shown a dormitory on the third floor where a hundred and fifty cots were laid out side by side, each with a grey blanket and white cotton pillow.

The day concluded with supper—potato and carrot soup, followed by a church service in a room with a stained-glass window that reminded Stephen of St Martin's in Birmingham. It was a routine they were not used to. Later that might, the brothers struggled to sleep, as their dreams were disturbed by the confusion and fear of the uncertainty that awaited them.

Stephen shivered in the swirling darkness and the crowded room of strangers snoring. He watched Albert's left eye flicker—a habit he had only recently developed—and his bottom lip tremble. Stephen reached out towards his cot and touched his brother's hand, trying to bring him comfort from yet another nightmare. He felt under his pillow for the book Miss Ratcliff had given to him and held it close to his chest.

*Annie, Annie . . . Annie, where are you?*
*I'm here.*
*I don't know what to do, Annie . . . I'm scared.*
*What are you scared of, the green-eyed monster?*
*This is no time for teasing. Can't you be helpful for once?*
*I'm here, aren't I? There's no need to be tetchy. You're safe.*
*Is there anything else I need to know?*
*When you want answers, read your book. It was given to you for a reason . . . no one's ever given me a book.*
*(Only then was he able to close his eyes and fall into the depths of sleep with a gentle dancing light shimmering just above his head.)*

# 4
# Tiger Lily

*"If a plant cannot live according to its nature, it dies; and so a man."*
— *Henry David Thoreau*

BEAMS OF LIGHT danced through the windows of *Peter Street Boys' Home*, as a brand-new day dawned in a different world. A light breeze rustled through the papery white birch, and the scaly grey-brown maple barks nearby—homes to unknown bird songs of the early morning. It was a joyful spring sound, in contrast to the empty, dark silence that ripped in synchronicity through Stephen and Albert's tormented, hollow hearts . . .

The boys awoke to stare at a chalk white high ceiling, a canvas of emptiness in a dormitory of strangers, with a twisted mix of fear and uncertainty piercing the nervous energy around them. Stephen reached for his brother's hand, and a gentle warmth tingled through their veins, as fingers entwined with a sense of familiarity. They shared a reassuring look from the depths of reflective fear spilling from their eyes.

A loud bell rang out into the silent, stifled room. Stephen and Albert forced themselves to get up and follow the other boys in line, like tin soldiers, waiting. They joined the back of the queue.

'Come along, boys, make your way to the washroom,' said Mr Sharp, a small round man with an elongated nose and thin lips lining crooked teeth.

'What's a washroom?' Albert whispered.

Stephen shrugged, unsure what to say.

The dormitory supervisor handed out cotton towels with a warm smile. Stephen saw a towel drop to the floor and noticed a freckled, ginger haired boy standing behind him, smiling serenely but reflecting a sense of something lost in his deep, misty eyes.

*I thought I was the last one out of the dormitory . . .*

'You dropped your towel,' said Stephen, handing it back to the boy.

'Thank you . . . I hadn't realised I was holding it,' he said softly.

'What's your name?' Stephen asked.

'I'm John.' The pale-skinned boy grinned.

Stephen quivered at the sound of the familiar name. His mind flashed back to England and the physical pain on his bruised and bloody face. But then a different sensation emerged as a stream of light shone halfway between their eyes.

'Did you come over on the boat?' Stephen asked, suddenly feeling curious and uplifted.

'Oh yes . . . I was there. Maybe you just didn't notice me,' said John.

'I don't remember . . .'

'It's Stephen, isn't it?'

Stephen trembled at the thought of a stranger knowing his name.

'I heard Mr Sharp call you earlier,' said John, reassuringly.

Albert snuggled closer to Stephen's chest, seeking the touch of skin that was so familiar.

'Oh, and this is my brother, Albie,' he said quietly, as he gently put his arm around him.

'Hello,' said John.

But Albert's eyes continued to stare downward, as if willing the floorboards to burn away and transport him back into a different time.

'Where did you live in England?' Stephen asked, curious.

'London . . .' said John.

'Come, come now, boys, let's not delay, move along the queue,' said Mr Sharp, in a very distracted way.

'I'll look out for you at breakfast,' said Stephen, turning back to John.

They both smiled, as if holding in mind an elated glimpse from an old friend . . .

Stephen and Albert made their way towards the next free washbasins. Stephen held the bar of soap tightly between his fingers and washed his face diligently, splashing the warm water over his closed eyes, as he felt a slight sense of exhilaration, and imagined himself back on the soil of his hometown, in the arms of his mother. But reality replaced the moment of fantasy, when he heard Albert cry out in pain.

'Albie! What's happened?' Stephen reached out.

But Albert's body lay on the tiled floor, trembling uncontrollably. Stephen knelt down to help his brother. Mr Todd, the boys' personal supervisor, rushed over to the incident. His right eye twitched, to mirror Stephen's, as his slim gaunt body bent over Albert.

'We need more towels, Mr Sharp. The boy's stone cold,' said Mr Todd, with a calm assertive edge to his voice.

'Albie . . . Albie . . .'cried Stephen.

Mr Todd wrapped Albert's shaking body in bundles of towels and carried him back to the dormitory. Stephen followed.

'He has a pulse . . . it's probably just shock, but I'll go and fetch Dr Hart, just to be sure,' said Mr Sharp, holding Albert's wrist.

Albert slowly drifted back into consciousness, unaware of his surroundings, as his frail body became still.

'Ma . . . Ma . . . I don't feel well . . . can I have some soup?' Albert cried.

Stephen's eyes burnt with the sensation of dry tears.

'The boy's gone mad . . . you're here at Peter Street . . . remember? Mr Sharp has gone to fetch the doctor . . . let me see your shoulder,' said Mr Todd.

'He's slipped on the floor, sir, I think he's just upset,' said Stephen, desperately trying to defend his brother, as the memory of John being whisked away to some unknown mental institution flashed before him.

But Mr Todd was far too focused on bringing Albert back to a world he thought he might be in danger of leaving behind.

'You'll have a fine bruise there . . . let's see what Doctor Hart thinks,' said Mr Todd, with a lisp and kind tone.

'Thank you,' said Stephen politely, grateful for the way Mr Todd supported his brother.

'What happened to your fingers?' Mr Todd asked, noticing Albert's phalanges missing from his left hand.

Albert's bottom lip trembled, and his voice fell into silence.

'The rag and bone man's horse crushed them by accident when we were playing at home on the street. It still upsets him to talk about it, sir,' said Stephen, answering for his brother.

*At home . . . on the street . . .*

Mr Todd discontinued his investigation, his curiosity satisfied. He pulled the cotton sheet and woollen blanket over Albert. The door opened swiftly, and Dr Hart entered the room, clutching a black bag, with a stethoscope wrapped around his bulging neck, where his chin rested from the weight of it.

'Is this the boy in question?' Dr Hart asked, squinting over round spectacles.

Dr Hart proceeded to examine Albert with an elegance that came with experience.

'He has a bit of a bump to the head and a few bruises, but he'll heal,' said Dr Hart, convincingly, as he reached into his black bag.

'Am I going to die and get thrown in the sea, Doctor?' Albert asked weakly.

'Eh . . . now we'll have no more talk of dying. I want you to take this, with water. It's just a Beecham's pill. It will make you feel better. And rest for a while.'

Albert choked as he sipped from the plastic beaker.

'He gets scared when he's alone. Can I stay with him, sir?' Stephen asked. 'Just for a while.'

Dr Hart left, with the shadow of Mr Todd behind him. Stephen sat on the edge of Albert's cot. He gently touched the top of his head and stroked his forehead with his thumb. His tears mingled with pearls of water dripping from Albert's dark brown hair, down his pale cheeks. But Stephen could only see the emptiness of the distant stare crawling from his brother's eyes.

LATER THAT DAY, Stephen helped his brother down the wide spiral staircase. Albert had realised he was hungry. The children gathered in the dining room below the grand staircase—boys queued sedately, with their heads bowed, staring at the unknown floor beneath their feet, as they waited. They had spent hours, days, and months waiting . . . to know their destiny. Were they any closer? Still weary from the long journey of the day before, they slowly found their voices.

Stephen put his arm around Albert and guided him towards empty chairs at the end of a long wooden table. They struggled to lift their tired feet, every step taking them further away from the life they had known. The brightly painted room echoed the sounds of quiet chatter and copper spoons clanging in rhythm against the basins full of vegetable soup. But Stephen could only hear his mother's voice, as an eruption of sadness continued to break his heart piece by piece. He felt heavy from an energy that weighed him down. Albert slurped his soup, unable to lift his head in fear of truly noticing the reality of this strange and unfamiliar place. Stephen was suddenly distracted from a lost world inside his head.

'Hello . . .' came a soft voice.

Stephen looked up to notice John.

'I missed you at breakfast. How's your brother?'

'He seems to have recovered. Just some bruises,' said Stephen.

John leaned forward across the wooden table, closer to Stephen, and whispered, 'Do you think you'll be happy in Canada? It's very different from England.'

'It just feels such a long way from home, everything we've ever known. Even the air feels heavy. I can hardly breathe.'

'You'll get used to it . . . things will start to become more familiar with time, you'll see,' said John.

'How can you know that? You've only just arrived yourself,' said Stephen.

'My Ma used to tell me I was an old soul . . . you've been 'round before, she'd say,' whispered John.

'What happened to your family?' Stephen asked.

'They died suddenly. It was cholera that killed them,' he said.

'I'm sorry, and yet you survived?' Stephen asked.

'Death comes to us all in the end,' said John.

'Are you by yourself now?'

'I never feel by myself . . . sometimes we walk alone when we least expect it, and we just have to keep walking, no matter how much it might hurt. There's a difference between being alone and loneliness,' said John.

'I don't know what I'd do without my brother. He's my last link with home,' said Stephen.

'Your brother will always be in your heart, no matter what happens.'

'That's comforting to know.'

'I always find it helps when I look up at the sky . . . it seems to speak back to me,' said John.

Stephen's eyes glistened from a reflective light shimmering between him and John, as they moved closer to each other. A warm tingling sensation flowed through his veins, as he felt lost in the hypnotic moment. And a transcendent strength reached into his heart that left him floating on air . . . until he heard the deep tone of Mr Griff's voice and noticed his dark eyes squinting over the top of his spectacles.

'Quiet children!'

Stephen turned his head to listen carefully to Mr Griff.

'When you've finished your dinner, I want you all to follow Mr Garner. Put on your coats and walk slowly towards the garden for some recreation time. The sun is shining brightly this fine afternoon,' said Mr Griff, smiling widely.

'Come on, Albie, let's get our coats,' said Stephen.

He looked across the table to continue his conversation with John, but found himself staring at an empty chair.

'Albie, did you see where John went?' Stephen asked.

'Who?'

Albert remained indifferent and shrugged.

Stephen was surprised to see that John had gone. He looked all around the dining room, in the hope of seeing his new friend again. But the pale-skinned boy had disappeared.

The children returned to their dormitory to fetch their coats. Albert struggled with his buttons. Stephen helped him, as he always did, easily sliding them into place, from the top of his purple, velvet collar down to just below his waist.

'There, don't you look the gentleman,' said Stephen, teasing.

They walked together down the staircase, through the hall, and out into the garden. The lawns stretched for miles in front of them. Flowerbeds edged their way across the boundaries of the land. Their eyes shone, capturing reflections from the bright sunlight that danced upon the yellow and orange blooms—later to become known to them as *Balsamroot;* petals ranging from blue, purple, and pink that they would come to recognise as *Lupine.*

Stephen bent down near the flowerbeds, with an intense curiosity.

'Look, Albie, I've never seen anything like this before. Can you see the orange petals with black spots and lines? It looks so different to the flowers in England,' said Stephen.

'Why don't the lines join the dots, so they are together?' Albert asked.

They both stared at the flower, almost waiting for it to speak back to them. But only silence returned as the sun danced its reflective light between them . . . until the quiet spell was broken.

'I miss the flowers in England. I want to go home, Stevie,' said Albert, crouching beside him, holding his stomach.

'Are you still in pain from when you slipped over, Albie?' Stephen asked looking concerned.

Albert's lips trembled.

'Why hasn't Ma written us a letter? She promised.'

'Listen, Albie, you're just feeling homesick right now. It will pass. Maybe Ma has written to us, and her letter's just been held up. We're a long way from home remember, anything could have happened to it. Let's just try and make the most of our time here, until we find out which farm we're going to,' said Stephen, as he put his arm around his brother.

'Shall we write another letter, just in case Ma missed the first one?' Albert asked.

'We'll do it later tonight when everyone's asleep,' said Stephen.

Albert found a small remnant of a smile hidden away behind the pain of grief.

'Ah, you've found the Tiger Lily,' said Mr Garner, bending down with his chest meeting the round belly that hung like elastic over his black trousers.

'Yes, sir, we were just saying how different it is, from any flower we've seen before', said Stephen politely.

'Well now that's interesting, because the Tiger Lily comes from a place called St Albert, a city in Alberta, Canada,' said Mr Garner enthusiastically.

'That is very interesting, sir,' said Stephen glancing at his brother.

But Albert didn't make the connection.

'So how are you both settling in, after your long trip from England?' Mr Garner inquired in a friendly manner.

Albert bowed his head, and silent words choked from the back of his throat.

'He's just a bit shy, sir,' said Stephen, a pink glow burning his cheeks.

'Ah . . . it might feel a bit strange here at first, but you'll both get used to it. I'll leave you to enjoy the garden,' said Mr Garner as he stepped away, carrying his weight like a bag of heavy potatoes waiting to be prepared for tomorrow's dinner.

'I don't like it here, Stevie. It's all mixed up. Why is everything so big?' Albert whispered.

'Let's not offend Mr Garner, Albie. He's just trying to be nice,' said Stephen.

But as Stephen stared at the Tiger Lily, the more his right eye twitched until it ached.

'Look, Stevie, what are they doing over there?' Albert asked, determined to pull Stephen away from the flowerbed.

Children mingled in small groups, playing different games—hopscotch, skipping, and marbles on the terrace, supervised by Mr Stretch, whose long lean body towered over the children, and whose hazel eyes shone beneath the sunlight.

'Stick to the path now, boys,' said Mr Stretch, as they beat their wooden hoops with sticks along a narrow, paved path that split the freshly cutgrass.

But Stephen was distracted as he strained his eyes at a shape that separated the green from the flower borders. 'Look, Albie! There's a heart in the grass!'

They both stared at the clear-cut silhouette, moving their heads slightly to the side, in disbelief.

'Is that what our heart looks like inside our chest?' Albert asked.

'I don't know Albie . . . maybe . . .' said Stephen.

'Does it mean our hearts are green?'

'Does it matter, Albie?

'Well, I like green, it's my favourite colour,' said Albert.

Then Albert's attention wandered to something he found far more interesting. Stephen followed his brother over to where a group of boys were playing leapfrog. Two lines of boys were bent strategically over their stomachs, almost touching their toes. They waited patiently for members of their team to leap over their curved back and race to the finish line.

'Can we play?' Albert asked.

Stephen smiled slightly as he noticed the first sign of interest his brother had shown in anything since they had started their journey together.

'Are you sure you're up to it, Albie? What about your bruises?' Stephen asked.

'Please, Stevie, I feel better now,' said Albert.

They joined the two queues and waited their turn.

'Watch me jump, Stevie . . . watch me . . . I bet I can jump higher than you . . .' said Albert.

Stephen breathed deeply as he gently removed his spectacles and put them inside his coat pocket to protect them, before the race began against his brother. But Albert wasn't quite tall enough to make the leap over the first boy bending down, and instead collapsed on top of him, which resulted in them both falling to the ground and rolling in the grass. The race came to a sudden halt, and the boys from both teams laughed loudly, beneath a line of invisible hysteria— louder than they had laughed in a long time.

Mr Todd appeared from the silhouette of the back door of Peter Street and called Stephen's name. It was a while before Stephen heard Mr Todd's voice, for the sound of laughter continued to echo round the garden as he helped his brother to his feet.

'Stephen Duckhouse! Follow me,' he repeated above the noise.

Stephen looked up to notice Mr Todd's stern expression as he tried to make himself heard. He walked across the lawn towards him and followed attentively, looking back at Albert, who seemed determined to conquer leapfrog.

Mr Griff was waiting in the main hall, at the reception desk, holding something in his hand.

'A letter has just arrived for you from England,' said Mr Griff.

'Thank you, sir,' said Stephen with an elated smile.

Stephen walked politely away, over the grey tiles until he reached the back door, holding the letter gently in his hand. As soon as he was outside, he stared at the weather-stained envelope, and the faded stamp with the head of the King staring back at him. But it was his mother's handwriting that made his fingers tremble and his heart beat faster than a steam train.

*I must find Albie.*

He made his way outside and into the slight breeze dancing with speckles of light from the falling sun on the horizon, and noticed his brother running in different directions, screaming, 'Stevie . . . Stevie . . . Stevie . . .'

Mr Sharp was trying frantically to catch him, but Albert was far too fast and determined to escape. Stephen's heart pounded through his chest as he ran towards his brother.

'Albie . . . Albie . . . I'm here,' shouted Stephen.

Albert's exhausted body suddenly crashed into Stephen.

'I thought you'd left me,' cried Albert hysterically.

'No, Albie, I'll never leave you. I promise,' said Stephen, holding him tightly until his breathing became calmer.

Mr Sharp appeared, gasping at their side, with his hands on his hips.

'Well, well . . . what happened to make you feel so upset?' Mr Sharp asked Albert.

But Albert continued to hide his face, burrowing against Stephen's chest, a place where he felt safe and protected.

'I think he just misses home, sir,' said Stephen.

'Yes . . . well that's to be expected,' said Mr Sharp, clearing his throat.

'I'll look after him, sir,' said Stephen.

'That shows a lot of maturity, Stephen, thank you,' said Mr Sharp.

He strolled back into the circle of children who were standing frozen on the green cutgrass.

Stephen led Albert towards the flowerbeds and the Canadian holly bush at the end of the garden, where they found a small wooden bench, out of sight. The maple tree beside them stretched over their heads and its leaves whispered their song on the wings of the breeze, reaching through the branches.

'Look, Albie, we've had a letter from Ma,' said Stephen.

Albert's tear-stained eyes suddenly found new life as he stared at the black ink in his mother's handwriting.

'It came. Ma said she would write. Stevie, read it . . . read it,' said Albert, trembling with excitement.

Stephen opened the letter slowly, not wanting to tear the precious leaf in his hand. He read the words with a voice that quivered from the back of his dry throat . . .

March 10th, 1910
c/o Barnardo's
Dear Stevie and Albie,

I can only hope this letter reaches you both, and you are safe and well. I cannot tell you how much I miss you, more than anything. Wherever you are in the world I want you to know that I will always love you, with all my heart. You are never far away from my thoughts. I want you to know that I hope and pray that one day you will understand how hard it was for me to make the decision to let you go. In the end I don't believe there was a decision to make. With decisions usually come choices. But I had no choice. Without money I couldn't provide for you. I fought so hard to keep us all together as a family, but it was an uphill battle, that I lost. I could no longer watch you suffer, without food or money. I wish our lives could have been different, and I had the chance to watch you grow up. But life doesn't always give us what we wish for.

Grandpa and Grandma send all their love. Fred is still working for Uncle James in the butcher's shop, and he comes over and reads me the newspaper at the end of the day. John hasn't found work yet and is sleeping on the floor in the shop until something turns up. It seems to be so hard to come by these days. George has just got some more shifts at the factory, which is a blessing, and Walter is growing up so fast. We all miss you every day. I would give anything just to have one more glimpse of you, and hold you close to me.

Stevie, I hope you receive this letter in time for your Birthday this month, because I want to wish you many happy returns. I don't even have to ask because I know you are watching over Albie, as you always have. I want you both to promise me that you will always be brave and strong and kind and remember me in your prayers at night. I will write again with more news as soon as I can. In the meantime, I am sending all my love, and I am so very proud of you both.

God bless you,

Ma

Albert snuggled closer to Stephen, as the image of their mother seemed to speak to them as if she was right there in that moment, sitting on the bench between them.

'Do you remember when Ma took us to the Bullring on Christmas Eve?' Albert murmured.

'Yes, Albie, and we sat in front of Nelson's statue.'

'I wish Ma was sitting on this bench with us now,' whispered Albert.

Stephen choked on the silence that got stuck somewhere inside his brittle throat as he fought to hold back the tears that fell like a waterfall behind his closed eyes.

'Read it again, Stevie . . . read it again . . .'

THE NEW MOON cast a light sparkle through the square window of the boys' dormitory, whilst the chaotic rhythm of snores, with the ticking oak-cased dial clock hanging from the wall, clustered in the stifled air. Stephen sat upright in his cot, staring at the million stars blinking back at him from the darkness of the black sky, with a streak of red across the horizon. *Ma would say it's going to be a nice day tomorrow.* His eyes reflected a determination to stay awake. He had promised Albert they would write a letter to their mother, but Albert had fallen asleep as soon as his head had touched the white cotton pillow. *Maybe tomorrow . . .*

Stephen reached inside his trunk beneath the cot and his fingers found the journal he had kept with him since he had said goodbye to his family in England. He wrote diligently on the next blank page with his sharpened pencil. His eyes strained a little through his round spectacles, but glimmers from the stars gazing through the window guided him.

March 22nd 1910

I met a new friend today, but he seems to have disappeared. I hope I see him again. I feel so alone here. I don't know what I'd do if Albie wasn't here with me. I'm trying so hard to be strong for him, but I don't know which one of us needs the other the most. I can't tell anyone how scared I feel. They might think I'm mad and send me away to some mental institution. I want to be all the things Ma said in her letter, but I don't feel brave. I have to hide how I really feel because if I start crying, then I don't think I will be able to stop. I miss everything in England. I didn't know you could feel this unhappy and still be alive. God please help me to accept the way things are and be strong enough to face another day.

Stephen hid his journal under clothes inside his trunk. He laid his head to the side and closed his dreary eyes as the last remnants of the night drifted away into the enclosing darkness.

THE NEXT MORNING after breakfast, all boys congregated in the small yard next to the garden with Mr Stretch for drill exercise. They extended their tired bodies up towards the pale blue cloudless sky as the sun rose to welcome a new day. The slow pace of the exercise suddenly moved to another dimension with star jumps on the spot.

'I want to go back to bed, Stevie, I don't feel well. I still feel sick and keep seeing the big waves from the sea come over my head. I can't breathe,' said Albert.

'Albie, we're not on the boat now. You're probably just tired. It was a long journey,' said Stephen.

But Albert started to retch from the depths of his stomach, choking in a corner of his throat where he had no control. Then the breakfast porridge appeared from his mouth and soared over Stephen. Everyone froze, like a slide from a silent movie.

'Oh, for goodness' sake boy, why didn't you go to the wash room?' Mr Stretch asked in an irritated tone of voice.

'Albie,' said Stephen, split between concern for his brother and what was sliding down his trouser leg.

'What's your name, boy?' Mr Stretch asked.

But Albert continued to choke with the stench of vomit seizing the air around him. The sound of synchronised moans echoed from other children's lips, as they turned their faces away.

'Shall I take him upstairs to the wash room, sir?' Stephen asked politely.

'Yes . . . yes, you better had. We'll leave it there for this morning. Everyone, make your way to the library for your history lesson. You boys come with me and we'll find Mr Todd. He can assist you,' said Mr Stretch.

Stephen helped Albert towards the back door where they met Mr Todd in the hallway.

'Well, this is a fine mess you've got yourselves into,' said Mr Todd.

'I don't think he's used to the food, sir,' said Stephen.

'Yes, well, it's not the first time, and I'm sure it won't be the last. It must all seem very different for you here,' said Mr Todd, guiding them upstairs towards the washroom.

'Yes, sir,' said Stephen, with his eyes burning every step he climbed to the top landing.

They removed their vomit-riddled clothing to emerge into a bath of warm silken water. Their bodies tingled at the touch of tiny splashes, their pent-up emotions spiralling inside, with the antiseptic vapours revitalizing them. Stephen held a bar of orange coal tar soap close to his nose and took the deepest breath . . .

When they had changed into clean clothes, Mr Todd agreed that Albert could lie down for a while and rest. Stephen stayed with him beside his cot, holding his hand.

'I miss Ma,' whispered Albert.

The words were like an electric current firing through the skin of Stephen's fingers.

'Me too,' Stephen whispered back.

Albert fell into a shallow sleep.

'Why don't you go downstairs and join the others in the library,' said Mr Todd, appearing at the dormitory door.

'Yes, sir,' said Stephen as he slowly let go of his brother's ice-cold hand.

STEPHEN ENTERED THE library on the ground floor, only to find an empty room as the lesson was over. He looked through the huge square window and noticed children playing outside, reading, lost in their own contemplation, lying in the freshly cut grass looking up at the pale blue sky. He turned his attention inside the spacious room with floor to ceiling books and felt millions of stories reflect back at him, from centuries of lost time.

He felt an arm reach over his shoulder.

'Hello . . .'

Stephen turned to notice John smiling through grey crooked teeth.

'Where did you come from?' Stephen asked curiously.

'I've not been well since the boat trip, so I've been resting,' said John.

'I didn't know where you'd disappeared to,' said Stephen.

'I've been here . . . I'm always here,' said John.

Stephen felt relieved to see his friend again, without understanding why. He only knew that a warm calm feeling filled his heart whenever he was near.

'Did you go to the History lesson?' Stephen asked.

'No . . . I've been waiting for you. Have you ever read Dickens?'

John removed the brown orange sleeve from the shelf and a spray of dust caught the chilled air between them.

'I don't remember,' said Stephen.

'Let's sit down, over here by the window,' said John.

Stephen glanced at the title of the book that John lay out on the small oak table, with the sunlight reflecting through the window and leaving sparkles in the eyes of the wood.

'*A Tale of Two Cities*. What's it about?' Stephen asked, peering through his spectacles.

'The French Revolution. Life and death . . . they're like two sides of the same coin,' answered John.

'Didn't they use a guillotine to chop people's heads off?' Stephen asked, remembering a lesson from his schooldays in England.

'They still do in France. The angled blade comes down onto the neck with such a force, the head falls into a basket below, with one swift blow. It must be a painless way to die . . . it would be over in a second,' said John.

'It sounds cruel to me. Why do we have to kill each other because we don't agree with someone else? It makes no sense,' said Stephen.

'Because sometimes we have no choice. We have to fight for what we believe in, even if it causes us the deepest pain . . . we're doing it for the greater good.'

John opened the sleeve of the book and flicked through, until he found what he was looking for. He cleared his throat, and Stephen noticed how his facial skin became paler like chalk dust in the strands of sunlight dancing through the window. He read from one of the pages within the book.

> Think now and then that there is a man who would give his life,
> to keep a life you love beside you.

'I don't understand,' said Stephen.

'Read the book,' said John.

The door flew open, and a gust of wind blew into the library, and carved a chill across the heated air. Two boys entered, waving sticks in their determination to win a sword fight, with a group of boys behind them looking disinterested, as they made their way towards the stained wooden shelves and feasted their eyes on the many sleeves before them.

'What's going on in here?' Mr Griff appeared.

The two boys looked downcast, as they murmured a weak apology and left without hesitation.

'Let's have some respect for the library area, boys. It's supposed to be a quiet space outside of lessons,' said Mr Griff, as he left with the door open behind him.

Stephen's focus became blurred as everyone faded away, until a dancing light around a silhouette smiled through crystal blue eyes. Her fair curls tangled around pure white skin shining from her face.

*Annie*

*I'm here, Stevie . . . I'm always here . . . Did you think you were rid of me?*

*I want to go home, Annie.*

*You have to try and accept that this is your home now. It won't be forever. Keep your journal close to your heart, and always hide it in a secret place. Don't let anyone read it. And when you write, that's the time when you can let go of your feelings, and write what you really think, instead of always asking me questions, like I can predict the future!*

*But it's not the same as being at home.*

*Nothing's the same in the real world.*

*What do you mean?*

*Get a grip!*

The pages of the book distracted Stephen, as if they opened with a life of their own, but he could only stare at the empty chair beside him.

*Where did John go? He must have left with the others.*

THE NEXT DAY Stephen returned to the library with Albert for their first History lesson. The room was full of children's rhythmic chatter until Mr Cartwright entered, clutching a leather-bound book to his chest. Everyone stood to acknowledge his presence.

'Be seated, children,' said Mr Cartwright, twitching his nose beneath the eyeglass balanced between his thick bushy brows and the top of his left cheekbone. The children did as they were instructed and sat down at the benched desks in three rows.

'Today, we are going to learn about the history of Canada, the Aboriginal people, which means the original inhabitants, the people who were here first. We are going to look specifically at the early settlers, the Inuit and the Metis . . .'

Mr Cartwright's voice became lost to Stephen as he looked around the room for John, but his attention soon returned when he noticed Mr Cartwright squinting through his eye glass, as if burning through his brain and down into his ears to make him listen. Stephen looked alert and focused, but his mind wandered until he heard, 'Now . . . The Indian Act dates from 1876 . . .'

He suddenly became interested in the tribes from Canada and their spiritual way of life, as if he resonated with them from a distant time he had long forgotten, planted deeply into the layers of his mind. The lesson moved towards its close, and Mr Griff appeared at the door, blocking the light from the hallway.

'Sorry to disturb you, Mr Cartwright . . . is Alfred with you?' Mr Griff asked, clutching a clipboard and an inked pen.

'Alfred . . .'said Mr Cartwright, addressing the children.

But only silence returned from within the walls of the library.

'Are you sure we have an Alfred? There's an Albert in the class,' said Mr Cartwright.

'No . . . no . . . it definitely says Alfred here, on my list,' said Mr Griff, wiping the pearls of sweat from his forehead with his handkerchief.

Mr Griff left the room. Stephen's right eye flickered as he looked at his brother, who stared into the empty space before him.


THE DAYS TURNED slowly through late March, until the twenty- seventh day. Stephen woke from his restless sleep to notice Albert half smiling from his cot next to him.

'I got you a surprise, Stevie. Look under your pillow,' whispered Albert.

Stephen lifted his head to pull out a white piece of card with black ink scribbled over it.

'Happy Birthday, Stevie, love Albie, with three kisses,' said Stephen.

When Stephen opened it up, his eyes widened at the tiger lily flower inside.

'I picked it from the garden when no one was looking,' said Albert, mischievously.

'Ah, thanks, Albie, but you must promise me you won't pick any more flowers. I don't want you getting into trouble,' said Stephen.

'I promise.'

'Have you scribbled ink on the flower?' Stephen asked as he squinted inside the card.

'I've joined up the dots,' said Albert.

Stephen reached out to put his arms around his brother. They held each other close, until their breath was ready to burst upwards into the cool air.

Later that same day Stephen and Albert returned to the bench at the end of the garden, as they had done since their arrival. They hid from sight behind the Canadian holly bush, the only place they found they could be alone and find some peace in their world of fearful uncertainty. Stephen opened the page of *A Tale of Two Cities* and continued to read to his brother:

*There is prodigious strength in sorrow and despair . . .*

Until the sound of Mr Todd's voice disturbed their equilibrium and they drifted away from their imagination and into the reality of their situation.

'Stephen Duckhouse . . . Stephen! Has anyone seen him?'

Stephen closed the book, placed it on the wooden bench between them, and stepped from behind their secret place.

'I'm here, sir,' said Stephen.

'Ah, there you are. Follow me, you're needed in the main hall,' said Mr Todd.

Stephen followed Mr Todd, with Albert behind him. But he shuddered as he stepped over the green heart at the side of the cut grass. He reached out for Albert's hand.

Inside the hallway he noticed Mr Griff scanning a clipboard, held upright and stiff in hands recently washed with coal tar soap. Mr Owen was standing next to him. The superintendent had clean-shaven white skin over thin chiselled cheeks, rose coloured, thin parted lips, and a few strands of hair combed over to the left side of his shiny head.

Mr Griff cleared his throat, put down his clipboard meticulously, and hitched up the material of his trousers that didn't know whether to go above or below his stomach.

'Stephen Duckhouse . . . you are to leave today for Eurach Farm in Wentworth, where you will live and work as a domestic for the McPhail family,' said Mr Griff with his usual serious tone.

'What about Albert?' Stephen asked politely.

'I only have your name here for Eurach Farm. I don't have an Albert on my list.'

Mr Griff scanned the clipboard, with his right eyebrow arched as he peered over his round spectacles. He scrutinised the black-inked handwriting, concerned he might have missed something.

'I only have your name down here, Stephen,' he said wiping his forehead with his white handkerchief. 'You will leave immediately by train.'

Mr Todd smiled kindly and wheeled Stephen's trunk from behind the counter. He tried to gently lead Stephen away from Albert, towards the front door, but Stephen clung to his brother.

'But, sir . . . I can't leave him here on his own . . . He won't cope without me. I promised I would look after him,' said Stephen, desperate to be heard, as tears burnt the insides of his eyelids.

'Come, come now. Don't make this more difficult than it is, Stephen. It's time to leave. Say your goodbyes,' said Mr Owen.

'But, sir, we were told we would stay together,' said Stephen.

Albert's lip trembled, and his body shook sporadically, as Stephen's fingers were gently prised apart from his brother's arm. But Stephen continued to plead, as he fell to his knees beneath Mr Griff's bursting stomach that towered over his head.

'Please, sir . . . Please, sir . . .' Stephen choked.

But his words disappeared into the dust of an unresponsive air. Mr Griff's curled moustache seemed to twitch over his pointed beard as he tried to help Stephen to his feet.

'Come now, boy, where's your sense of dignity? Mr Todd, give me a hand here, it's like trying to lift a dead weight,' said Mr Griff.

'Now, listen to me, Stephen, you need to leave, or you will miss your train. Your brother will be well looked after, you needn't worry . . . and you can always write,' said Mr Todd, in his usual gentle manner.

Stephen raised the sleeve of his woollen coat to wipe the wet stream from pallid cheekbones, as he felt a shooting pain cross his right eye. He turned to face his brother, as he was slowly led towards the open door.

'Love you,' his mouth moved to form the words without sound.

Albert slowly realised the distance between them, and found his voice and screamed, 'Stevie!'

He ran towards Stephen and clung to him with both arms.

'Stevie . . . don't leave me . . . don't leave me,' he cried out.

The brothers held each other. Stephen cried out into the ice cool air between them, unable to control his emotion. His strength drained from his quivering body and left him feeling hollow inside, unable to comprehend the reality of the situation. He could no longer be strong for Albert, and all he had left was to collapse in his arms, terrified of letting him go.

'Come now . . . say your goodbyes. It's time to go.' Mr Griff shuffled awkwardly as he waited.

The boys only held on tighter together, as if their bodies were locked in a mass of glue. Their acid tears mingled on their wet cheeks as they cried out. The Grandfather clock towered majestically in the corner of the staircase hall and chimed ten times. The sound boomed in synchronicity with the thumping sensation of the boys' hearts. Seconds passed, and still no one moved—until Mrs Griff appeared from the side parlour.

'What's all this bother out here?' she asked, wiping her hands on her apron.

'Mrs Griff, I have to go and attend to some important business,' said Mr Owen, hurrying towards his office.

Mrs Griff strolled over to the boys, and gently put her hands, on Albert's shoulders.

'It's time for Stephen to leave,' said Mrs Griff.

'Mr Todd, take Stephen to the station now, or he will miss the train to Hamilton,' said Mr Griff.

'Alfred, your time will come. You will be fine here with me for now,' said Mrs Griff in a quiet but firm tone.

'I'm not Alfred . . . I'm Albert,' he cried.

'Yes, yes . . . of course . . .' said Mrs Griff, raising her eyebrows with a confused expression that stuck to her rosy complexion.

The boys were separated slowly—each part of their body being forced apart until they only had each other's hand to let go of. Their fingers finally surrendered to the energy pulling them in opposite directions. Stephen was dragged away from his sobbing brother, as Mrs Griff held Albert close to her. Their arms remained held out into the empty air between them, as if they were still holding each other.

'Stevie!' Albert screamed, as he fell to the floor on his knees.

Stephen suddenly felt a surge of energy that enabled him to struggle free from the tight and forceful grip of Mr Griff, and he ran back towards his brother. He threw his arms around Albert. The sweat from their cheeks mingled with tears, whilst the sound of two hearts pounding echoed in synchronicity with each other. Again, their frail bodies stuck together—skin next to skin, brother in front of brother.

The hand of the Grandfather clock moved slowly through the torturous moments and still they held on, determined never to let go. But the firm-gripped fingers of Mr Todd and Mr Griff overpowered them and Stephen was suddenly wrenched away from his brother.

'No . . .' screamed Albert.

His arms thrashed around in mid-air as he wriggled out of Mrs Griff's arms and ran back to Stephen. He clung to his brother's coat but struggled to hold on due to the missing phalanges on his left hand.

'Please . . . please . . . please . . . don't leave me here on my own . . .' wailed Albert, as his body shivered sporadically on the tiled floor beneath him.

'He's having some kind of fit . . . fetch Dr Hart,' said Mrs Griff.

Mrs Griff gently pulled Albert's trembling body away, until all that was left of his brother was a small gold button from Stephen's coat that fell into his right hand. Stephen was dragged in the opposite direction, leaving Albert collapsed, his body distorted from the agony of grief.

'Albie . . .' Stephen whispered from the empty silence of the fear that cut his dry, mangled throat.

The front door of *Peter Street Boy's Home* closed. Stephen had the strongest urge to look over his shoulder as he was escorted away and saw John waving from the library window. He lifted his weighted free arm, and his hand reached up to touch the empty air between them.

'Who are you waving to?' Mr Todd asked, as he looked in the direction of Stephen's swollen, red eyes.

But Stephen's voice was lost in the darkness that clouded his mind as he walked the empty path before him.


THE TRAIN ARRIVED on time and filled the station platform with white clouds of steam that only aggravated the daggers in Stephen's eyes. Mr Todd shuffled his feet.

'Work hard, Stephen, and you will do well.'

But Mr Todd's voice was lost, somewhere in the hollow shadows of the memory of his brother. He remained in a daze as he watched strangers slowly disappear into the distance of a now deserted platform. The steam from the engine blurred his vision and the tears in his eyes still stung so deeply he was convinced it was blood running down the side of his taut face.

He climbed into the second-class carriage with Mr Todd, and sat upright, desperate to keep masses of tension contained inside his body, for fear of collapsing into insanity. He stared into the window, where all he could see was the reflective light from his eyes.

The jilted sound of Mr Todd's voice became lost to him as he fell even more deeply into his own tortured silence. And the train moved him further away from all that was left of his family—his brother.

*How will Albie survive without me? What will I do without him?*

When they finally arrived at Hamilton Station, a thunderstorm rumbled over the town. Heavy rain lashed down from the grey black sky, and lightning flashed intermittently with the crashing of thunder. A nervous energy moved through the crowds as they prepared to step on to the platform and into the rain. Mr Todd carried Stephen's trunk and guided him towards the exit. Stephen stopped, unable to move any further, as if his whole body froze in mid-air. His feet felt stuck like glue, unable to go forward or back, until his dried-up throat found its voice again.

'Wait! I need to go back, sir. I've forgotten something.'


THE STORM CONTINUED to thrash in turmoil, outside the windows and closed doors of *Peter Street Boy's Home*. It took both Mr and Mrs Griff to carry Albert up to the third-floor dormitory. There was no escape. He lay in his cot, defeated and numb as he choked on guttural sobs that writhed from the pit of his aching stomach. When he tried to reach out to the cot next to him, praying that this was all a dream, he saw Stephen in the empty space, smiling back at him. But his brother's face kept disappearing into a blurred distance. When it became too painful to look anymore, he covered his head with his grey blanket, closed his red swollen eyes, and continued to cry himself to sleep.

> *(Annie sat at the edge of Albert's cot and sang the familiar words of a song from home.)*
> *Hush, little baby, don't say a word . . .*
> *(Although Albert couldn't hear her soft, distant voice, his husky breath became calmer from the warm comforting velvet light she shone into his heart . . .)*
> *(Annie then slowly transcended back to Stephen, as she heard him cry out for her.)*
> *Annie . . . Annie . . . where are you?*
> *I'm here . . . I've been on singing duty.*
> *Have you been singing to Albie?*
> *You know me . . .*
> *What will happen to him? I know he won't cope. I have to get back to him. Help me Annie . . . please help me . . .*

*I can't change time, Stevie. I'm not a magician. Although sometimes, I wish I was.*

*Did you know this was going to happen?*

*(Silence.)*

*How could you Annie? Why didn't you warn me?*

*It was out of my hands.*

*What do I do now? I'm not giving up.*

*When night falls, look to the sky and know that the brightest star is reflecting its light through the eyes of both you and Albie. No one can ever take that away.*

*This isn't a time for poetry, Annie! It's not the same . . . you don't understand.*

*Why would I? I'm not you.*

# 5
# Eurach Farm

*"Where there is great love there are always miracles."* — *Willa Cather*

STEPHEN'S MIND CLOSED down, aware only of the empty space in the forest. The pathway to Eurach Farm was lined with towering maple trees, side by side, and wings of their shadowed leaves fluttered in the gravel below. It was a pathway that led to a beautiful white-washed stone house with steps leading up to a narrow terrace and a white, painted oak door. A small white gate was attached to a wooden fence that went all around the house. The square Georgian windows ensured light, especially during summer time. The surrounding acres of land were occupied by well-cared-for animals—horses, cattle, and sheep grazed serenely in the open fields. Behind the stone house, a huge barn dominated the yard, towering over the tips of yellow-green corn waving in the light breeze, stretching for miles to meet the clear blue horizon dancing with shadows from the late afternoon sunshine.

The horse and cart came to a standstill at the side of the stone house. In contrast to the light breeze surrounding the tranquil air, Stephen's heart continued to race with the uncertainty of what lay before him. He sat with his head lowered between his feet, clenching distorted muscles, like elastic, stretching with no way back. Mr Todd sat by Stephen's side, occasionally turning his head to attempt a reassuring look. Until the silence cracked and the need for words broke into the cool air.

'You can write to Mr Owen anytime, Stephen. If you have any questions, or need anything, then you can contact us at this address,' said Mr Todd, handing him a piece of white paper with the official Barnardo's stamp.

'Thank you, sir,' he whispered.

'We've arrived at last. Are you ready?' Mr Todd asked.

'Yes, sir . . . I think I am,' said Stephen, struggling to find his lost voice from the back of a dry, husky throat.

Stephen breathed from the depth of his stomach, and slowly stepped down with the one possession that reminded him of England—his trunk. His feet touched the gravel beneath him, his legs trembled, and his tired eyes blinked back hidden tears. He had never felt more alone.

*Please don't leave me . . .*

Stephen heard footsteps. He slowly lifted his head to distant voices moving closer.

'Good afternoon, I am Walter Todd, from the Barnardo's home in Toronto. I would like to introduce you to Stephen Duckhouse, one of our Home boys,' he said, shuffling his heavy feet forward.

'A pleasure to meet you, sir, I'm Edgar McPhail. Thank you for bringing the boy.'

Stephen struggled to clear blurred eyes behind his round spectacles as the two men shook hands. He slowly noticed the stranger before him as he came into focus for the first time. His dark brown hair receded on top of a shiny head to meet thicker layers neatly cut beneath linear earlobes set slightly away from carved cheekbones. His elongated moustache curled at the edges and looked like it was ritually trimmed each morning, beneath a slightly pointed nose. And his deep-set brown eyes with layers of firm kindness turned their focus on Stephen.

'Welcome to Eurach Farm, Stephen,' said Edgar, in a strong tone.

'I'm pleased to meet you, sir. Thank you for having me.' Stephen politely held out his hand, an automatic gesture with yet another stranger.

They exchanged a gentleman's handshake.

'Let me introduce you to my wife, Ada McPhail,' said Edgar.

At his side was a small woman with brown hair parted down the middle, curled over her ears, and tied back in a roll. Sparkles of light shone from her watery blue eyes and an unfamiliar scent tapered the air around her from a handkerchief she held elegantly close to her side.

'How was your journey, Stephen? You must be exhausted. Come inside,' said Ada.

Ada put her arm around Stephen's shoulders, and he felt a warm glow penetrate into the depth of his closed heart from the tenderness of her touch. She guided him through the gate and alongside flowerbeds full of colourful petals in bloom. But Stephen's feet suddenly immobilised like they were trapped beneath melting ice as he stared into the reflection of his own memory.

*Why don't the lines join the dots, so they are together?*

'Stephen . . . do you know this particular flower?' Ada asked.

'Eh . . . yes . . . I've seen it before,' said Stephen quietly, unable to hear the sound of his own voice.

Ada held Stephen's hand and led him towards the side door of the farmhouse. The mumbling sounds of Mr Todd faded into the distance between them.

Stephen entered an open-plan kitchen. His eyes lingered on the steel pans of mixed sizes hanging in sequence from a horizontal pole below the ceiling. He felt a sense of peace from a room of warm vapours. He shivered from the change in temperature that stuck to his chilled skin and wanted to scratch ice-cold air away and leave behind the old shell, where he felt drowned in the depths of invisible tears, sinking beneath a waterfall.

He unbuttoned his black double-breasted coat, until he stared at the missing gold button and the empty space it left behind. His mind flashed back to Albie's last choked scream as it echoed in his ears, and his fingers froze in motion . . .

*Please . . . don't leave me here on my own.*

Ada helped Stephen with his coat and steered him towards the long oak dining- table.

'Come now, sit near the oven stove and get warm,' she said, with a soft tone.

'Thank you,' Stephen whispered politely as he wondered why there were two oven stoves with two chimneys in the kitchen.

Stephen's eyes flickered from the stone floor to a blue cupboard near the window, where Ada was putting away plates and dishes.

A small boy entered and grinned mischievously. His fair, tousled hair parted at the side and was neatly cut to meet linear earlobes. But it was his sparkling deep blue eyes with a hint of secrecy, that captured Stephen.

'I would like you to meet our son John,' said Ada.

Stephen trembled as the sound of the familiar name draped in the mellow air like a silent pause waiting for its next moment.

*I know you . . .*

John climbed onto a chair opposite with a familiar effort. He was smaller and younger than Stephen and had to sit on a cushion to reach the table. Stephen felt comforted by his kind face, which held an expression overflowing with curiosity.

'How old are you?' John asked with his head drooped to one side.

'I'm eleven,' said Stephen.

'You talk in a different way . . . where are you from?'

*Just like Albie . . . always asking questions.*

'Stephen has come all the way from England,' said Ada.

'Yes but . . .' John's hand clasped his right cheek as he leaned his elbow on the table, holding the weight of a mixture of thoughts swirling around his brain.

'John, that's enough now, let Stephen settle in . . . We've prepared a sandwich for your supper. We were not sure what time to expect you, and you've missed dinner,' said Ada.

'Thank you,' said Stephen.

Ada placed homemade bread with cheese, a muffin, and a glass of milk on the oak table. Stephen drank the white liquid slowly, quenching his dry throat, and noticed the thud from his heartbeat become quieter. He was shown to a small room on the ground floor at the left-hand side of the kitchen, where he bathed in a tin bath with sweet, unfamiliar aromas around him. The warm water helped him feel a little calmer from the spiking ache in his head. Later that evening, he followed Ada to a bedroom behind the kitchen, with stone white washed walls and a square window overlooking the yard that led to a two-storey barn.

'I hope you find it comfortable here, Stephen. There's a pipe that leads from the oil burning stoves through the wall and into this room, so it's always warm in here. After the fall, we get very cold winters. This small cupboard has three drawers for your clothes, when you feel ready to empty your trunk. There's a jug of water, a lamp, and Bible beside your bed. We rise at six. We'll see you in the morning. Sleep well . . .' said Ada softly.

'Thank you, you are very kind,' said Stephen.

Ada's left eyebrow arched over vibrant shades of light leaving her eyes, like the stars ready to meet twilight. They exchanged a familiar gaze, as if recognising the other for the first time, but having no comprehension of where they had met before.

The latch door closed. Stephen sat on the edge of the bed and stared at the white canvas of the wall before him. His mind emptied into oblivion as his body immobilised like Nelson's statue, hundreds of miles away overlooking his hometown. In the stillness of the unnerving silence, he allowed time to move on, without him.

Seconds, minutes fell into the hour, until Stephen blinked and noticed the hand of the small mantel clock near his bedside pass midnight. He slowly moved towards his trunk, leaving behind the frozen air that had locked him into a motionless waking sleep. He reached inside to retrieve his journal. He undressed, put on his nightshirt, and lay under the cotton sheet beneath a woollen patchwork blanket. The light from the full moon beamed through his bedroom window, like the face of an old familiar friend, and he wrote . . .

Albie, I've arrived at my new place in Hamilton. I don't understand why you aren't here with me, and why we've been split up. I miss you. Where have they taken you? I wish you were here with me. I know you'd like it here. The farm is very nice and has lots of rooms. I hope you are somewhere like this, with open spaces and fields that seem to go on for miles. I've never seen so many tall trees with green leaves. It all seems very different from England.

I'll find you! I promise I'll find you, Albie. I won't give up. I'll write to Mr Owen and ask for your address, and maybe we can visit each other. We just have to wait until we can be together again. I hope you remember to look up at the moon tonight and know I'm watching it with you.

Stephen stared at the circle of light reflecting back at him, set amongst a canvas of stars, as if speaking to each other above the realm of darkness in the vast velvet sky. He diligently put his spectacles on the wooden ledge next to his bed, laid his head on a soft white pillow, and turned down the small oil lamp. With relief, in the solitude of the night, he was able to release some of the hollow grief that stirred like a sickness inside him, as he cried out in silence for his lost brother.

*A rickety wooden door creaks open to a sparse, chilled, stone walled room with a bucket in the corner catching drops of water leaking from the roof above. Albie shivers as spirals of draft from the cold wind outside seep through the cracked windows and tingle down his spine. He lowers his red, swollen eyes, unable to comprehend this strange and desolate place . . .*

STEPHEN'S RIGHT EYE flickered from the rays of light curving through the square window and a hollow breath swept out of his mouth as his body shot upright from the wet sheet beneath him.

*It was just a dream.*

Early April sunshine danced away the shadows of the night before. Sounds that Stephen would come to know as the lemon-breasted warbler and the white-throated sparrow, echoed their sweet songs from the protective branches of the towering maple trees nearby.

Stephen gazed around an unfamiliar room and remembered the arrival at Eurach Farm. A heavy ache weighed down a corner of his heart, and his stomach tingled with nervous uncertainty, not knowing what to expect from the first day. He looked at the clock on his bedside table . . . *it's only five . . .*

A slight breeze touched the branches of the maple tree outside the small square window. He had the urge to touch something familiar and reached inside his trunk for the book Miss Ratcliff had given him. Stephen put on his spectacles and stared at the blue sleeve. *Duchess of Renee: An Episode in the History of the Reformation by Sarson C.J. Ingham.* It was like looking in a mirror with no reflection, entwined with orange flowers. He opened the pages carefully . . .

She observed the branches of the trees thrill with the life that was astir with them, and burst into blossoming beauty; the catkins dangle on the hazels; the blackthorn assume its delicate vesture, suggesting the idea of an Ethiop in white: all these had charms for her; and when she saw the corn begin to kern, the fruit to drop from the boughs, the landscape to blush and bronze beneath the golden pencil of nature's great painter, she sighed pensively, "Why is the beauty all there? Why has nature been so much kinder to these unconscious things then to us . . . ?

Stephen removed his spectacles and rubbed his eyes as his bottom lip trembled. *Why couldn't Albie come with me? I don't understand.*

He stepped onto the tiled stone floor and quickly removed some clothes from inside his trunk. He poured some water from a jug into a crock basin and washed his hands and face, then got dressed with unthinking haste. The sound of a horse in the nearby distance suddenly reminded him of Daisy pulling the cart to the shout of 'any old iron' in the streets of his hometown. He felt impelled to go outside and explore his surroundings.

Stephen opened the back door and closed it quietly behind him, not wanting to disturb anyone else in the house. He noticed the two-storey barn ahead of him with stables on the left-hand side. He opened a small gate at the back of the house and stopped by the outside privy in an enclosed shed. There was a pile of newspaper and an Eaton Catalogue inside.

When he emerged from the privy, there were six horses watching him from the stables with a gaze that shone from their eyes, as if they had always known him. He moved closer and gently patted their manes one by one.

'Hello . . . what's your name?' he whispered.

Stephen had a strong sense of knowing the answer, without knowing. He felt a warm feeling of comfort tingle through his bloodstream as he resonated with these animals. He continued to whisper softly, 'You're strong, I can feel your strength, I think you are the leader.'

He moved from one to one with a sense of a quality that he felt with each . . . wisdom, gentleness, curiosity, mystery, and a tendency to be slightly irritable.

Stephen breathed in the warm air as he snuggled towards the leader. He felt a heavy bolt that had locked his heart open slightly, to let in a lighter feeling. It compelled him to sway gently in a space where he was able to smile. But then he felt a slight breeze force his energy towards the entrance of the barn. His right foot reached out for the gravel beneath him, but a cold chill tingled down his legs, leaving him frozen like a stone statue waiting in time. A black cloud closed down his eyes, whilst he fought to grasp the next breath, until he heard Annie's voice calling him. He stepped further inside the barn and followed the dancing light.

*Stevie . . . Stevie . . .*

*Annie . . . where are you?*

*I'm hiding in the barn. Come and find me.*

*Oh . . . there you are.*

*Well, about time! Hope you had a good night's sleep in your warm cosy room.*

*Annie, I've missed you. I thought you'd left me. Where've you been?*

*I'm here Stevie . . . right here in the barn, with the cows mooing in one ear and the horses neighing in the other? Or are your eyes and ears deceiving you?*

*I had this horrible dream last night, Annie. I dreamt . . .*

*I know, Stevie.*

*But what if . . .*

*I don't want you to worry about Albie. You need time to settle in here. This is your home now. What do you think of Eurach Farm? I love it here. But I think I'll sleep in the house tonight.*

*I like my new home, Annie. The family are treating me well. But I feel troubled about Ada. I feel like she can read me, the way you do, but it's as if she's hiding something.*

*Ada does feel a strong connection with you, and things will come to light, sooner than you think. She will help you understand many things whilst you're here. You can trust her with your secrets.*

*It feels as though I've met her before but can't remember. But what about Albie . . .*

*It's time for you to go back, Stevie. The family are rising and it's almost six.*

*I'll come back later. Will you be here?*

*I might be.*

Stephen found his way out of the barn and returned to the horses. He had a distinct feeling they had been listening and heard every word he had spoken to Annie.

'I have to go now, but I'll come back later and see you again,' said Stephen as he moved away from the stables.

As he walked away, he turned and could see each horse bow their long mane with their eyes remaining on him. He smiled and strolled towards the door of the farm house.

He removed his boots and stepped with trepidation towards the kitchen. The sound of an unfamiliar melody, loud and out of tune, but with a voice on the brink of great conviction, echoed in the distance. He rested his ear against the solid latch door and listened.

> One sweet solemn thought
> Comes to me o'er and o'er;
> Nearer my home today am I
> Than e'er I've been before . . .

Stephen's eyes streamed with the thought of home—distant memories fading into a blind space somewhere in the avalanche of his mind, like a maple tree in front of the glare of a falling marigold sun. And the bristling sound of the leaves dancing with the breeze.

> Father, perfect my trust!
> Strengthen my pow'r of faith!
> Nor let me stand at last, alone
> Upon the shore of death . . .

He trembled at the sound of the word *death* and rubbed his eye in an attempt to remove a piece of dust from behind his spectacles. His hand reached for the latch door. He hesitated, unsure of whether to disturb the unknown life that seemed to have taken over the space in the kitchen.

> Be Thee near when my feet
> Are slipping o'er the brink;
> For it maybe I'm nearer home,
> Nearer now than I think . . .

Stephen rested his tongue on a spot of blood from his lip where his teeth had grazed, took a deep breath, and gently opened the kitchen door. He flinched as the hinges creaked alongside the vibrant tones of the song, desperate to go unnoticed. But his feet slipped across the recently polished tiled floor.

A rotund woman busting out of her apron, with grey hair tied in a neat knot on top of her head and pink rosy cheeks, wiped the beads of sweat from her forehead with a cloth. She had a slight stoop and walked with a wooden cane. She lifted her head above one of the oil burning stoves in the far corner of the room.

'Ah . . . you must be Stephen? Well, that was quite an entrance. Come in and sit at the table. I'm Catherine, Edgar's mother.' Her voice still held a melody, as if the tone of the song was still warbling from the back of her throat.

'I'm pleased to meet you,' said Stephen as he sat down and rested his arms on the solid oak table in an attempt to contain the tension rising from his unsettled stomach.

'I believe you're a long way from home,' said Catherine with a distinctive, curious tone.

'Yes, I'm from England,' said Stephen quietly, lowering his head.

A mirror image of low cast eyes on the tiled stone floor prevailed through a moment of time.

'My family came over from Ireland, you know? Not that far from England,' she said through crooked teeth, rubbing her hip and grimacing.

'Do you miss your home?' Stephen asked tentatively.

'This is my home now. There's always a part of you that will miss your homeland, Stephen. It's where life begins,' she said, staring into the reflection from his round spectacles.

'Is the song about your home in Ireland?' Stephen asked.

*Why am I asking so many questions? I'm beginning to sound like Albie.*

'The song is about everyone's home . . . you can make a home anywhere in the world, Stephen, as long as it is in your heart to do so,' she said.

Stephen felt a warm glimpse into the life of someone he had known only minutes of time as he stared at the face of the mahogany carriage clock on the window ledge.

'Well, now, are you ready for some breakfast? There's scrambled egg, bacon, and tomatoes and bread with maple syrup. Ada baked it herself this morning,' she said briskly.

'I would like that very much, thank you,' said Stephen, casting his eyes over every dish placed neatly on the white cotton tablecloth.

'Well, aren't you a polite young boy, now? I think you'll be happy here, Stephen. It might take some time for you to settle in, but if you're not sure about anything, then just ask,' she said.

The inner door that led from the ground floor hallway suddenly opened, and John entered, followed by his mother, Ada. Sweet rose oil from her handkerchief surrendered to the rising smells of Catherine's breakfast creation.

'Good morning, Stephen, I hope you slept well during your first night with us?' Ada asked softly.

'Yes, very well, thank you,' answered Stephen.

'Can we play a game later?' John asked.

'Both you and Stephen have school today, John,' said Ada, with her left eyebrow slightly raised.

John smiled mischievously as he looked through the reflection of his glass of orange juice. Stephen felt a warm glow in the midst of the sadness that pined for his lost brother.

Whilst Catherine attempted to lift a ceramic pot from the stove with a sturdy cloth in her hand to protect her from the heat, Ada intervened.

'I'll do that,' said Ada as she took the cloth and the pot from her mother- in-law's hand.

Catherine smiled, bustled over to the oak table, leaning on her cane, and sat next to John.

Ada poured some brown liquid into rose-laced china cups. Stephen sniffed slightly as the unfamiliar aroma forced his nostrils to twitch.

'Would you like some coffee, Stephen?' Ada asked.

'Eh . . . no, thank you,' said Stephen as his eyes flickered from the light steam lingering in the air, from the smell of coffee beans.

*What's coffee?*

'There's plenty of water here. We have a well outside in the white shed and a cistern underneath the kitchen and the summer room,' said Ada.

'What's a cistern?' Stephen asked.

'It catches and stores the rain water,' said Catherine.

The side door creaked open with a gust of cool breeze gushing in from the outside. Edgar appeared. He removed his soft felt hat and sack coat to reveal a button-down shirt underneath overalls.

'Good morning,' said Edgar, as he made his way to the washroom to wash his hands. He poured water from the jug into a crock basin neatly placed next to the tin bath.

A respectful silence lingered until Edgar was seated at the head of the table, opposite Ada. Stephen watched Edgar clasp his fingers together and close his eyes. Everyone mirrored him like reflective impressions waiting, until the customary words were murmured.

'Bless us, O Lord, and these, Thy gifts, which we are about to receive from thy Bounty, through Christ, our Lord, Amen.'

'Amen,' was echoed around the table, with the sign of the cross, like a shadow of peace, always present.

Stephen ate his breakfast quietly with his head slightly bowed, trying desperately to look grateful for his new position within the family, but his mind continued to wander to Albie. Flashes of memory from the dream he had the night before struck his mind whenever he tried to focus on the conversation around the table. And all he could hear was the voice of his brother, and all he could see was broken grief, cutting like a razor-sharp knife into his lost eyes.

*What if it's not a dream?*

Stephen shivered from the warmth from the log burning stoves, and Ada reached out her hand across the table towards him.

'Are you cold, Stephen?' Ada asked.

'No . . . I'm fine, thank you,' said Stephen.

Their eyes held each other locked into an energy invisible to the others around the table. But then Stephen's mind wandered to a different realm, a secret place he felt he couldn't speak about . . .

*Annie . . . what are you doing here?*

*I said that I would be, I'm always here. Besides, it's warmer inside the house compared to the barn . . . so draughty! And as for the mice . . . they have lazy cats!*

*I feel lost, Annie. I need to talk to you about Albie.*

*Not now, Stevie. You need time to settle in.*

*But I feel cold when I think of him.*

*You're just missing Albie, in the same way he's missing you. What do you think of your new family?*

*They've been very kind to me. But what if they don't like me and send me back to Peter Street?*

*Just be yourself, Stevie, and they will love you for who you are, as I do . . . of course. Because you know I always tell the truth . . .*

'I've planned for us to have a walk around the farm later this afternoon, Stephen, so you are familiar with the grounds,' said Edgar.

Stephen's drifting thoughts fell into oblivion as he returned to the sound of Edgar's voice.

'Yes, sir,' said Stephen, blinking away the moments that had gone before.

'We hope you enjoy your time with us, and you are comfortable here,' he said, clearing his throat.

'Thank you, sir,' said Stephen.

Ada smiled with a serene gentleness that seemed to reach inside Stephen's soul and caress a part of him that had craved for so long for the lost love of his mother.

'You will get used to things around here, Stephen. It will just take a little time. We hope that you start to feel at home with us soon,' Ada said tenderly.

Stephen nodded slightly and attempted a smile, but his voice vanished into the dry choked throb at the back of his throat.

'John, it's time for school. I want you to walk with Stephen and show him where the schoolhouse is. They are expecting him today,' said Edgar, removing his pocket watch.

'You will need your coat, Stephen,' said Ada.

'Yes, I just need to get my boots from the back door,' said Stephen.

When Stephen returned, he reached inside the cloakroom near the side door, retrieved his coat, and noticed something different.

'I've replaced the missing button for you,' said Ada.

'Thank you, that's very kind of you,' said Stephen.

'It was no trouble,' said Ada.

He felt a sense of hope flutter through his stomach as he realised the new button would always remind him of Albie. In that moment, he knew that no matter how far apart they were, he was determined never to forget him. He vowed they would be together again because he was going to do everything he could to make that happen. His hand gently stroked the new shiny gold button that filled the empty space at the front of his coat.

Edgar opened the side door, and Stephen and John followed into the cool brisk air. Stephen looked up at the towering maple trees lining the path that had brought him to Eurach Farm the day before. He felt the warmth of a velvet cloak around him as if the leaves were gathering a welcome with the sound of their soothing whisper, echoing from the other side of a different world.

Stephen walked with John to the end of the lane, where they both turned left to head towards Valens School.

'Don't be late home now,' said Edgar as he turned and strolled towards the barn.

As they walked casually to school, Stephen wondered if they would ever reach it. The long road stretched before him and seemed to never end.

'This is quite a long walk,' said Stephen.

'You get used to it,' said John, looking up at Stephen, smiling.

'What's the school like?' Stephen asked.

'I don't like it much. I'm glad you're here,' said John as he moved closer to Stephen.

They finally arrived at a small building on the right-hand side of the road. Stephen noticed children of different ages staring at him with a distinct curiosity. He felt an uncomfortable tinge of nerves flutter inside his stomach as he entered the school gate. John held his head high and looked proud beside him. Hushed whispers followed Stephen inside the building until he found himself standing before the schoolmaster—his skin creased with rugged lines on his face, grey hair, and clear brown eyes that seemed to have a faded sparkle that still shone with old age.

'Good morning, John. I believe this is Stephen Duckhouse?'

'Yes, Mr MacNally. Pa said you were expecting him,' said John.

'Welcome to Valens School, Stephen,' said Mr MacNally.

'Thank you, sir,' said Stephen as he cleared his dry throat.

A group of boys pushed past Stephen as they rushed towards the assembly hall, and a book dropped to the floor near his feet.

Stephen bent down to pick up the brown leather-bound book. *War and Peace* by Leo Tolstoy. He handed it to a ginger-haired boy, whose cheeks were flushed and eyebrows knotted in the middle.

'Slow down, Hamish. No need to push your way forward, you're not marching on to war,' said Mr MacNally.

'No, sir, I mean yes, sir, thank you, sir,' mumbled Hamish as he walked slowly down the hallway.

Stephen noticed Hamish look back and grin widely in his direction. There was something familiar about him as if he had met him before.

'John, take Stephen to the assembly hall for morning prayers,' said the schoolmaster.

'Yes, sir,' said John eagerly.

Stephen followed John into a hall brimming with children, and three schoolmasters looking very serious, standing at the front. He joined a line near the back. Two square windows overlooked a small garden with a maple tree in the corner. Stephen put his hands together and followed the Lord's Prayer. His mouth moved but no sound came, trapped somewhere in the back of his throat. There seemed to be two versions of the prayer, as some were behind others rushing to catch up.

Following the assembly, Stephen followed John. He sat at the back of a classroom behind a wooden desk. John sat close by and kept turning his head to look at Stephen.

'This is Stephen Duckhouse. It's his first day, and he's from England. I hope you make him feel welcome, and you enjoy your time with us, Stephen,' said Mr Mac Nally.

'Thank you, sir,' said Stephen.

It felt like a million faces turning around as children stared at him with wide eyes.

*I feel different . . . I don't fit in here.*

Stephen struggled to settle into reading, writing, and arithmetic from the chalked blackboard in front of the classroom. Mr Mac Nally's voice became lost to him as he gazed into a distant oblivion where time was frozen in the silence of his closed heart.

'What's that big round ball?' Albert asked.

'It's a globe ball with a map of the world on it, can you see?' Mr Bains spun it around slowly for the boys.

'I didn't know the world was so big,' said Albert.

'This is where we are . . . England,' said Mr Bains.

'We look so small, compared to the rest,' said Stephen.

'Yes, and this vast country here, is what we call Canada,' said Mr Bains, as his eyes drifted into the empty space beyond the globe.

'I don't think I'd like to go to Canada, I think I might get lost,' said Albert, peering up at the globe on Mr Bain's desk.

'But you'd have your brother to look after you, wherever you go,' said Mr Bains.

Stephen blinked away his blurred vision as if waking from a deep sleep and felt the warmth of a hand nudge his arm. He turned to look into sparkles of light that shone from John's eyes.

Stephen and John walked home together, later that day.

'Do you enjoy school, John?' Stephen asked.

'I had a good time today. No one picked on me. I like having you to go to school with,' said John.

'Has anyone ever hurt you?' Stephen asked.

'Some boys punch each other when the schoolmaster is not looking, but not me. Ma says they just tease me, and I should ignore it. I had something called diph . . . em . . . emia, when I was a baby, and sometimes my ear runs,' said John.

'I don't know what that is, but you're right to ignore them. If anyone does try and punch you, be sure to come and tell me,' said Stephen.

'Okay,' said John, smiling up at Stephen.

Gradually more children joined Stephen and John on their journey home from school. There wasn't much conversation, but a lot of silent curiosity around Stephen. With Stephen's first day at school over, he strolled with John towards the side door of the farmhouse. Edgar was waiting.

'I thought I'd show you around the farm, Stephen,' said Edgar.

'Yes, sir,' said Stephen, politely.

'John, go inside, your mother wants you.'

'Can I come?' John asked.

A stern look from Edgar was enough for John to rush into the house.

'This way, Stephen, I want to show you the barn, first,' said Edgar, proudly.

They walked through the gate behind the farmhouse and stepped into mud that splashed around the edge of Stephen's boots.

'Are those apple trees, sir?' Stephen asked as he pointed towards an orchard at the back of the farm.

'Yes, we pick them when they're ripe. We go to market a couple of times a week in the wagon and sell vegetables, honey, bread, and eggs,' said Edgar.

'Do you sell the fruit, sir?' Stephen asked.

'No, we keep the fruit,' said Edgar.

They headed towards the stables where Stephen had explored earlier.

'Do you know anything about farming?' Edgar asked.

'No, sir, but I'm willing to learn,' said Stephen.

'We have a small live stock of sheep, cattle, pigs, and chickens. Six working horses, used to prepare the soil for planting, with the plow and harrow. I'll show you,' said Edgar.

They stepped out of daylight and into the shadows of the inside walls of the barn. The air was tinged with warmth as it touched his skin. A slight breeze mingled with Stephens's uncertainty, and the sweet smell of fresh hay tingled around the outside of his nostrils.

Stephen's mind closed down as a spark of light flashed through like a shooting star in a desolate sky.

*There were four shredded woollen blankets in the far corner amongst the hay. Albie slowly slid down the ice-cold wall and observed his unfamiliar surroundings—he gasped at the closed off animal pens and the high-beamed roof, which only added to his loneliness and fear of being so far away from home. The pungent smells of hay and manure made him cough to an echo of three other boys beside him as they continued to wonder how or why they had ended up in such an isolated place that seemed frozen in time . . .*

'Over here, Stephen . . . Stephen . . .' Edgar called from the far corner of the barn.

Stephen's right eye flickered as the vision cleared, and he returned to the present moment.

Edgar pointed to a piece of unfamiliar machinery. Stephen hesitated, feeling disorientated in the huge space that made up the ground floor of the barn.

'What do you think?' Edgar asked.

'Eh . . . it has big teeth,' said Stephen, his head falling to one side as he wiped beads of sweat from his forehead with his sleeve.

'That's what loosens the soil and breaks up clods just before we plant the seeds,' said Edgar.

'How do you know when to do that, sir?' he asked.

'Farmers have to work with the seasons, Stephen. In spring, we prepare the soil for planting and spread manure on the fields to help make the soil richer and produce better crops,' said Edgar.

'Can I ask what happens in summer, sir?' Stephen asked.

'The fields are cultivated to keep weeds from growing between the rows of plants. We also harvest the hay in summer, which is used to feed the horses and the cattle. Are you taking all this in, Stephen?'

'Yes, sir, so what kind of crops do you grow?' Stephen asked.

'Potatoes, corn, wheat, barley, and oats, that sort of thing,' said Edgar.

'What happens in winter, sir?' Stephen asked.

'Well, we have to work hard in the spring and summer, because we have to prepare food for the winter. In the fall, the crops are harvested,' said Edgar, looking pleased with Stephen's interest.

'What's the fall, sir?' Stephen asked, feeling confused.

'I believe you call it autumn in England,' said Edgar.

Stephen wiped away a dry tear from just beneath his spectacles at the mention of his home.

'Are you all right, Stephen?' Edgar asked.

'It was just a piece of dust, sir,' said Stephen.

'There's a lot to learn about the farm. But together, I'm sure we'll manage,' said Edgar.

'Yes, sir,' said Stephen.

They walked side by side past the stables and further on to the milking rows until they entered the straw mow. Stephen looked through the granary at the open door on the second floor and noticed the cornfield beneath the falling sun. It was as if the tips of the corn danced with joy and greeted him for the first time. But there was also a sense of being here before, something he didn't quite understand. It gave him a warm feeling, which he knew he would get used to.

He took a deep breath and felt this would be a place where he could feel closest to home and remember. He never wanted to forget all that he had left behind.


EDGAR ENTERED THE kitchen from the side door, and the cool, outside air followed him like a shadow of mist, stuck to the outside of his knee-length overcoat. He cradled a basket, weaved with wood splints, like a child in his arms.

'Stephen, can you take some of these logs into the kitchen and I'll come and put them in the oven stoves,' said Edgar.

'Yes, of course, sir,' said Stephen.

'Take the basket, it will be easier for you to carry,' said Edgar.

Stephen removed his boots outside and entered the kitchen and placed the basket near the oven stoves. The logs crackled with gentle sparks of flames twirling from the embers beneath, ready for their next feed, waiting to breathe out circles of warmth. He wandered into the back parlour where the early evening sunshine filtered through fluorescent green curtains with gold cords to play with shades of twilight—casting their shadows over leather-encased books, lining the oak and walnut library bookcase across the side wall. Stephen looked curiously around the room and noticed framed oil paintings hanging from the white washed walls. But he had to squint through his round spectacles to make out the details that seemed to fade in the distance. A round bronze table with a leather top was situated near a silver cushioned sofa. He could hear muffled snores nearby and remembered that Catherine's bedroom was next door in the front parlour, and she usually had an afternoon sleep. He crept quietly back towards the kitchen and heard Ada calling him. He followed the sound of her voice and entered the side parlour.

Ada sat at a long table with a small piece of tapestry and a needle and cotton in her hand. Stephen noticed a china doll on top of a baby grand piano in the corner of the room.

'Come over here, Stephen, and sit with me,' Ada said, as she gently patted the chair next to her.

Stephen carefully stepped around what he thought was some kind of statue without a head and did as he was asked. He couldn't help but look confused.

'Don't mind the mannequin, Stephen. I use it when I'm making my clothes,' said Ada, smiling.

Stephen smiled with relief.

'I want to talk to you before the others come in,' said Ada.

'Have I done something wrong?' Stephen asked.

'No, Stephen, why would you think that?' Ada asked gently.

'I'm not sure,' said Stephen.

'I just want to tell you something. I know there was someone with you at breakfast,' Ada whispered.

'How do you know?' Stephen asked as he stared behind her to notice Annie smiling back at him.

'I see them too,' said Ada.

'Oh, do you really?'

'Yes, but we must never speak about it in front of Edgar. The community is very religious, and we must respect their beliefs. I talk to John because I've known from the day he was born that he's like me. I knew from the first time I saw you, that you were different,' said Ada, with rays of light reflecting from her eyes and penetrating right into his heart.

'I've never spoken about it to anyone before, because I didn't think they would believe me,' said Stephen.

'Well, I do. You can talk to me anytime, but it must stay between us. You must promise me, you will keep this to yourself,' said Ada.

'I promise,' said Stephen.

'I won't ask you any questions, Stephen. But if there is anything you are not sure about, and want to ask me, then I'm here. I don't want you to ever feel alone,' said Ada.

'Thank you,' said Stephen as he touched his cheek to hide a fallen tear.

He felt a heavy weight lift from his shoulders as his secret was shared for the first time in his young life. The relief that spiralled through his body almost shot outside into the energy between them and fixed like matted electricity as he found himself leaning towards her.

'Can Stephen read me a story?' John asked as the door creaked open and he stumbled through it.

'Not tonight, John, you know how your Pa likes to read a psalm,' said Ada.

They shared a smile. Catherine entered, holding a cup and saucer close to her chest.

'There's cocoa on the kitchen table,' she said, smiling, as she limped back to the armchair closest to the log burning oven stove.

'Oh, thank you. I was just about to come through to make it,' said Ada as she glided towards the kitchen.

Stephen followed, with John beside him.

'Be careful not to spill it, John,' said Ada.

They sat at the kitchen table, watching the brown liquid gently dance around the edges of the cups.

'Come and sit next to your grandmother, John. I've hardly seen you all day,' said Catherine.

The family gathered together and waited patiently for Edgar.

'It's gone cold tonight,' said Catherine, shivering slightly.

'Yes, the air is cooler. Here's your shawl, you left it at the side of the sofa,' said Ada, wrapping it around her shoulders.

Edgar appeared in the doorway with only the sound of the log burning stove daring to rise above the silence. Stephen remained by Ada's side and felt safer than he had done since he left the shores of England. He noticed John looking at him with a curiosity that almost fell out of his eyes as he snuggled close to his grandmother. The peace in the kitchen continued as the family waited for Edgar as he tended to the log burning oven and then prepared himself to speak.

'I've been asked to read this psalm at the next Sunday service,' said Edgar.

'That's wonderful news,' said Ada.

'We go to church every Sunday, as a family, Stephen. Religion is very important in our community,' said Edgar.

'Yes, sir,' whispered Stephen politely.

Stephen gulped to quench his dry throat as the memory of his visit to St Martins Cathedral with his mother and brother flashed through his mind—his only experience of a church service. The flames of the log-burning oven drew him closer . . .

*Ellen smiled at both her boys, led them to the entrance of the church, and stepped inside. Overhead wooden arches towered down the sides of rows of pews. They sat a distance from the pulpit, where stained glass images of an unforgotten past, reflected back a stillness of unspoken peace captured in the surrounding cool air . . .*

Edgar opened a black leather Bible with gold edged leaves at Psalm 2. He sat upright and coughed slightly. His voice was deep as it seemed to move into the depths of his heart.

Why do the nations rage,

And the people plot a vain thing?

The kings of the earth set themselves,

And the rulers take counsel together . . .

In the stillness of the parlour, the words from the Psalm spilled out into the air between them. The crackling of the logs continued to burn sparks of delight, casting a warm orange glow, to dance with shadows of flickering candlelight.

Against the Lord and against His

Anointed, saying,

"Let us break Their bonds in pieces

And cast away Their chords from us."

But Stephen's eyes could only reflect the memory of the last touch of his mother's hand, leaving a burning sensation, twisted like a coil inside his heart, as the cord between them was broken. Stephen continued to stare into the flames of the fire, as an invisible knife cut into the scar of his soul, leaving it to bleed into the abyss from an open wound . . .

*'Don't make us go . . . please let us stay,' Stephen choked on his dry mangled throat.*

*The sound of multiple cries fell into a chorus of no return. But Stephen remained dazed, trapped in his own silence, as if he was watching from a distance.*

*Ellen took the deepest breath . . .*

*'Listen to me. I love you with all my heart, but you won't survive if you stay with me. I can't look after you, and God knows I have tried. I want you to be safe and well and have a good life . . . and stay together. I promise I will write to you often. But you have to be strong now and go with Mr Davies.'*

*It took the remains of whatever strength she had left to unclench their fingers, from the palm of her hands, and let go.*

*'The train's about to leave,' said Mr Davies, clearing his throat.*

Edgar cleared his throat before moving into the next verse, and Stephen's right eye ached as his mind returned to the reality of the moment.

I will declare the decree:

The Lord has said to Me,

You *are* My Son . . .

Stephen noticed that John had fallen asleep in the arms of his grandmother. He thought he looked small, held at her side, and so loved. Edgar continued his close relationship with his Bible, as if an old friend he could never let go of. Stephen felt Ada's hazel eyes shine flashes of light whilst watching him closely. From the touch of a warm and gentle energy of her soothing presence, Stephen had a sudden urge to be held in the arms of a stranger.

Today I have begotten You.

Ask of Me, and I will give You

The nations for Your inheritance,

And the ends of the earth for Your possession.

Stephen found the courage to let go of his trance to look up from the small flames of the log burning oven. He noticed Ada smiling with soothing kindness in recognition of his deepest heartfelt loss, and her eyes reached out to him.

'It's time for bed now, John, it's getting late,' said Ada softly as she stood and drifted across the floor towards her sewing box, as if elevated from this world.

Stephen noticed John stir himself awake, but only silence returned in the hope that Ada might forget what she had just said and become distracted with something else. Elegantly dressed in a long flowing cream gown, holding a scented handkerchief close with its sweet aroma surrounding her, she glided back to her cushioned velvet armchair.

'It's been a long day. I think we could all do with some rest,' said Ada.

'Can I stay up a little longer with Stephen?' John asked.

'Do as your mother has said, John,' said Edgar, without lifting his down-cast eyes from his Bible.

John immediately obeyed his father, said goodnight, and disappeared.

'Have you enjoyed your first day with us, Stephen?' Ada asked.

'Yes, thank you, I feel very welcome. I like the open spaces here. It's a very peaceful place,' said Stephen.

Ada's eyes had a way of capturing Stephen's heart whenever she looked at him. It was if they had always known each other, without knowing one another.

'I think you'll do well here, Stephen,' said Edgar.

'Thank you, sir,' said Stephen, relieved to hear that he just might be good enough.

Stephen retired to his bedroom and lay beneath the comfort of his cotton sheet and woollen blanket. Alone with his own thoughts, he cried out for Annie from the silence of his unspoken voice.

*Annie . . . Annie . . .*

*I'm here, Stevie . . . there's no need to shout!*

*I've got my first day over, Annie.*

*You've done well, Stevie. But I must say, I couldn't be doing with all that learning at school . . . so boring! That Mr Mac Nally sent me to sleep.*

*Everyone's been so good to me. Do you know that Ada can see you?*

*Yes, Stevie . . . I know everything.*

*She speaks to me in a kind way, but sometimes I notice her staring into space and she looks sad.*

*You're right to pick up on her sadness, Stevie. Ada has insomnia and lies awake at night with memories of losing their stillborn twin boys and son, Clarence, who died of a cot death shortly after his first birthday.*

*How do you know all of that?*

*Really?*

*So, John is their only remaining son?*

*Yes, that's why she's very protective of him.*

*That explains so much . . . but I still need to talk to you about Albie, I keep getting the strangest images in my head . . .*

*Do you remember anything about Aunt Rose?*

*Who?*

*Will you stop acting stupid and bring her back into memory. Oh, all right, I suppose I have to help you . . . again!*

*Oh, I remember now . . . she's Ma's sister and she moved to Canada.*

*Well, expect a letter near Christmas, because sometime in the future, she's coming to the farm to see you.*

*Is she?*

*Yes . . .*

*Why?*

*Questions . . . questions. You know some patience wouldn't go amiss. When did I become the font of all knowledge?*

*You're just teasing me now, Annie.*

*It's time to close your eyes, Stevie . . . enough for one day, and I'm sleepy. It's hard work playing with the sheep.*

*But I'm not tired, Annie.*

*I am!*

# 6
# The Barn

*"Everything is made out of magic, leaves and trees, flowers and birds, badgers and foxes and squirrels and people. So it must be all around us."*
— *Frances Hodgson Burnett*

STREAMS OF LIGHT shimmered upon the rooftop of the barn from behind clouds resting in the gaze of a violet sky.

'Hey, Steve, can we play hide and seek?' asked John as Stephen filled the straw mow with fresh hay.

'I'm working, John.'

'But you can have a break . . . please.'

'Okay, you go and hide whilst I just finish off here.'

'Oh, but I've still got my suit on from school.'

'Be careful, it's dusty in here.'

'I'm still going to hide. I'm sure it will be all right. What do you think?'

'It's up to you, John. I don't want you to get your clothes dirty.'

'I'll find the best place where there's no dust,' said John as he ran off into the straw mow.

Stephen continued with his task whilst he counted to twenty.

'Coming,' Stephen yelled.

He wandered amongst the milking rows, calf pens, stables, and straw mow until he found John hiding in the granary, behind a barrel with his knees tucked around his chin. He could hear the muffled chuckles of laughter.

'I wonder where he could be?' Stephen asked himself as he bent down to face his captive.

They both giggled with a sense of freedom they always seemed to find when playing in the barn. John crawled out of his hiding place and remembered to dust down his smart suit.

'Can you see any dirt on me?' John asked.

'You've got some straw in your hair,' said Stephen as he gently removed it.

Stephen swung open the granary door and looked down at the six feet drop beneath them. They sat down together at the edge and swung their legs out into the open air where they could see acres of land stretched out beneath the sunset.

'Let's watch the sun come down,' said John.

Stephen smiled and looked beyond the horizon . . .

*If only you were here, Albie, with us. You'd love it, with all this open space. I wish I could find you hiding in the barn.*

It was during these times that Stephen found a way to heal some of the hurt that bled within his aching heart. Through playing with John, he found a way to mask some of the pain he felt when he missed his brother.

'Are you happy here, Steve?' John asked.

'Yes, I can't think why anyone wouldn't be happy here,' said Stephen.

'Only, I wanted to ask you something,' said John.

'Okay, I'm listening,' said Stephen, staring at the reflection of the sun falling from the sky.

'It's just that, I've never had a brother, and I was just thinking whether you might like to be . . . my brother?' John asked.

Stephen nudged his shoulder gently and smiled.

'It would be an honour,' said Stephen.

'Really?'

'Yes,' said Stephen.

'Does this mean, as my brother, you'll read me a story and come skating with me every day?' John asked, with a mischievous glint in his eyes.

'Only if there's time, when I've finished my chores, after school,' said Stephen.

'You promise?'

'I promise,' said Stephen.

Let's shake on it,' said John as he held out his hand.

The light from the late afternoon sun faded in the shadows to rest on the leaves of the maple trees as they whispered their sweet song with the breeze.


THERE WERE MANY times when Stephen enjoyed John's company, playing games in the barn, but also other days when he continued to write down his feelings, whenever he was alone. He still had his journal in his trunk, so it was easy for him to slip it in his pocket when he headed for the barn. On this day he opened the latch door of the granary and sat swinging his legs. The glistening yellow cornfields and the endless views beyond, which seamlessly met the blue sky in the far distance of the green and peaceful land surrounding the farm captured his gaze. How he felt inspired to write!

Or he would climb further up and shuffle across to the straw mow, where he burrowed in a corner. He nestled blissfully beneath the swallows' nest in the overhang from the roof above, where he listened to the sounds of new life. During these solitary moments, his journal expanded into what he referred to as his bible.

*I need a hiding place, where no one will ever find it.*

He noticed a beam to the right side of the barn. He climbed up to discover a small platform, where it was easy to hide his most precious possessions. He had retrieved a grey cake tin that Ada had thrown out. It was big enough to put things inside he wanted to contain. He soon discovered the tin fitted neatly into the empty space behind the beam. It was here that he placed photographs of himself and Albie, and his mother, with the most precious leaves of his journal. He was now content that his writing was safe and secure, as he felt at Eurach Farm.

THE SEASONS CHANGED from harsh, heavy snowdrifts freezing the winter air, to blossoming springtime, hot blistering summers and misty falls, as time echoed the rhythm of Stephen's unspoken feelings . . . Christmas cast its sparkling light upon the shadows of the ice-cold winter breeze, swirling around the edge of Eurach Farm.

One cold, frosty day, when Stephen was least expecting it, he received a letter from his mother. He returned to the barn climbed high into the straw mow, and settled in what became his secret place. Here, he found solitary contentment within a space he fondly called his own. As he tentatively opened the envelope, a Christmas card fell into his hands, with a serene angel overlooking a glittering tree with sparkles of gifts and berries hanging from each branch. Stephen opened the card to read his mother's writing.

1st December 1912

Dear Stevie,

We are all thinking of you and hope you have settled into your new home. I've enclosed a money order for you to change, for Christmas. My gift to you during this coming season is to ask you to read a passage from Corinthians 13:4-8 Love is patient, love is kind . . .

We will all be reading this passage on Christmas Day and remembering both you and Albie. I pray you will always know how much I love and miss you, and how much I patiently wait for the time when we are all together again. Remember to be kind to strangers; you never know when you might need their friendship.

I have some wonderful news, Stevie. Aunt Rose has written to Barnardo's to request that she visits you and Albie. She lives in Canada and is waiting to hear that her request has been granted. I am very excited about her visit, and she is looking forward to seeing you both.

God bless you always and sending lots of love for a Happy Christmas and New Year.

Love Ma

Stephen's hand trembled as he read the words from the letter over and over again. He carefully removed his spectacles to wipe escaped tears with his sleeve and called out into the empty space around him.

*Annie . . . Annie . . .*

*I'm here, Stevie.*

*You were right. I've had a letter from Ma, and she says Aunt Rose wants to visit. What does this mean, Annie? Is she coming to take Albie and me away with her?*

*Why don't you wait and see what she has to say? She's not even here yet!*

*Only . . . I want to see Albie again, more than anything, but I also like it here, Annie. I love the McPhail family. I can't imagine my life without them. Do you think she might bring Albie here?*

*Try not to think about what might or might not happen, Stevie. You're doing really well here.*

*Okay, but I just don't know what to think right now.*

*Why don't you write to Mr Owen?*

*Yes, then I can buy Christmas presents for the family.*

*Don't forget me!*

Stephen reached for his journal, removed a sheet of paper, and began writing.

MR OWEN IMMEDIATELY responded to Stephen's letter and enclosed thirty-six cents, the equivalent value of 18d in English money. Stephen smiled as he folded the letter and put it carefully with other correspondence he had received from Barnardo's, always returning it to the same secret place. This was somewhere special that he knew no one could ever take away. It belonged only to him. He knew that he was loved and accepted by the McPhail family, but he still needed this time alone—and cherished it as secret time with memories of his family in England and his spiritual world where he spoke to Annie. Although he had long accepted she could also be really annoying! He never felt lonely. Stephen was always aware of Annie beside him, gently guiding his words, and listening to his unspoken voice, even when she pretended to be asleep.

*Annie . . .*

*I'm still here, Stevie. But not for long, it's milking time soon, and you know how I like to watch the cattle.*

*I have a feeling that something's wrong with Albie. It's such a strong feeling and I can't let it go. I need you to show me where he is. Take me to him . . . please take me to him.*

*I don't think that's a good idea, Stevie.*

*Why?*

*You won't like it if I take you there.*

*I need to know, Annie. I keep getting a shooting pain in my leg, and at the side of my head, whenever I think of him. He needs me . . . I know he needs me.*

*Oh, all right, if you're sure, Stevie, but be prepared. You must accept this is out of your hands for now. Close your eyes and follow me . . .*

Annie gently touched the space between Stephen's eyes and transported him to a farm in Muskoka, miles away. An image of light showing Albert's life, flashed through his mind like a moving picture on a blank canvas. Annie stayed with him . . .

*Jane, the mistress of the house, pulled her headscarf off to show straight brown hair greased back and wiped her wet hands on her grey, worn apron. Their three daughters—Eudora, the eldest at twenty-four, Marjorie, who was twenty, and the youngest Mabel, who had just turned seventeen, sat 'round the oak table and enjoyed potato soup for supper. John, Head of the household, scratched the bristles gathered on his unshaven, chubby face and smiled with relief, whilst he sat back and delegated tasks to his new farm labourers—four young boys, who shivered near the creaking door as the rain pelted the windows from outside.*

But it was all a blur to Albert as the kitchen table reminded him of home, and his mind flashed back to his mother.

Why? Why did you leave me? Albert cried out from the silence in the darkest corner of the room . . .

Stephen reached out his hand towards his brother.

'Albie, come with me. You're safe now,' said Stephen.

But Albert remained still, like a ghost, frozen from a different time, unaware of Stephen's voice beside him . . .

'Steve . . . Steve, where are you?'

'I'm here, Albie,' whispered Stephen.

Stephen's eyes glazed over as the moving picture, somewhere in the whirl of his mind, changed back to the reality of his present situation, to find John at the bottom of the straw mow, calling his name.

'I'm here,' said Stephen.

'Hey, Steve, that's a great hiding place. I've been looking for you all over,' said John.

'Oh, I'm coming,' said Stephen as he climbed down from the top of the haystack.

'Who were you talking to up there?' John asked.

'You know me, I like to talk to myself sometimes,' said Stephen.

'Did you think I wouldn't find you?' John laughed.

'Now I'll have to find a different place to set you a new challenge,' said Stephen.

'Dinner's almost ready, and Pa's waiting to say prayers,' said John.

Stephen rushed forward with long strides, with John running by his side, into the late afternoon shade. They headed towards the house, leaving Annie waving from the barn.


STEPHEN HAD INTUITIVELY felt his brother's pain, and now Annie had shown him a glimpse of Albert's reality. He waited until he had time alone, where he allowed himself to cry silently in the granary of the barn where no one could hear, feeling helpless despair. Annie held Stephen in her arms.

> *Annie . . . I need to know more about Albie. I need to know that he's safe.*
> *One step at a time, Stevie . . .*
> *But I can feel he needs me. Will you help him, Annie?*
> *Always . . . but all this time-travelling is very tiring.*

Stephen found consolation the only way he knew how. He continued to write his feelings in his journal. Writing gave him a sense of comfort, his only way back to some kind of connection with his brother.

With Annie by his side, whenever he called out for her, Stephen settled into family life with the McPhail Family. With time, following their secret pact to be brothers, he looked upon John as a brother—although he knew that Albie could never be replaced, John filled an empty space in a corner of his heart.

'Stephen,' Edgar called from outside the stables.

Stephen closed his journal and ran to his secret hiding place, climbed up, and quickly placed it behind the beam, near the straw mow. Then he rushed down to the ground floor and followed the sound of Edgar's voice.

'Yes, sir.'

'Ada wants to speak to you. She's waiting for you in the side parlour. Then I need you to help me bring the horses back from the field,' said Edgar.

'Yes, sir, of course,' said Stephen, as he hurried on his way.

He stopped by the washroom, before finding Ada sat in the parlour, mixing some sweet-smelling potions between small glass containers. She smiled serenely as Stephen entered the room.

'Ah, there you are Stephen, come and sit with me,' she said softly.

Stephen waited patiently for Ada to speak.

'We've had a letter from Mr Owen, letting us know that you have an aunt living in Canada,' said Ada.

'Yes, my mother wrote to me at Christmas,' said Stephen.

'Well, she would like to come and visit you here at the farm. We were just wondering how you might feel about that?' Ada asked.

Stephen hesitated, not wanting to hurt Ada's feelings. He had come to look upon her as the mother he had lost.

'I would like to meet her. I only know that she's my mother's sister. I don't know anything more about her,' said Stephen.

'Then it shall be arranged. I just wanted you to know that she's been in contact, and to make sure that you are okay about her coming here to see you,' said Ada.

'Thank you, for letting me know,' said Stephen.

They shared a smile that seemed to glow within the walls of the room. But Stephen could feel Ada's unease about the situation, and he felt compelled to reassure her.

*I don't want to leave you.*

Ada reached out and held him close, as if Stephen represented all the parts of the children she had lost in childbirth. Then she slowly and gently let him go.

'Stephen, your hair has grown. Let me find my scissors,' said Ada, wiping her eyes with her handkerchief.

Ada began trimming Stephen's hair. The door opened suddenly, and John rushed in.

'Can I have my hair cut?' John asked.

'Yes, of course you can,' said Ada.

'I'd like Steve to cut mine,' said John.

'Do you want to have a go, Stephen?' Ada asked, smiling.

'If you'll show me what to do,' said Stephen.

Ada handed Stephen the scissors as John made himself comfortable on the chair. Stephen was then guided in his first lesson in cutting hair, with Ada by his side, watching over him.


THE WEEKS PASSED with the movement of seasons, from spring to summer, until the day came when Stephen's aunt arrived at Eurach Farm. Stephen got dressed in the suit that Ada had skilfully made him to wear to attend church. He slowly buttoned up the jacket, but his hand hovered over one of the buttons as his mind flashed forward . . .

Albert spent his days working long hours from five in the morning to seven at night, milking cows, feeding animals, ploughing fields, and wearing socks in replacement of gloves when the ice and snow fell during the long, chilled winter season. The sleeves of his coat almost reached his elbows, and he had long given up trying to make his buttons reach, to stop the draft from the blustering wind outside, that swirled around him in the isolation of his loneliness.

Stephen blinked, and rubbed his right eye that ached from a shooting pain echoing inside his head. He took the deepest breath made his way towards the parlour, and found Ada waiting for him in the kitchen.

'There you are, Stephen. You look very smart,' said Ada, as she turned the collar down from his jacket.

'Thank you,' said Stephen.

'Are you ready to meet your aunt?' Ada asked. 'She's waiting in the front parlour.

'Yes, I think so,' said Stephen, suddenly realising how nervous he felt.

Ada put her arm around his shoulder and walked with him into the room used for visitors.

The door opened, and Stephen gasped when he saw a woman with features he recognised sitting in the armchair near a small stove. He stared into her blue eyes to make sure it wasn't his mother looking directly at him.

'Good morning, Stephen. I'm your Aunt Rose.'

'Good morning, it's nice to meet you,' said Stephen.

'I'll leave you two to get acquainted. There's coffee on the table, if you would like some, Stephen,' said Ada, as she turned and left the room.

Stephen watched the door close behind her.

'Come over here, Stephen. Let me look at you,' said Aunt Rose.

She stood upright with her arms held out. Stephen moved towards her and allowed himself to be held by a stranger. It could have easily been his mother, but something felt different.

'Sit down, and tell me, are you keeping well?'

'Yes, thank you. The McPhail family are kind, and they're good to me,' said Stephen.

'I'm pleased to hear that, Stephen. They do seem nice people and appear very fond of you, the way they talk about you,' said Aunt Rose.

'Have you been in contact with my mother?' Stephen asked.

'Your mother writes to me and tells me that everyone is well. The police still haven't found your father, and it seems unlikely that he will ever be found now,' she said.

Stephen bowed his head towards his chest, trying to stop the erratic beating of his heart, in an attempt to block the memory of his father leaving.

'Your mother does miss you, Stephen, they all do,' said Aunt Rose.

Stephen tried to smile and hide the wet tears blurring his vision behind his round spectacles.

'I miss them too,' said Stephen.

'Is there anything you need?' Aunt Rose asked.

'No . . . thank you . . . I'm provided with all I need here,' said Stephen.

'I'm pleased to hear that,' she said.

A long silent pause prevailed in the unfamiliar air between them.

'Have you been to visit Albie?' Stephen asked, shuffling his feet.

'No, but I'll be arranging to go soon. He's quite some miles away, I believe. It's a shame you're so far apart. It would have been good for you both to have been placed in the same farm, or at least be able to visit each other from time to time,' said Aunt Rose.

'Will you write to me and tell me how he's getting on?' Stephen asked.

'I'll do what I can, Stephen. But I'm sure he's fine and well looked after, just like you,' said Aunt Rose.

'Thank you, only I worry about him sometimes,' said Stephen.

'Well, you're his older brother, and I hear from your mother that you've always looked out for him. I just don't understand why you were split up. There seems plenty of work here for both of you,' said Aunt Rose.

'Do you think it was a mistake, and he was meant to come here with me?' Stephen asked.

'I don't know the answer to that question, Stephen. We can't change what's happened. But how would you feel about you and Albie coming to live with me?' Aunt Rose asked.

Stephen hesitated, feeling torn between his deepest heartbreak over the separation from his brother, and his love for the McPhail family.

'I would say that is very kind of you to offer,' said Stephen.

'I shall contact the Barnardo office in Toronto, and will let you know the outcome,' said Aunt Rose.

'Thank you,' said Stephen, suddenly feeling agitated, but unsure why.

'Are you happy here, Stephen? I mean really happy?' Aunt Rose asked.

'I miss Ma and everyone in England, and Albie. But yes, I'm happy here,' said Stephen.

The door creaked open, and Ada appeared with a tray in her hands.

'I thought you might like some hot buttered muffins,' she said.

Stephen jumped up, took the tray from her, and placed it down on the table.

'Thank you, Stephen, that's very thoughtful,' said Ada.

'Stephen's been telling me how much he's settled in since he came here,' said Aunt Rose.

'Yes, we're very pleased with him; he's like one of the family. Will you be staying in Hamilton long?' Ada asked.

'No, I'm returning home today. It's been very kind of you to let me visit. Stephen looks so grown up,' said Aunt Rose.

'Yes, we're all proud of Stephen, he's doing so well,' said Ada.

'I believe your mother-in-law lives here with you?' Aunt Rose asked.

'Yes, Catherine McPhail. She sends her apologies for not being here, she's gone to lie down, she struggles with her hip from time to time,' said Ada, offering the hot muffins on china plates with roses elegantly painted around the side.

'Please give her my regards for a return to good health,' said Aunt Rose.

'Thank you, that's very kind of you,' said Ada.

A silent pause returned with only the sound of the pendulum swinging from left to right, contained inside the grandfather clock in the corner of the room.

'I really must be going, if I want to get home before nightfall,' said Aunt Rose.

'Oh, you don't have to leave, why don't you stay for dinner? Stephen can show you around the farm?' Ada asked.

'No, really, thank you. It's time I headed back. It was only meant to be a short visit anyway,' said Aunt Rose.

'Then I shall leave you to say goodbye,' said Ada, and she glided towards the door.

'Look after yourself, Stephen. I'm so glad we've had this opportunity to spend some time together,' said Aunt Rose.

'It's been good to see you,' said Stephen.

'Why don't you write to Mr Owen, and ask for Albie's address? Then you can write to him,' said Aunt Rose.

'Do you think I might be allowed to have it?' Stephen asked.

'I don't see why not, he is your brother,' said Aunt Rose.

She put her arms around Stephen and held him, as if afraid to let him go. Stephen watched Aunt Rose leave Eurach Farm in her horse and carriage. He waved from the bottom of the tree-lined path, that led onto the road that took her back in the direction of her home in Port Arthur. Ada stood by Stephen's side and put her arm around his shoulders.

'Did you enjoy your visit from your Aunt, Stephen?' Ada asked.

'Yes, thank you. It was very nice to meet her,' he said.

They shared a familiar smile and walked side-by-side back into the house.


STEPHEN WAVED TO John as he watched him run towards the barn at the end of the school day. But just for a moment he thought he saw Albert coming towards him. Stephen blinked and rubbed his right eye.

'Steve, come and look what I found. I have this great idea,' said John,

Stephen followed John to a quiet, secluded spot behind the barn out of sight from the main house and noticed a maple tree about to grow into its mature stage of life.

'Don't you think it's perfect?' John asked with a wave of mischievous excitement.

'For what?' Stephen asked.

'A tree-house!'

They shared a knowing smile and immediately began the task of retrieving some wood from the barn, and building a den, hidden away behind the leaves of the tree. They covered the floor with an old horse blanket they found at the back of the stables.

It was here, in their tree house, that they spent most of their time together at the end of each day. They filled their secret place with objects that would go missing from the main house and return days later.

'Look what I found?' John giggled, as he held up two pieces of cake from one of Ada's baking trays.

But their new game created havoc in the McPhail household.

'Has anyone seen my cigar, I left it on the mantelpiece?' Edgar asked at the dinner table.

'No, but I can't seem to find my lavender oil,' said Ada, bemused.

'A funny thing happened the other day. I turned my back for just minutes from the chopping board, only to return to find the carrots had disappeared . . . completely!' Catherine said, with a wry smile.

Stephen and John remained silent in their dual secret, with only Catherine perhaps guessing their mischief. It was in their tree-house, where Stephen would whisper some of the stories that used to help his brother, Albert, sleep.

'Tell me the story of Black Beauty again . . . please . . .' said John.

Stephen never once tired of repeating stories he had told from a very young age. John trusted Stephen, and as their relationship developed they shared secrets that they dare not tell anyone else.

It was one particular day, when they both shared a special secret, that they became even closer. Amongst the many games they played, Stephen and John loved to skate. They would often skate together on the iced pond between the farm and a neighbour's farm belonging to the Fletcher family. It stretched across the field behind the cornfield, at the side of the stone house and across the acres of land, especially during the freezing, blustering winter months. It was easy to forget the minutes, hours that passed by in the late afternoon.

'It's getting late, Steve, we better head back, in time for dinner,' said John as he skidded into a wooden fence.

'Okay, I'll race you. I might even let you win.' Stephen laughed.

The boys removed the skating blades from their boots and ran back towards the farmhouse. John celebrated entering the barn first, with his arms raised in ecstasy. They sat near the calf pens in front of the manger in the hay, concentrating diligently on untying their laces. The smell of hay lingered through the air to embrace the sweet scent of the groomed horses behind them. And synchronised laughter echoed, as they shared the memory of John colliding with the fence, until . . .

'Look, John,' Stephen whispered, staring at the wall in front of them.

'A horse is running?' John murmured, as he was about to run in the opposite direction.

Stephen put his hand gently on John's shoulder as he felt the energy from his trembling body spiral through his fingers. John remained mesmerised as he continued to stare at the wall.

'But where is it going?' Stephen asked, confused.

They took a deep breath simultaneously as their wide eyes became transfixed on the horse. A gust of light wind entered the barn. The two boys shivered as they looked behind them and saw none of the horses moving in the stables. And as they slowly turned back—the image before them faded on the wall before their eyes.

'What just happened?' John asked.

'I'm not sure. Did you see that horse?' Stephen asked.

'Yes . . . did you?' John asked.

They sat, as though in a trance, unable to move, wanting to investigate behind the wall. But instead they remained frozen in the hay.

'We can't tell anyone about this. They wouldn't believe us,' whispered John.

'Let's wait and see if it comes back,' said Stephen.

And so, they waited together, too scared to do anything else . . .

Eventually, Stephen got up and walked over to the wall. He looked behind it and shrugged. John followed him, remaining close by. Stephen touched the white stonewall with his hand.

'I don't understand. I definitely saw a horse moving,' he said, bemused.

'Do you think it was a spirit horse, come back from the dead?' John asked.

They looked at each other, their eyes wide.

'Whatever just happened here, it was real, wherever it came from,' said Stephen.

They promised to keep their magical horse a secret but were unable to hide it from Ada. She had a way of looking into their eyes and repeating their thoughts back to them.

'You two are hiding something,' said Ada, whilst the three of them were gathered in the kitchen one evening, waiting for Edgar.

'What do you mean, Ma?' John asked.

'You've both seen something, haven't you?'

Stephen and John shuffled their feet and stared at the floor.

'We saw a horse moving on the wall in the barn,' said John quickly, shrugging at Stephen.

'A horse?' Ada questioned.

'Yes, we both saw it at the same time. We thought one of the horses had got out from the stables behind us, but they hadn't. It was definitely there, running across the wall near the cow pens,' said Stephen.

'What happened next?' Ada asked.

'We looked behind the wall, and there was nothing there. It was like it just vanished,' said John.

'Has anyone seen anything like that before, in the barn?' Stephen asked.

'I've not heard of a story about a horse. But you must never be afraid of what you see or hear. If you feel scared about anything, you must promise me you will come to me,' whispered Ada in her soft gentle voice.

'Promise,' said the boys together.

'But why was the horse running?' John asked.

'There is always a message in what they choose to show us. You will come to know what it means, in time,' answered Ada, trying to reassure them as her hand trembled beneath her tapestry.

Stephen and John listened attentively.

'If you have any other visions, I want you both to write them down and hide them away somewhere safe. Then come to me, and we'll talk about them together,' said Ada.

'What visions are you talking about?' Edgar asked as he entered the room with his Bible in hand.

'We've seen a horse moving on one of the walls in the barn, sir,' said Stephen.

Ada lowered her head.

'A horse moving?' Edgar asked.

'It was running, Pa . . . and suddenly it faded and just vanished,' said John, separating his hands.

'Now, John, you've always had a vivid imagination. Stephen, I'm surprised at you, I thought you had more sense,' said Edgar.

'Yes, sir,' said Stephen, bowing his head.

'But Edgar, they've both seen . . .' said Ada.

'I won't hear of it. Visions on walls. You must stop encouraging them to tell such stories,' said Edgar.

'Yes, dear,' said Ada, clasping her hands together in prayer.

Edgar sat down in his usual armchair, opposite Ada, and opened his Bible; clearing is throat as he did so.

> There shall not be found among you anyone who burns his son or his daughter as an offering, anyone who practices divination or tells fortunes or interprets omens, or a sorcerer or a charmer or a medium or a necromancer or one who inquires of the dead, for whoever does these things is an abomination to the Lord. And because of these abominations the Lord your God is driving them out before you. You shall be blameless before the Lord your God . . . Deuteronomy 18: 10 to 13.

Silence fell in the kitchen with only the crackling sound of the flames burning through the logs in the oven stoves.

Ada continued to encourage Stephen and John, despite Edgar's convictions. A triangle of secret meetings developed that had to be protected and kept from Edgar. It was a time to ask questions and share their experiences. Stephen was able to talk openly about spirituality for the first time. He came to realise that he was not alone and so different from other people, as he had always thought. When he was with Ada and John, he learnt to trust like he had never done before.

But he still deeply respected Edgar and enjoyed listening to his Bible readings in the evening, when the family gathered around the log burning oven stoves, in the kitchen. He was attentive to Edgar's deep, clear voice and vowed that one day: *I will make you proud.*

THE MCPHAIL FAMILY made their way towards Kirkwall Presbyterian Church in the horse and sleigh. Buffalo blankets covered their laps to protect them from the chilled ice air. The sleigh easily glided over the deep white snow, whilst leaf shaped flakes continued to fall from the grey hollow sky. The family never missed a service at the rural church in Cambridge, Ontario. But today was a special service, just prior to Christmas Day.

Stephen looked up at the grey-slated roof, which covered a triangular fronted brick building with elongated spiral windows.

'Why is it we're always a little late for church?' Catherine muttered, as Edgar helped her down from the horse and sleigh.

Edgar bit his lip as he breathed deeply and seemed to ignore his mother's comment, as the family made their way through the entrance door.

'Would you like to lean on my arm, Catherine?' Stephen asked as they approached a wide flight of stairs.

'You're a good boy, Stephen,' said Catherine as her cane led the way.

Stephen followed Edgar and Ada, with John by their side, until he noticed bright beams of sunlight flooding the first floor of the church.

'Good morning,' said Edgar as he held out his hand to Reverend Ivan standing at the top of the stairs.

'Good morning, Edgar, it's nice to see you and your family looking so well', said the grey- haired man, clutching a bible and peering at his pocket watch.

'Thank you, Reverend,' said Edgar.

'The Elders have congregated near the pulpit, they're waiting for you,' said Reverend Ivan.

'We will go and sit down,' said Ada.

Stephen continued to support Catherine until they found their usual pew to the left of the church. Ada smiled serenely at familiar faces as she gracefully sat down. Stephen watched Edgar approach the Elders and listen attentively to their conversation before speaking. There were lots of nodding and shaking of heads and raised eyebrows.

'Do women ever become Elders?' Stephen whispered to Ada.

'Not that I know of, Stephen,' said Ada.

'Do you think we should tell the Elders about the horse running on the wall of the barn? Pa always says we should tell the truth, especially when we're in church,' said John.

'No, I don't think that's a good idea, John. You must keep quiet about that, promise me?' Ada whispered, wiping his nose with her handkerchief and smiling at the congregation to her right.

'I promise,' said John.

Ada breathed deeply as she shared a look of relief with Stephen. Edgar made his way towards them and sat with his family.

'Why do they call it a Presbyterian church, sir?' Stephen asked.

'Presbyterian represents the sovereignty of God and the authority of the scriptures through faith in Christ,' said Edgar, pleased with Stephen's interest.

'Did this type of Church begin in Canada?' Stephen asked.

'The history of Presbyterian churches can be traced back to Scotland, from where my family originally came over to Canada in the eighteenth century. It's Scotland, where the name McPhail comes from, you know?' said Edgar, proudly.

'I believe Scotland's not so far away from England,' said Stephen.

'That's right, Stephen,' said Edgar.

Reverend Ivan asked the congregation to stand as the first hymn was announced, and the words filled the air with harmonious voices chiming together.

> Silent Night! Holy Night!
> All is calm, all is bright
> 'round you virgin mother . . .

Stephen choked as the words stuck somewhere at the back of his throat, and he was left with no voice . . . and all he could do was mime, in the hope no one noticed.

> . . . and child!
> Holy infant, so tender and mild,
> Sleep in heavenly peace . . .

Stephen held his Hymnbook close to his chest and felt a sense of belonging to a family he had come to love, but there was still part of him missing. It was like a hollow, empty hole inside where his wounds of loss and separation were hidden from the outside world. Only he knew the true meaning of his own pain that remained his deepest secret.

THE SEASONS PASSED with heavy, snowdrift winters and scorching hot summers. Stephen continued to escape into the barn and hide amongst the straw mow, where his writing slowly expanded from his own general thoughts and feelings upon the pages of his journal.

> Sunday: I went to church today with the family. I love them very much, and they are good to me. But I can't help but notice there's tension between Edgar and Ada when it comes to their religious beliefs. Edgar won't allow us to talk about anything that he says is not written in the Bible. Ada seems uncomfortable in church, especially when members of the community gather around her and ask her questions. I feel that I want to protect her, but I don't want to offend Edgar, by speaking out of turn. So, I must stay quiet. I'm glad I spend time with Ada and John, when Edgar leaves the house to go to his church meetings. At least then we can talk openly and honestly about things that are not religious.
>
> It seems that when I'm in church I miss my Ma and my brothers, especially Albie, the most. I pray that one day we will all be together again.

As Stephen sat, covered in straw, he spoke softly to Annie, about how deeply he missed his brother. He worried for Albert's safety, and his mind closed down into a black spell, until a light flashed through . . .

*As the dark and painful years passed, Albert pined for his brother and desperately missed his mother. He could only remember the affection he once knew and longed to be held again. And so he held himself during the isolated hours from dusk to dawn when he was allowed to rest in the freezing barn—trying hard to remember the stories his brother once told him, that brought him comfort before sleep. Albert became tired and slower at completing his chores. He struggled due to his young age and the missing phalanges from his hand. Mr Thompson beat his legs with a stick, until he cowered in the corner of the barn and screamed, Please . . . please stop!*

Stephen kicked out his legs in the hay and cried out . . .

*Where am I?*

He rubbed his aching right eye in an attempt to make the pain go away.

*Annie . . .*
*I'm right here, Stevie.*
*I just had another of those bad dreams.*
*You're safe now.*
*But Albie . . .*
*It's time to go back to the house, Stevie. They're waiting for you.*

Talking to Annie was a source of great comfort to Stephen, a way of feeling close to those he had left behind. During these precious moments, he was with his own family. All he had to do was go inside his imagination and remember, but he couldn't understand why he kept having dark nightmares about his brother.

STEPHEN'S UNSETTLED HEART reflected the general unrest on a much wider scale in Europe. The world was changing with the threat of war pending. Stephen sat close to Ada as the family gathered in the kitchen listening to Edgar's clear and deep voice as he read sombrely from the local newspaper.

'Great Britain declares war on Germany. King George V has sent a personal message to the troops of the British Expeditionary Force, on August 12th, 1914: You are leaving home to fight for the safety and honour of my Empire. Duty is your watchword, and I know your duty will be notably done. I pray God to bless you and guard you and bring you back victorious.'

The crackle of the log-burning oven stoves merged into the silence of the dark and starless night. Ada's breathing became heavier as a weighted fear locked down her heart. She never spoke of her deepest and most hidden secret. But now she had to face the unwanted truth. Although she could not deny the torturous horror stories she heard across the globe, she was also unable to deny her true heritage.

Edgar's curled moustache twitched beneath a falling shadow over his eyes as they lingered in the space between him and his wife. Ada picked up her embroidery and used it as a shield to hide the slight tremble in her fingers. She continued in quiet contemplation, with the serenity of her countenance becoming frozen in contrast to the heat from the log-burning oven stove.

A long, loud yawn broke the silence. John stretched his arms over his head as he sunk deeper into the chair.

'What does war mean?' he asked.

'I think it's time for bed,' said Edgar.

John screwed his face beneath his tousled blonde hair but knew not to defy his father.

'Edgar, why don't you read a psalm before we retire,' said Ada gently.

The black-covered bible by his side was opened almost immediately. He cleared his throat, as usual.

> Psalm 31 . . . In You, O Lord, I put my trust: Let me never be ashamed; Deliver me in Your righteousness. Bow down Your ear to me. Deliver me speedily; Be my rock of refuge, A fortress of defence to save me. For you are my rock and my fortress; Therefore, for Your name's sake, Lead me and guide me. Pull me out of the net, which they have secretly laid for me, For You are my strength. Into Your hand I commit my spirit; You have redeemed me, Oh Lord God of truth.

'You always know the right words to say, at the right time,' whispered Ada, as ripples of light shone from her eyes.

Edgar returned her loving smile. John fell asleep peacefully in the chair. Stephen stared into the dying flames of the log-burning oven stove . . .

As the beatings continued, Albert's heart broke into shattered pieces that reflected the sleets of ice that he always believed fell from the light of the moon . . . And one day, Albert spoke back to him . . .

Later that evening, Stephen lay awake in his room, unable to read, write, or sleep. He looked out of the small square window and tried to count the stars glowing in the endless purple sky, like eyes watching over him. But all he could do was call out from the silent corner of his heart.

> *I don't know what to do, Annie. I need to find a way of getting back to Albie, he's in trouble, I can feel it.*
>
> *Just as I'm here with you, I go to Albie, when he needs me. The only difference is, that Albie doesn't know I'm there. But he does feel the comfort of my touch in his dreams. One day we will all be together again.*
>
> *But what will become of everyone at home, now my country is at war? Will they be safe? Tell me what to do?*
>
> *You will know what to do when the time comes, Stevie. It's called intuition! Besides, I've never left you alone yet have I?*
>
> *Well . . . you do tend to come and go.*
>
> *That's because I'm busy, flying here and flying there. It's a full-time job being invisible!*

*But, Annie . . . can't you be serious for once?*

*Rest now . . . close your eyes and wait for the sun to rise. All will become clear, as you open your heart and listen. But listen well, Stevie. Because whatever decisions you make . . . there will be no going back.*

*There you again with the poetics. Is this you being serious?*

*I'm bored now!*

# 7
# The Great War

*"Any coward can fight a battle when he's sure of winning, but give me the man who has the pluck to fight when he's sure of losing."* — *George Eliot*

IT WAS A clear morning, with rays of early sunrise shining brightly from the vast blue sky over the town of Hamilton. The light danced with shadows from the maple trees and wings of warmth gently touched the square windows of the kitchen.

Ada blinked away her sleepless night as she scrambled eggs with an elegant twist of her wrist. Edgar sat at the oak table reading the *Flamborough Review,* his eyes locked within a distance that no one could penetrate. John's legs dandled over the chair next to his father as he gathered his books ready for school, sighing deeply at having to face a day without playing with Stephen. Ada gently smiled at her son. Stephen's socked feet touched the stone floor beneath him as Ada never allowed boots inside the house. The face of the *Herschede* mantle clock looked back at Stephen as the second hand moved slowly through time. It reminded him of home, where shapes and colours were different but the deep, sweeping tone of the tick radiating from the clock was the same.

The clink of cutlery against the bone china plates harmonised with the words that Edgar read from his folded newspaper.

'A large- scale offensive has been launched against the German Front Line on both sides of the Somme River.'

'Where's the Somme?' John asked.

'It's a river in a country called France, far away from here,' said Ada, quietly.

'It's been two long years and still the war drags on,' said Edgar.

'Is there no end to all this fighting?' Ada asked an unanswerable question.

'I've heard lots of men are enlisting in Dundas, sir,' said Stephen tentatively.

'Mm . . .' said Edgar as he continued to read his newspaper.

'Well, thank goodness you're too young, Stephen. I don't know what we'd do without you.' Ada smiled gently.

Stephen finished his breakfast in silence, until Catherine appeared from her bedroom, leaning on her cane.

'I think I need my cane seeing to,' she muttered as she pulled her shawl closer around her neck with her free hand.

'Come and sit down and have some breakfast. It looks like your back has bent a little further forward,' said Ada, gently supporting her arm.

'I'll shorten it for you again,' said Edgar.

'I can do it,' said Stephen

'You're a good boy,' said Catherine.

'Right, there's work to be done,' said Edgar.

'John, it's time for school,' said Ada as she helped him put his school books inside his bag.

Stephen jumped to his feet and pushed his chair under the table. He reached for Catherine's cane and rushed across the stone floor as Edgar strolled behind him. They pushed socked feet into their boots waiting for them near the outside door. Stephen stepped out into the early morning sunshine, greeted by Ned, an old English sheep dog—retired from farm work. He held Ned's lifted paw and stroked the top of his head.

'Come on, Ned, we need to go,' said Stephen.

Ned followed Stephen, watching him curiously with sleepy brown eyes.

'He's certainly taken to you, Stephen. Ned doesn't follow anyone else around the farm,' said Edgar as he continued to stroll behind them.

'I'll shorten the cane, and then get the horses ready for the plough, sir,' said Stephen.

'We need to finish at least one of the fields today, or we might not have a chance of harvesting in time,' said Edgar.

'Yes, sir, I'll be as quick as I can,' said Stephen.

He entered the shed, stepped round the well, and found a handsaw near a pile of logs. Stephen cut the end from the cane and ran back to the house.

'How's that?' Stephen asked, placing the cane in Catherine's hand.

'That feels a little better,' said Catherine as she slowly stood up and walked more easily.

'Thank you, Stephen,' said Ada, as she cleared the table.

'You know what they say about good deeds. What you give, always comes back to you,' said Catherine, as she looked up at Stephen.

They shared a smile, and Stephen hurried back to the barn. Ned slowly followed, found a spot in the hay, and lay down for a snooze.

Stephen entered the stables and the horses shook their manes to greet him.

'Morning, Del, you seem calmer today, and look at you, Delwyn, full of life. There's something different about you two, are you trying to trick me?' he whispered in their ears and smiled as he patted them gently.

Stephen recognised a sense of peace inside his heart whenever he was inside the barn. He led four of the horses to the side field where they were left to graze in the sunshine. Then he quickly returned to fit collars over the shoulders of Del and Delwyn, to make sure the drag of the load was distributed. He hooked the bellyband to the traces. The movements were automatic, and so natural to Stephen, like putting on his skates and playing with John.

'Right, Stephen. Let's head out and get an early start. I've never seen Delwyn so calm. You work well with animals,' said Edgar.

'Thank you, sir,' said Stephen.

'Do you think you might go into farming when the time comes?' Edgar asked.

'Yes, sir. I enjoy the work here. I feel like I'm learning a lot about things I never knew before,' said Stephen.

'I want you to know, you will always have a home here,' said Edgar.

'That means a lot to me sir, thank you,' said Stephen.

Edgar opened the rickety green gate that led onto the far-left field opposite thousands of speckles of corn sparkling in the flow of the light breeze. The burning sun reflected beads of sweat gathering on the brows of Stephen and Edgar as they worked side by side, turning over the upper layer of soil, creating long trenches of furrows. The work continued whilst the day moved slowly towards flecks of shade, and it was time to rest.

'Take the horses back to the stables now, Stephen. I'm going to walk over to the Fletcher farm. Tell Ada I'll be back for dinner,' said Edgar.

'Yes, sir,' said Stephen.

Stephen removed the harness from the horses' collars and climbed up on Delwyn's pure white back whilst holding Del's rein. He steered them slowly and gently back towards the barn.

'There now, you've both worked hard today and deserve a break. Don't you?'

They shook their manes proudly as they listened to Stephen's voice. A spark of electric heat ran through Stephen's veins, and he felt the close connection with Delwyn as he sat astride the white horse. He knew Delwyn understood every word he said. He had always felt an affinity with animals, but especially Delwyn.

'We've met before, Delwyn,' he whispered as he learnt towards his ear.

Stephen knew that all he had to do was close his eyes, and in his dreams, Delwyn would fly him high into the stars where he was free to be whoever he wanted to be. The fantasy always returned when he needed to escape, and

Delwyn never let him down. He was as steadfast and courageous in flight as he was grounded and strong, when needed to plough the fields.

Stephen smiled and looked up into the velvet sky. A sense of silent peace overflowed his heart, a protective flame warmed his body, and a beam of violet light guided his way, surrounded by angelic love. He travelled past the resting clouds and into the realms of other dimensions, where the stars blinked back at him and lit the way into a magical place. He laughed with joy, until . . .

Delwyn's hooves suddenly returned to earth, and Stephen opened his eyes. He leant forward, closer to Delwyn's ear.

'Thank you, Delwyn,' he whispered.

When they returned to the barn, Stephen brushed the horses' coats and used a towel rag to remove sweat marks as the horses drank intermittently from the water barrels. He patted them affectionately and filled the stables with clean hay. When he had finished his work, Stephen stretched and yawned widely. He made his way towards the granary. It was quiet up there on the first floor of the barn with no one around. He climbed up to a beam on the right-hand side and reached for his journal in its secret hiding place. Stephen sat down and dangled his legs outside the wooden framed door, and his pen glided across the blank page.

> I travelled with Delwyn today, higher into the realms of the velvet sky. He took me to this magical place where I could only feel love shooting through my heart. I swam in warm turquoise water beneath a flowing waterfall. Exotic flowers opened their petals as if to speak to me, as they floated by. I could see my own reflection in the white cliffs surrounding me. Delwyn waited patiently on the golden sand dunes, until it was time to leave. I wish I could dream like this all the time and the nightmares would leave me.

Stephen looked down at the ground below, and then lifted his head to the blue, cloudless sky and the horizon beyond the cornfields. The orange glow of the resting sun cast shadows in darkened spaces to meet the late afternoon. He turned over the page in his journal, but the black ink remained within as the pen hovered over the white paper. His mind wandered . . .

*Come closer, Annie (he whispered).*

Stephen rubbed his right eye until he could clearly see the familiar light beside him. The girl's fair hair curled beneath her shoulders, and her blue eyes shone brightly like a torch of light from another time. Stephen felt the warmth from her velvet aura, and his mind became focused. They shared a gentle, loving smile. Then the light danced away.

*Annie . . . Annie. (Stephen whispered, reaching out for her.)*

Stephen noticed a shadow move across the hay and looked up to see a familiar light across the beam at the top of the straw mow.

*Oh, Annie, don't start playing games now. I need to talk to you.*

But Stephen could only see a dark shadow behind the beam. He put his head in his hands and sighed deeply. A light breeze blew across the pages of his journal, flickering them towards the end of the brown book. Stephen stared at the empty page, until the light returned beside him.

*Do you think you can stay in one place whilst I talk to you?*
*(Stephen's ears tingled with the echo of distant laughter.)*
*I feel confused, Annie. What's the purpose of my life? I have a place here, on the farm, and I love what I do. So why doesn't it feel enough?*
*You've grown so much, Stevie. Open your mind . . . You need to learn to trust yourself. Look deeper within. What can you see on that empty page?*
*It's blank.*
*Look again . . .*

A spark of light flickered across his journal until he saw himself walk off the page and fall into a ditch. Stephen screamed at his torn muscle. He retched into the blood, which sucked at stained mud, concealing his ice-cold body. His right eye flickered. A blurred figure moved closer. Who's there?

Stephen's body jolted. He gasped for breath as the surrounding barn came into vision. Yellow tips of the cornfields stretched out, bowing gently with the breeze. The falling sun reflected the shimmering glow beside him. Stephen swung his legs in rhythm with Annie's as the dark shadow lifted from the top of his head. A violet light swirled around him, and he realised how much he had changed.

*It's time for my lesson. Ada will be looking for me.*
*(Annie danced around him determined to slow his footsteps.)*
*Don't leave yet, Stevie, let's play.*
*I have to go, I can't be late.*

*So, you'd rather read from a German textbook than stay and have fun with me?*
*Don't be disrespectful. Ada's good to me.*
*Well . . . if you must go . . .*

A small bale of hay suddenly moved across the floor. He tripped, but regained his balance to the sound of Annie's giggles.

*That wasn't funny, Annie.*

Stephen rushed towards the barn door. He looked back and saw Annie's light fade in the distant corner until the darkness returned.

*I'll be waiting (Annie whispered from inside the white stonewall.)*

BRIGHT RAYS OF sunlight glimmered between the branches of the maple tree, contrasting with the shadows, which invaded the side of the farmhouse. Stephen ran towards the back door of the house and removed his boots. He entered the washroom and poured some water from the jug into the bowl. The splash of the water cooled his face, then he washed his hands with coal tar soap. As he entered the kitchen he noticed Catherine sitting near the log-burning oven stove. Her knitting needles clinked as they caught the red wool in a rhythm determined to finish her scarf.

'Would you like some coffee, Stephen? I've just made a pot. Help yourself,' said Catherine.

'Yes, thank you,' said Stephen as he poured the dark liquid into a china cup and placed it gently upon a saucer.

Stephen made his way into the side parlour where Ada was waiting patiently, holding a leather-bound book. Her sweet perfume contrasted with the smell of burnt embers from the log-burning oven.

'There you are, Stephen. Close the door and come and sit down,' said Ada.

'I'm sorry I'm late. I forgot the time,' said Stephen.

'You're here now. I thought we'd look at *Hymnen an die Nacht* today, translated as?'

'*Hymns to the Night*,' said Stephen.

'The book is by Novalis, a poet, author, mystic, and philosopher. He was born 1772 and died in 1801 at the age of twenty-eight,' said Ada.

'That's a young age to die,' said Stephen.

'Maybe not in that time, but we can die at any age, Stephen. I lost twins at birth before John was born. John had diphtheria when he was very young, and we thought he was going to die. I made his funeral gown in preparation for what we thought was to come. But a miracle happened. Our local doctor did a procedure on his throat that saved his life,' said Ada.

'John told me he had something. But I had no idea he nearly died,' said Stephen.

'Some things we keep close to our hearts. We don't need to speak of them, to remember,' said Ada.

'So, John wasn't an only child?' said Stephen.

'We had a son, two years after John was born. His name was Clarence. He died a year later. We don't know why. We have to accept and be grateful to the grace of God for what we have. I pray for my children every day, including you, Stephen. I believe a gracious spirit is watching over all of you,' said Ada.

Stephen listened attentively. Ada continued to talk about life and death and the connection of the spirit world between a human life and God. His eyes widened as he became hypnotised by the gentle tone of Ada's voice.

'But what's interesting about this book, Stephen, is that the six hymns are based on Novalis' own life. He wrote it whilst he grieved for the loss of his young fiancée. She was only fifteen when she died of consumption. We all face loss in our lives. It's how we learn to live with it that counts,' said Ada.

'I miss my family in England, and I know my brother is here in Canada, but he seems so far away. I feel like I've lost him too,' said Stephen.

'No one is ever lost to us. Novalis writes about a loving union with our loved ones in the presence of God, when it is our time to go home. You will know when that time comes. The universe will call you by your name, and don't ever be afraid, Stephen. Death is but a pause to eternal life,' said Ada, as a glimmer of light shone from her eyes.

'Novalis is an unusual name,' said Stephen.

'That was his pen name. He was born Georg Philipp Friedrich Freiherr von Hardenberg,' said Ada.

Stephen mirrored Ada's smile as she opened the book and turned to a particular page. She placed it in Stephen's hands, and he held it out in front of him.

'Now let me hear you read,' said Ada.

Stephen looked across at the closed door to the parlour.

'Edgar's still outside working. He knows you're here and does approve of us having some time to read together. But you know that the community here is not aware of my German heritage, and with the situation in Europe, we are determined to keep it secret,' said Ada, slightly biting her bottom lip.

Stephen nodded with respect and lowered his head.

'Lift your head up, Stephen. Don't ever be ashamed of who you are and where you have come from,' said Ada.

A glow of warmth stirred inside Stephen as he felt the urge to hide away in the comfort and safety of Ada's arms. But he knew she was waiting patiently for him to begin. Stephen cleared his throat.

> Oh ziehen an m . . . meinem,
> Herzen L . . . liebe ziehen,
> bis ich weg bin,
> da e . . . entschlafen ich kann immer noch lieben auf.

'Translated?' Ada asked.

> Oh draw at my heart, love,
> Draw till I'm gone,
> That, fallen asleep,
> I still may love on.

Ada rested her head against the soft purple velvet cushion behind her head and breathed deeply as she raised her eyes to the white stone ceiling above. Stephen paused.

'Go on, Stephen, you read beautifully,' said Ada.

Stephen continued to read the German language, translating to English from one verse to the next.

> I feel the flow of
> Death's youth—giving flood
> To balsam and ether
> Transform my blood . . .

Stephen's voice faltered as he rubbed his right eye . . .

He stared into the flames of a sizzling fire, where he saw a flash of charcoal mud streaming with purple blood gushing from the mouth of an unknown warrior. He gasped for air as he sank deeper into a silent scream . . .

'Stephen, what is it?' Ada asked.

He shivered as flashes of light coiled around twisted logs.

'I . . . I'm fine,' faltered Stephen, resting inside the warmth from Ada's gaze. He tried to swallow the dryness from his throat.

'Well, only continue if you're sure. These are very powerful words,' said Ada.

> I live all the daytime
> In faith and in might
> And in holy fire
> I die every night.

Stephen's fingers trembled slightly, and the pages from the book slowly turned. Ada reached out and touched his hand gently. The silence in the room seemed to drown out the ticking of the clock on the mantelpiece. Stephen felt a warm glow radiate through his body as he smiled with gratitude. Ada had a way of making him feel at peace with himself.

'Your German has really improved since you first arrived here, Stephen. I can see you have been practising,' said Ada, looking pleased.

'Thank you, I like learning,' said Stephen.

'I enjoy us spending this time together since you left school. You're doing really well,' said Ada.

'It's not easy,' said Stephen.

'Nothing in life is easy, Stephen,' said Ada.

Stephen's eyes caught Ada's as he looked back from the doorway.

'Just remember not to discuss these texts or speak the German language to anyone else, especially in this time of war,' said Ada.

Stephen nodded respectfully. He returned to the barn and continued to clean out the stables and feed the horses. Thoughts of Novalis whirled in his head.

'Hey Steve . . . Steve,' John called from outside the barn.

'Here, John, in the stables,' Stephen responded.

John rushed into the barn, struggling to catch his breath, cheeks flushed with the run home from school. He tossed his schoolbag into the hay, grinned widely, and patted the horses.

'I don't understand why I have to go to school every day. It's boring. I'd much rather be here with you, Steve. I miss you since you left. It's not the same,' said John.

'Yes, but you can leave when you're fourteen. In the mean time you get to learn all that clever stuff you need to get by in the world,' said Stephen.

'You don't have to go to school now, and you know lots of things. Besides, I want to be a farmer, so why do I need to learn to read, write, and do sums?' John asked, lowering his head and kicking a cluster of hay out the way.

'Maybe one day, you'll be glad you did learn, and you'll have no regrets,' said Stephen.

'Okay, but it's still boring.'

Stephen laughed as he finished his work in the stables. John grinned mischievously and looked directly at Stephen.

'Shall we go skating?'

'It's not cold enough, the pond won't be frozen yet.'

'How about the tree house?'

'That's a good idea. Come on, I'll race you.'


STEPHEN LISTENED TO the trees whisper through the breeze as the sun lifted its pure light above the quiet stillness inside the farmhouse. Flickers of sunlight played on his eyelids. He stretched his arms over his head as he yawned and headed slowly to the washroom. He stared in the mirror hanging from the wall, above the jug of water and small basin. As he looked at his own reflection, his hand touched a surface of bristles growing from his chin outwards towards his ears. Stephen picked up the razor that Edgar had given to him on Christmas Day and shaved diligently. It was over in seconds. He couldn't remember how his features had changed over time, but the young boy, who had first arrived at the farm feeling like an empty sack inside, had long disappeared.

Stephen knew there was no need to rush this morning, so took his time in getting dressed. He stretched into his only suit and took a deep breath. He opened the latch door to head towards the kitchen and smiled to himself.

'Oh, Stephen, that suit's starting to look too tight. You're growing out of it. It will have to do for today. Give it to me when we get back from church and I'll see what I can do,' said Ada.

'I remember the first day you arrived here, quiet as a church mouse, now look how tall you've grown,' said Catherine, peering over her spectacles.

Stephen sat at the oak table, pulling at the sleeves. The smell of freshly baked bread lingered in the air, mixing with the aroma of strong coffee. He reached for the toast and eggs, plated neatly in the middle of the tablecloth and noticed Edgar staring at his naked wrists.

'I might have a jacket that fits you,' said Edgar.

'Thank you, sir,' said Stephen, wondering what the jacket might look like.

'We can't have you going to church in a suit that's starting to look too small for you,' said Ada.

'I think I might be growing out of *my* suit,' said John.

Stephen noticed Ada smile at John as he attempted to pull down his sleeves.

'Mm . . . I think your suit fits you well enough,' said Edgar from behind his newspaper.

'What's the latest news in France?' Ada asked.

'John, can you go and look for my bible, I think I may have left it in the front parlour?' Edgar said.

Stephen watched John sigh heavily as he excused himself from the table and slowly disappeared. Stephen lowered his head. He shivered as he rubbed the itch from his right eye.

Edgar cleared his throat to speak and shook his newspaper gently in an attempt to bring it closer. 'April 26, 1915. Ypres, Belgium—Troops of the 1st Canadian Division have fought hard here against fierce German attacks. The enemy offensive began four days ago with clouds of poisonous chlorine gas. The Canadians attempted to counter the clouds of noxious gas by breathing through handkerchiefs soaked in urine . . .'

'Oh . . . my goodness, how have they survived?' Ada asked as she brought her scented handkerchief closer to the air she breathed.

Stephen moved his hand across the table and gently touched Ada's arm as he noticed Catherine remove her spectacles and wipe tears away. Edgar continued reading.

'Canadian officers learned a lot about the "the fog of war." Battles are confusing affairs to manage, orders are misunderstood or changed, and both sides make mistakes. In some cases, confused troops dug in facing the wrong way. Artillery and machine-gun fire have been deadly, and losses have been terrible. Some 5,000 Canadians have been killed, wounded, or taken prisoner . . .'

'I've found it,' said John as he rushed into the kitchen, holding Edgar's Bible above his head like a trophy.

But only silence prevailed as Stephen stared into a carved eye on the surface of the oak table, and even the sound of the *Herschede* clock seemed to fall away into stillness. A quiet pause lingered around the table as Edgar diligently folded his newspaper, placed it in front of him. and gently touched his curled moustache with his thumb and forefinger. Stephen noticed Ada stare into the coffee pot as if she was searching for something inside that couldn't be found. John buttoned up his jacket and breathed out, still convinced it didn't quite fit. Catherine excused herself and made her way to the armchair near the log burning oven stove, where she retrieved her knitting needles from down the side of the cushion and began the click of the entwining wool, coordinated with the tick of the clock, passing time on the mantelpiece.

'It's time to leave for church,' said Edgar, interrupting the silence and disappearing upstairs.

'We mustn't be late,' said Ada.

'That'll be a first,' muttered Catherine from behind her knitting needles.

The family slowly stirred from the table. Stephen helped Ada clear away the dishes, whilst John struggled to put his boots on, and coats were passed around.

'This should fit you, Stephen,' said Edgar, as he appeared in the doorway.

'Try it on,' said Ada.

Stephen put his arms into the sleeves of a black jacket that fitted perfectly.

'Look at you, quite the young gentleman. I don't know where the years have gone,' said Ada, brushing away some light dust from his shoulders.

'Come and help me prepare the horse and carriage, Stephen,' said Edgar.

'It's time we were setting off, but we do need some more water brought in from the well,' said Ada.

'I can do that when we get back from church,' said Stephen.

Ada smiled, with sparkles of light falling into the distance between them.

Stephen followed Edgar outside and headed towards the stables.

'We'll take Del and Delwyn today,' said Edgar.

Stephen helped Edgar with the task of attaching the collar and harness onto the horses' shoulders. Then he held out his hand to help Ada and Catherine board the carriage.

John tripped over his foot as he rushed to climb inside and claim his seat.

'Can I sit next to Steve?' John asked.

'John, you always sit together anyway,' said Ada, smiling.

When the family were settled inside, Edgar steered the carriage along the pebbled path, leaving behind the green leaved maple trees for the road that would lead them to Cambridge, Ontario. Whilst the carriage rumbled towards its destination, John looked up at Stephen with a mischievous light shining from his eyes.

'Why is it called Kirkwall Presbyterian Church? It doesn't have a wall around it,' said John.

'I've often wondered where the name came from,' Stephen said, looking in Ada's direction.

Ada gazed towards Edgar as he steered the carriage with an expertise that came naturally to him.

'Many years ago, six families from Scotland came here,' said Edgar.

'Because their soil wasn't good to plant crops,' said Ada.

'The soil is really good here,' said Stephen.

'They built a log house,' said Edgar.

'That's why they chose this land. The spaces between the logs were stuffed with moss from the trees,' said Ada.

'So, was that the original building where the church stands now?' Stephen asked, as he felt John lean his head into his shoulder.

'No, they set out to build their own homes on the land. Our colony doubled by the arrival of more families from Scotland, England, and Northern Ireland,' said Edgar.

'Is that why Charlie always tells me his great grandfather saw a leprechaun once in the Irish countryside? I've never seen one here,' said John.

'I think you mean Charles, not Charlie. Don't believe everything you hear, John. And as for the girls, always giggling between them. It's time they were married and settled down,' said Catherine, squinting over her spectacles beneath her bonnet, looking like she was ready for sleep.

'I think Flo, Ettie, and Sophia have plenty of time to think about marriage, they're still very young,' said Ada.

Stephen lowered his head, afraid someone might see his flushed cheeks.

'The original log building was sometimes used as a place of worship, where they first met with God on this land,' said Edgar.

'Those early pioneers formed the basis of the present congregation. It was a little later when the lower floor of the church was built in Kirkwall, and then the second floor was added,' said Ada.

'Will we all be buried in the church yard alongside those early pioneers?' John asked.

Stephen's eyes reflected an unspoken sadness falling from Ada's as they stared into their own hidden grief.

'One day, when our time comes. When God decides to call us home,' said Ada gently.

Stephen noticed Catherine with her back slightly stooped forward, her crinkling skin on her hands as they clutched each other, and her eyes closed. He wondered what his life might be like on reaching Catherine's age, and was curious how she could sleep almost soundly inside the carriage as it swayed from side to side. But she always seemed to find a way.

The carriage finally arrived outside the two-storey building. Stephen followed the family inside. They climbed the steps up to the first floor, where the early sunrise shone rainbows of light through the long, tall windows. Edgar moved towards the elders congregated in the far-left corner of the pulpit and began the usual ceremony of hand shaking, nodding and quiet conversation, whilst the large wooden cross looked like it was lit from within against the white stone wall.

Stephen's eyes scanned the pews until they rested easily on the figure of a young girl he recognised. He found himself moving slowly towards her with Ada and Catherine leading the way and John by his side. Stephen felt his stomach move like a wave as he struggled to breathe. A sensation similar to an electric current sizzled through his head, as he noticed her fair hair fall into wisps of curls around her high cheekbones. Her small, slim demeanour was upright and graceful. A touch of elegance reminded him of a young Ada. But it was the violet light from her eyes that forced Stephen's heart to pound as if it might rip open his chest and dance towards her.

'Good morning, Flo,' said Stephen, smiling.

The inside of the church seemed to fill with clouds of mist as the young girl smiled and bowed her head. They were close enough to touch.

'It's good to see you, Steve,' said Flo.

Stephen felt determined to continue the conversation, but Flo's mother suddenly appeared by her side. He always saw her hat first, decorated with a combination of feathers, artificial flowers, and fruit, and knew it was a sign to move on. She bustled forward and grasped her daughter's hand as it reached to meet Stephen's, smiled politely in his direction, and whisked Flo away to be seated.

Stephen was left standing in silent disappointment until he heard John whisper.

'Steve . . . come and sit next to me.'

Stephen lifted his head and turned to join John, Ada, and Catherine who sat in their usual places on the left-hand side of the church. He wanted so much to look back at Flo but was afraid he would see her mother or at least her hat with a stuffed bird perched at the side, with eyes looking back at him. So, he stared into the empty space before him, dreaming of the touch he had missed by only seconds.

The service began when the elders were seated, and the congregation settled into Sunday morning service. Reverend Ivan invited all to stand to sing the opening hymn.

> Abide with me, fast falls the eventide
> The darkness deepens Lord, with me abide
> When other helpers fail and comforts flee
> Help of the helpless, oh, abide with me . . .

Stephen's right eye flickered as the light shone through the long windows and rested gently across the shadows of the wooden cross on the white stone wall. His mind flashed back to his mother in England and his brother Albie. From a hidden corner of his heart where he held his secret grief, and in the serenity of this place of worship, he prayed that one day they would all be reunited.

Hold Thou Thy cross before my closing eyes;
Shine through the gloom and point me to the skies;
Heav'n's morning breaks, and earth's vain shadows flee;
In life, in death, O Lord, abide with me.

The congregation sat down. Stephen was determined to listen attentively to the morning sermon, but his mind continued to wander back to his homeland.

The service moved towards a close.

Families mingled, slowly left the pews behind, and made their way down the stone steps to the ground floor for refreshments. An orderly queue formed in front of a long table covered in a pure white tablecloth, with china cups and saucers, pots of tea and coffee, and maple leaf cookies. In the congregated groups of chatter and movement towards friends, Stephen found himself once again in the presence of Flo, who had managed to slip away from her mother's watchful eyes.

'You look very nice today,' said Stephen, feeling a blush of heat burn his cheeks.

He noticed her long narrow skirt that almost touched the top of her flat shoes, a white blouse with the cuffs fringed with lace underneath an ankle length woollen coat that was fitted into her waist, and a small rimmed bonnet decorated with white feathers.

'Thank you, Steve. Is that a new jacket you're wearing? It looks very smart,' said Flo, smiling.

But before Stephen could answer, he found himself forced gently towards Flo where he could feel the breath from her mouth on his lips.

'Whoops . . . sorry about that, Steve. It's busy in here.' Giggled Ettie, untying the ribbon from around her bonnet.

Within seconds, Sophia arrived by her side, wearing an identical bonnet and ankle length linen skirt, white blouse with lace around the collars and cuffs, and a blue shawl draped across her shoulders.

'I've never been able to tell you two apart,' said Stephen.

'Can you imagine how our husbands will feel when we're married? We could get up to lots of tricks,' said Sophia, laughing.

'Oh Phia, I can't believe you've just said that. Who are you intending to marry I wonder?' Ettie teased.

'Well, I can't say right now . . . but have you heard about Charlie and Hamish?' Sophia asked.

'No, what's happened?' Stephen asked, feeling concerned.

'They've enlisted to join the Canadian Army. I'm so proud of them,' said Sophia.

'They do look really smart in their uniforms,' said Flo.

'Are they here today?' Stephen asked.

'Yes, they're here somewhere. It's all happened very quickly. What do you think about that, Steve?' Sophia asked.

'I think it's a very brave decision. This war seems to be dragging on. But they're both Homeboys. Have they been given permission to go from their farms?' Stephen asked.

'I don't believe they need permission to enlist. They're doing their duty, and I guess that's what counts,' said Flo.

'Yes . . . yes, of course,' said Stephen.

Stephen felt a hand touch his shoulder from behind. He turned and noticed Charlie smiling back at him, standing upright in Canadian uniform.

'Hi, Steve,' he said. His hazel eyes shone with excitement.

'Charlie, it's good to see you. Phia's just told me you've enlisted,' said Stephen as he shook his hand.

'Yes, I've joined the 129th Battalion with Hamish. We leave for England for training next month,' said Charlie.

Stephen noticed Hamish's head appear from behind Charlie and his green eyes sparkle with intrigue.

'Did I hear someone mention my name?' Hamish asked, laughing.

'Hamish, what's happened to your hair?' Stephen asked, looking surprised.

'I couldn't go to war with ginger curls now, could I? The Germans would spot me a mile away,' said Hamish, grinning, and showing a gap in his teeth.

The sound of giddy laughter echoed around them as chatter of war filled the air. And a new venture called across the miles of ocean, far from the peace and safety of Kirkwall Presbyterian Church.

# 8
# Goodbye to Love

*"Imagination is the only weapon in the war against reality."*
— *Lewis Carroll*

FOLLOWING SOME OF the most extreme seasons that commanded this particular corner of Canada—Puslinch, Ontario—Stephen reached the age of seventeen. He had grown into a young man. The fair hair of his youth had turned brown, and his blue eyes shimmered deeper, or maybe it was the way the light shone through them.

The conversation in church replayed through Stephen's mind. He continued to reflect in the quiet of the barn—where it was so easy to hide away with what had become a trustworthy friend, his journal. His tears reflected sparkles of light from the resting sun, slowly disappearing on the scarlet horizon beneath the array of maple trees. Annie stayed close beside him, and the ink glided across the white paper.

Stephen wrote diligently, his mind wandering back to the first day he arrived at the stone house. The warm welcome he received when he had felt so afraid and uncertain of his future. But six years had passed of playing and working on the farm, and now war had come.

> I feel a deep sense of duty to fight for my country. I still miss my hometown, in England, my mother and my brothers, especially Albie. My heart wants to break when I think of them. Sometimes I can't bear this separation. I feel like I'm sinking in the mud on the edge of the fields. Falling deeper and deeper with nowhere to go but to the bottomless pit beneath the earth. I wonder if I will ever see them again? Hold them close to me? Hear the sound of their voice? I'm forgetting. I'm forgetting what they look like ...
>
> But Edgar and Ada have been so kind to me. And Flo was so impressed with Charlie and Hamish for enlisting. I feel an allegiance to Canada. I'm scared. Is this the right thing to do? I

want to give something back to a family who have loved me like their own son. If only I could make Edgar proud—that would make me happy. I feel so torn. I love Ada and Edgar, but I still want to see Albie, and return to England and see my family again. I miss them. God help me to find the courage to do the right thing.

'Steve . . . Steve,' called John from the other side of the barn.

Stephen put his journal in the tin where he had contained it since he first arrived at the farm. He climbed quickly up to the beam to lodge it safely behind and out of sight.

'There you are. Dinner's ready. We're having your favourite,' teased John.

'Stuffed baked potatoes.' Stephen's eyes widened with the remembrance of the taste.

'Have you been up here all by yourself? Only I thought I heard someone,' said John.

'There's no one else here, just me,' said Stephen.

He smiled secretly to Annie as she danced her way back towards the mellow orange light of the late afternoon sunset, shimmering over the horizon, bringing closure to another day.

The next morning, Stephen rose early from a sleepless night. He listened to the uplifting song of the hummingbirds, whilst his heart remained heavy, like a lead stone weighing him down, further into what felt like a bottomless pit of quick sand.

*I don't know what to do . . . please God, tell me what to do.*

Stephen sat on the edge of the bed and rubbed his right eye, only to stare into an abyss of emptiness. He eventually went through the motions of getting dressed, physically appearing for breakfast whilst his mind continued to stare inwardly.

'Can you pass the sugar, please?' John asked politely.

But his words were lost in the haze around Stephen.

'Stephen . . . where's your head today?' Ada asked kindly.

Edgar rattled his newspaper to get Stephen's attention.

'Oh, sorry, sir, I was just thinking,' said Stephen as he felt his cheeks flush pink.

'You look tired, Stephen. Are you not sleeping well?' Ada asked softly.

'Yes, I'm well, thank you,' said Stephen.

Stephen felt the light from Ada's eyes shine into his. Ada sensed something was troubling him. She was astute enough to wait, knowing he would go to her when he was ready. His lips parted into a smile of reassurance—that was enough for now.

Later that morning, when Stephen had taken the horses out into the field, he returned to the barn and raked the hay into a linear heap in the straw mow. But his mind wandered back to the purpose of his life. *What am I doing here?* The swing of his arm stopped when a piece of dust settled on his eyelid. He blinked and rubbed his right eye. Stephen took the deepest breath, threw the rake into the hay, and left the barn. His footsteps hurried their way to the washroom at the back of the kitchen. He could hear Catherine's mellow voice singing in the distance and the clanging of pots out of tune with the song. But Stephen paid no attention to the familiar sounds as he quickly washed and changed his clothes. He then closed the door quietly behind him and walked along the tree-lined path. The leaves of the maple trees bowed their heads towards him, catching the breeze gently in the shaded air. Memories of leaving England, separation from Albie, and arriving at the farm flashed through his mind like grains of sand swirling back and forth with the ocean. Stephen's right eye flickered as he felt the urge to stop at the end of the path. He looked over his shoulder. *All I need to do is go back.*

'Afternoon lad.'

Stephen turned towards the main road and noticed Mr Fletcher from the neighbouring farm, on his horse and wagon, passing by.

'Good afternoon, sir,' said Stephen, bowing his head politely.

'Need a ride into town? The sky's changing, it looks like rain is on the way.'

'No, thank you, sir,' said Stephen.

'Give my regards to Mr and Mrs McPhail.' He smiled and encouraged his horse to walk on.

Stephen stared at the back of the wagon, and Mr Fletcher's flat cap as both slowly moved away into the distance. His feet left footprints in the dusty road as they plodded one after the other with no connection with his whirling mind. His eyes stared into the clouds of powder disturbed by Mr Fletcher's horse and wagon. He suddenly jolted as he noticed three young women walking on the other side of the road, dressed in calf length skirts and cotton blouses, with small flat, ribbed bonnets. He felt his cheeks blush as he realised it was Flo, with Ettie and Sophia at her side. He watched the three women giggle and whisper in each other's ears as he cleared his throat to speak.

'Good afternoon,' said Stephen, removing his cloth cap.

Ettie and Sophia stared in his direction, and Stephen waited in anticipation. Flo smiled gently beneath the flat rim of her small bonnet, and a spark danced between them. Her blonde curls surrounded her oval face, and Stephen noticed her gaze lower in what looked like an attempt to hide the heat rising through her cheeks. Stephen wiped beads of sweat from his forehead with his sleeve and replaced his cloth cap.

'May we ask where you're going, Steve?' Sophia asked.

Stephen hesitated before answering. 'I'm heading towards Dundas, to enlist.'

'Oh, I'm sure Mr and Mrs McPhail are so proud of you,' said Ettie, as her eyes widened.

'We've heard Charlie and Hamish's Battalion have been sent out to the Somme in . . .' Sophia paused as her eyes looked towards the cloudy sky.

'France,' said Ettie.

'Does this mean we get to see you in uniform in church on Sunday?' Flo asked.

'I'm not sure,' said Stephen, feeling nervous.

'It's a very brave thing you're doing, Steve,' said Flo.

'We'll say good day to you. We mustn't be late back, and the market was so busy in town today,' said Ettie, changing her basket full of groceries from one arm to the other.

'Whatever happens from here . . . Come home soon, Steve,' said Flo.

The three women continued to walk by in the opposite direction. Stephen watched them, hoping for another glimpse from Flo. Then she turned and looked back. Stephen's heart beat faster and his mouth felt dry as he struggled to swallow. The glimpse soon became lost in the distance between them but stayed in Stephen's mind as he continued his journey.

His eyes blinked to miss the pellets of rain that fell from the matted grey sky. He turned to look behind him when he heard the hooves of a horse close by and recognised Mr Elliot, the milkman in his wagon.

'Going my way, lad?' Mr Elliot asked, his unshaven face showing grey stubble.

'Yes, sir,' said Stephen as he climbed up and sat next to the milkman.

'Here, drink this,' said Mr Elliot as he poured some milk from a jug into a tin cup.

'Thank you, that's very kind,' said Stephen.

'Where're you heading, on this fine 4th July?' Mr Elliot asked.

'Dundas, sir,' said Stephen, as he slowly sipped the cold milk.

'Walk on,' said Mr Elliot.

The two black and white horses obeyed their master's command. The wagon continued, along the deserted, dusty road, with the sound of their hooves and the creak of the wagon, out of rhythm with the pellets of rain that hit the ground without mercy.

The milk wagon finally arrived in the town of Dundas. Stephen climbed down, and his boots stepped into a puddle of mud.

'I wouldn't stay out too late now. It looks like a storm's coming. I reckon there'll be thunder and lightning before tea time,' said Mr Elliot.

'Thank you, sir, I appreciate the ride,' said Stephen.

He hesitated whilst he watched the milk wagon move away. *What shall I do now?* Stephen ran towards a three-storey building to shelter from the rain. He sat down in the doorway and turned to face his own reflection in a glass door. He blinked with his right eye that ached more when he had to make a decision. His memory floated back to the day he first arrived in Hamilton six years before, wearing his trench coat and spectacles.

*How did I get here? I don't know what to do. I've no money. Maybe this is the answer, but what if. . .*

Stephen's thoughts whirled, as if tearing himself inside out.

*I'm going to turn back. I'll be home for dinner and no one will know I've left. If only. . .*

Stephen's mind suddenly jolted to the present moment as the glass door swung open, and a young boy with sallow cheeks, a shaved head, and tortured blue eyes, glided past him. There was a moment of recognition as Stephen froze, in the late, dark afternoon.

*Albie?*

He turned to scream his brother's name, holding out his right hand . . . but there was only the swirl of dust in the road and an empty pathway. He felt a cold shiver vibrate through each vertebra as he stared further towards the edge of darkness . . . until . . . his eyes flickered towards the light, and he noticed the breath leave his body.

Stephen lifted himself up from the doorway, and without hesitation, entered the glass doorway, passing through his own reflection. The large square room was full of an aroma mixed with ink, paper, sweat, and hay from the surrounding farmland. Young men with mud on their boots filled the crowded stuffy room. Stephen noticed a tall soldier in uniform, sniffing loudly from a long pointed nose above a curled moustache.

'What's your name, lad?' he asked in a deep voice, not looking up from his clipboard.

Stephen hesitated. He coughed nervously before answering the question.

'Age?'

'Eh . . . nineteen, sir,' said Stephen, as he swallowed hard and almost choked from the back of his throat.

'Join the lads on the right-hand side for medical and fitness tests. Move along now.'

He was directed towards an orderly queue, where he waited in silence. But as each step brought him closer to a blue door, his feet felt like lead weights. Beads of sweat fell from his chest, down onto his stomach, where he felt his heart had fallen and wanted to rip its way out. Whenever someone moved towards him to speak, he lowered his head further to the floor; for fear of screaming *this is a mistake.*

But Stephen didn't have to wait long before he found himself entering the blue door. He noticed two soldiers in uniform, one sitting, writing at a desk with his head lowered, and one standing in front of him.

'Take off the top half of your clothes lad and leave your trousers on,' said the soldier indifferently.

Their faces were blurred within a blue mist that filled the room. Stephen blinked, determined to see clearly, pulled his braces down and did what was required. He then performed an eye test and a series of fitness tests. Stephen struggled to read the smaller print as his right eye flickered.

'Grade one for fitness,' said the soldier as he completed his series of tests.

'Passed,' said the soldier at the desk as he continued writing.

Stephen was asked to leave the room and was directed towards a different queue in the main hall on the left-hand side, where he waited patiently to enter a green door. His head whirled with fuzzy sparks of pain as his eyes glazed over. It was as if the blue mist thickened around him as he prepared to wake up from a dream.

'Come along, lad, quick step forward,' said a soldier, resting his hand on Stephen's shoulder.

Stephen opened his eyes wide to see clearly in front of him and followed three others from the queue across the threshold of the green door. There was something different about the soldier in uniform standing behind a wooden round table in the middle of the room. He wore medals across his chest, looked important, and stood proudly with his head held high.

'Take a Bible, raise you right hand, and repeat after me,' he said clearly from the back of his throat.

Stephen reached for a Bible, and his fingers tingled as he held it close to his chest. Dark shadows forced light out of the small square window. The blue mist returned as his words echoed out of tune with other voices, whirling round the warm room, stifled from lack of air.

'I, Stephen Duckhouse, swear by Almighty God, that I will be faithful and bear true Allegiance to His Majesty King George the Fifth, His Heirs and Successors, and that I will, as in duty bound, honestly and faithfully defend His Majesty, His Heirs, and Successors, in Person, Crown, and Dignity against all enemies, and will observe and obey all orders of His Majesty, His Heirs and Successors, and of the Generals and officers set over me.'

Stephen took a deep breath and rested his right hand on top of the Bible. *God help me.*

'Well done, lads, now sign your names here,' said the high-ranking soldier.

The mist cleared and the pen in Stephen's hand felt real as he found himself signing his name on paper, his writing slanting towards the right, and all he could see was the word *Attestation.*

'You've been enlisted with the 129th County of Wentworth Battalion. Here are copies of your Attestation papers,' said the highly ranked officer.

The task was completed, and all Stephen could see before him on the paper he clutched in his hand was 784602 Private Stephen Duckhouse. He walked out of the recruitment office and into the late afternoon darkness. He looked up at the moving grey clouds overhead and ducked as a flash of lightning suddenly struck the walnut tree at the side of the building. *What have I done?*

Stephen slowly made his way back to Eurach Farm along the quiet and dusty road. His eyes were dazed, and muddled thoughts turned around in his head like the wheel of a wagon. His footsteps became even slower as the rain beat down faster.

*It's not too late. I can go back and tell them I lied about my age.*

Stephen remained still in the road, closed his eyes, and felt a warm ray of light dance across his face.

*Well, Stevie, what have you gone and done that for?*

*Annie . . . what are you doing here?*

*Don't you know by now . . . I'm always here.*

*Maybe I should go back.*

*You've done it now, signed your name and everything. Who am I going to play with now?*

*I don't know what to do, tell me what to do Annie.*

*Pack up your troubles in your old kit-bag, and smile, smile, smile. (Annie sang out loud).*

*Annie . . . you're not helping.*

*What's the use of worrying? It never was worthwhile, so pack up your troubles in your old kit-bag, and smile, smile, smile . . .*

*(Annie giggled as she danced in front of Stephen, the sound of the song filling the air between them.)*

*Really, Annie, I don't need you playing games right now.*
*Well what do you want me to say? There's no turning back now, Stevie.*
*The deed is done.*


Stephen continued walking with Annie by his side, and another verse of the song echoed in his ears. He arrived back at the farm and made his way down the tree-lined path to the side of the stone house. Stephen entered the back room through the latch door and removed his muddy boots. His heart felt like cast iron weighing him down. *Is it too late to go back?* Thoughts raced in and out of his jumbled, heated mind as he whispered, 'Ada . . . Ada . . . Ada . . .'

'Stephen . . . is that you?' Ada called from the side parlour.

He trembled from the wet ice seeping through his clothes, stuck to his skin.

'Yes, it's me,' choked Stephen as his damp socks left footprints on the tiled floor.

He desperately tried to make his way to his bedroom unnoticed. But the door from the kitchen opened, and Ada appeared with the reflective light from the oil lamp shining from her wide eyes.

'Oh, Stephen, where have you been? Edgar has gone out looking for you. We've been so worried. Look at you, you're wet through,' said Ada.

'I'm sorry,' whispered Stephen as tears mingled with the splattered rain on his face.

'What's happened to you? It's not like you to go missing for hours?' Ada asked softly.

'I . . . I've done something,' murmured Stephen, rubbing his right eye.

'We need to get you out of these wet clothes. Come and sit in the warm, and then you can help me fill the bath with some hot water,' said Ada as she gently guided him into the kitchen.

Stephen sat next to the log burning oven and immediately felt the heat tingle against his ice-cold body. But he couldn't stop trembling. His eyes were blurred but he helped Ada pour water from the outside well, into two pans and heat them both on the oven stoves.

'There's some tea in the pot, Stephen. It's still hot,' said Ada.

Stephen picked up the teapot in the middle of the kitchen table. His hand shook as he poured the brown liquid into a cup. He sighed as the tea relieved the brittle dryness at the back of his throat.

'Right, Stephen, the water's hot enough now. Help me fill the bath and when you've washed and changed into dry clothes, come into the side parlour, and we can talk. I have some sewing I need to finish,' said Ada.

Stephen soaked his weary body in the tin bath and felt chills turn to a warm glow. But his head ached like prickling nettles stinging his brain.

*What if I just duck my head under water? I wouldn't have to think anymore.*

Stephen slowly slid further down into the bath until his face was beneath the surface of the water, and he held his breath . . .

A familiar energy took hold of his hands and forced his body to rise.

*Stevie . . . Stevie*

*Annie?*

*You can't see me, Stevie, I've got my eyes closed.*

*What are you doing in here?*

*Making sure you don't do something stupid.*

*I'm just tired . . . I just want to sleep.*

*Sleep you can do. But not in the bath—it's not your time, Stevie. You have work to do.*

*You need to leave now. I want to get out and get dressed.*

*I was never here.*

Stephen felt a hollow emptiness in his heart. He made his way to the side parlour where he found Ada, sitting near the baby grand piano with her sewing needle entwined between her fingers like an extension of her elegant hand.

'Ada, can I talk to you?' Stephen asked respectfully as he slowly moved closer.

'Yes, of course, Stephen. I've been waiting for you.' She gently reached for his hand. 'You're still trembling.'

Stephen sat beside her and lowered his head. He tried to speak but the words got stuck in the back of his throat.

'Stephen, what's happened? Has someone upset you?' Ada asked.

He shook his head as tears stung the inside of his eyes.

'I've just been to Dundas and enlisted in the Army.'

'Oh . . .' Ada's breath shot through her heart like a spear in full flight. Her hazel eyes widened as she gazed into the clouded darkness of Stephen's.

'I don't know if I've done the right thing,' whispered Stephen.

'But you are too young. You are only seventeen. How could this happen?'

'I lied about my age. They believe I'm nineteen. I want to fight for my country and do my duty. I thought it was the right thing to do, but now I'm not so sure.'

'Oh, Stephen,' she choked as she held him close to her heart.

THE SUN CLIMBED high in the sky over Eurach Farm as it had done the first morning of Stephen's arrival. Now he was facing his last. He sat in the barn near the straw mow with his journal open, staring at a blank page, empty of words like the feeling inside his heart. The pages of his journal flickered beneath a slight breeze, and the pen he was holding tightly fell from his hand. A dancing light shimmered between the shadows like lines and dots across the hay.

> *Annie . . . is that you?*
> *Who else would it be, Stevie?*
> *Tell me what it's really like . . . I need to know.*
> *Oh . . . you mean the war? I don't think that's a good idea, Stevie. (Annie drifted away.)*
> *Tell me . . . I need you to be honest with me.*
> *Well . . . if you're sure?*
> *I am.*
> *Close your eyes.*

Stephen was transported to a world far away from the peace and tranquillity of the straw mow . . .

A lot of people thought it would be over by Christmas! That was the misguided belief of most during the early months after the declaration of War. Three long, bloody, death-soaked years later, saw the German attack on Verdun—the largest battle of the War, defended by the French.

In synchronicity with Verdun, the battle of the Somme began on the 1st July 1916, culminating in one of the most horrific bloodbaths of the century—with the greatest number of casualties in British military history. More than a million men were wounded or perished—ordered across the enemy lines like cannon fodder, flailing towards a destiny of torn flesh and battered limbs, across a path of lost, lifeless souls trapped within the blood-stained darkness that emanated from a black tortured sky. Still, they continued to fall into a dungeon of breathless sleep, with shadows of grey mist lurking over a mass of locked coffins, awaiting burial.

There seemed no escape for the thousands of men who fell—limbs ripped to splintered pieces, burning flesh meshed with the dripping mud, blinded from the scorching heat of the constant spiral of bombs, shells scraping and tearing skin into open wounds. Left to bleed into the purple-red river, ever flowing, ever dying. And still they charged forward, with honour in their hearts, duty bound to an inevitable demise, sinking deeper into the layers of mud, cascading its brown, slippery slime with broken, savaged blood riddled bodies, embalming the suffering and the dead.

Across the ignited rivers of the Somme, in between battles, an eerie silence cast its shadows across the plains where the cries of men were still heard, long after the agonising pain of death . . .

Stephen opened his eyes and gasped for breath. He looked around at the familiar walls of the barn and felt his right eye blink away beads of sweat from his forehead.

> *Annie . . .*
> *Well, you asked, Stevie, and now you know.*
> *Is it really that bad, or are you playing tricks on me?*
> *In contrast to the ceaseless gunfire and stench of death in France, the August sun trickles through the maple trees at Eurach farm—shining its light amongst the shadows on the rooftops of the stone house in the peaceful town of Wentworth.*
> *Have you read that somewhere?*
> *Who, me?*

Annie danced away into the shadows from the falling sunlight. Stephen climbed up into the eaves of the barn and remembered the many times he had played mischievously with John, and the quiet, when he had sat writing his journal alone. These were his most treasured and secret thoughts.

*I must hide the journal for now. When the war's over, I'll come back for it.*

He put his brown leather-bound journal inside the rusty tin, climbed the ladder, and pushed it behind one of the beams, in his secret place, convinced that no one would ever find it.

*Why would they?*

There had been many hiding places for his journal since he arrived at the farm—in the granary with other tins, or up high behind the beams in the straw mow. But he felt this final secret place was the safest and the most difficult to reach. He was sure it would be there when he returned.

But for now, it was time to leave this safe haven that had given him shelter over the last few years, protecting him from any outside dark forces—such as growing up in the workhouse, dying of hunger in the streets, being lost and alone without comfort or guidance—that may have turned his world upside down, showing him a very different experience. He felt deeply grateful to both Edgar and Ada, for their genuine kindness. He knew it wasn't going to be easy to say goodbye, but before he left the barn he entered the stables for the last time to be with the horses he had come to love. Stephen whispered softly in their ears and gently patted their manes. He knew they understood every word he said.

'I don't want to leave you. But I must go to do my duty. You understand, don't you? I know you do. I'll think of you sometimes. I promise.'

He walked away from the barn, and as he looked back, he noticed Annie waving from the granary.

Stephen entered the kitchen through the side door and removed his boots. The room was thick with silence. Ada looked up from the pot of beef stew she stirred over the oven stove.

'Stephen, would you go and talk to John, he's waiting for you in the back room,' said Ada, wiping her eye with her apron.

'Yes, of course,' said Stephen.

Stephen found John sitting near the window, with wet cheeks and red eyes. He sat next to him and put his arm around his shoulders.

'Why do you have to leave? I won't have anyone to play with. I'll be all alone,' said John.

'You're not alone. You have your family and school friends,' said Stephen.

'It's not the same. Who will I go skating with, play hide and seek in the barn with, and go to the tree house with?' John asked.

'I don't want to leave you. But I must go to do my duty. Please try and understand, John. I'll come back and visit, after the war, and whilst I'm away I'll write to you whenever I can,' said Stephen.

'You promise?'

'I promise.'

'Are you taking your trunk with you? I guess I could help you pack,' John said, trying to be brave.

'No, I won't be able to take it with me. I thought I'd leave it here and give it to you to take care of for me,' said Stephen.

'Really?' John asked.

'You go and find a pen and I'll bring the trunk in here. We'll write inside it, so everyone knows I've given it to you,' said Stephen.

Stephen noticed John's eyes become slightly wider as he forced a smile. He disappeared to get his trunk from his bedroom. It was the only possession he had when he arrived at Eurach Farm, and it was all he had to give to John.

'What will you write?' John asked.

'Let me think . . . Why don't you write something?'

In the top right-hand corner inside the trunk, John wrote in blue ink.

'Steve gave me his trunk when he enlisted for war. John McPhail.'

'Now anyone who opens the trunk will know I gave it to you,' said Stephen.

They shared a smile from a distant look of sadness. Stephen held out his arms and drew John close to his chest. They held each other like brothers, not wanting to let go. Until the silence between them was suddenly interrupted.

'John . . . Stephen . . . come and look at this,' Ada called from the kitchen.

They rushed towards Ada's voice and followed her out of the side door.

'What do you think?' Ada asked, smiling.

'What is it? I've never seen anything like that before,' gasped John.

'It's a Gray-Dort,' said Edgar proudly, polishing the bonnet.

'What's all the commotion about,' grumbled Catherine as she appeared in the doorway, leaning on her cane. 'Heaven preserve us, what on earth is that contraption?' she asked with her mouth wide open.

'It's our first car,' said Ada with a hint of excitement in her voice.

'What does it do exactly?' Catherine asked, leaning further down onto her cane, peering at the wheels over her spectacles.

'It means Edgar can drive us anywhere we want to go, like church on Sundays,' said Ada.

'Why would we need it to take us to church when we have the horses?' Catherine asked.

'Well, maybe in the car, we will arrive on time,' said Ada.

'Really?' Catherine's eyes squinted with suspicion.

'What colour is it, Pa?' John asked. 'It looks like a kind of purple?'

'It's maroon,' said Edgar.

'Can we sit in it?' John asked, touching the door.

'Eh . . . just be careful,' said Edgar.

'Shall we go for a short drive before dinner?' Ada asked.

'I think I need a lie down,' said Catherine as she headed back inside the kitchen door.

Ada sat in the front seat next to Edgar, and Stephen and John sat behind them. The engine roared and the car rumbled down the lane behind the house, past the orchard, and towards the road at the back of the farm.

'Look, Pa, the cows are going around the straw mound again, scratching their backs.' John laughed as he looked to the left-hand side of the barn.

'They keep doing that,' said Ada.

'It will be the flies irritating them,' said Edgar.

Stephen felt a rush of exhilaration as he sat in the back of the car, gazing at the cornfields, stretching for miles to meet the orange glow from the horizon, and the clear blue sky above. He felt a sense of freedom and a deep love for a family he had come to call his own.

*I wonder what would happen if I told the Army I had changed my mind?*

The wheels of the car turned faster along the dusty dirt track until it arrived at the main road.

'Left, or right?' Edgar asked.

'I think it has to be right,' said Ada.


THE FOLLOWING DAY, the family gathered at the side door to say goodbye. Edgar climbed into the driving seat of his new car, his upper body remaining erect, whilst he put on his gloves.

'You will always be welcome at the farm, Stephen,' said Edgar, clearing his throat as he spoke.

'Thank you, sir. I appreciate you driving me to the train station,' said Stephen.

Ada held Stephen in her arms as she fought to breathe. Her acid tears burnt the side of her cheeks whilst she crumpled into his right shoulder.

'I will always love you, Stephen. Come back safe,' she whispered gently in his ear.

Stephen was too choked to speak. The familiar smell of her perfumed handkerchief comforted him until he wanted to run back to the barn and hide in the straw mow.

*Then maybe the war won't be real, and I could stay.*

He slowly pulled away, but Ada only held him tighter. The hand of time moved seconds into minutes. A light gust of wind jangled through his spine and left him tingling with an ice chill.

Catherine silently touched Ada's arm until she was able to let Stephen go and hold herself upright.

'Now you remember to come back safely,' said Catherine as she held out one arm whilst balancing on her cane with the other.

Stephen bent his knees to hug her, whilst Catherine patted him gently on the back.

'Yes . . . yes . . . well, off you go,' said Catherine.

Stephen turned to hug John who had grown tall for twelve years old.

'Don't forget to look after my skates and my trunk . . . and don't get into any mischief whilst I'm gone.'

'I promise,' murmured John with his head bowed.

'Remember, you've signed your name inside my trunk. It's a responsibility to keep it safe, until I come back,' said Stephen as he gently lifted John's chin with his hand.

'Come back soon,' John said through a muffled broken voice.

Stephen climbed into the car and sat next to Edgar. He turned to wave to a family who he knew, in the deepest corner of his heart, loved him like their own son. Edgar started the engine and drove the Gray-Dort sturdily down the long, maple-tree-lined pathway, leading Stephen towards an unknown destiny for the third time in his young life. The car turned left at the end of the lane, and Stephen looked back at Ada, Catherine, and John. They were still waving, but became smaller in the distance between them, like dots on the Tiger Lily flower.

*England*

STEPHEN'S BATTALION LEFT Canada on the SS Olympic to train in England during August 1916. He was based in the military training area, covering half of the Salisbury plain, in the county of Wiltshire. He spent the long summer days in intensive exercises, learning the new principles of fire and movement, and the late evenings watching over the Neolithic burial mounds and Stonehenge nearby.

He was popular with his battalion and found it easy to make friends through his inspirational skills as a storyteller and his mischievous sense of humour. He could reassure the most fearful soldier . . .

'You will return to your home and family because the war is sure to be over soon.'

Stephen continued to write. His insomnia allowed him quiet time in the barracks, whilst his comrades snored into the early hours of the morning. Here in the stillness of the night beneath the black-purple sky, he was able to write letters to the McPhail family to reassure them of his safety. It was here he eventually found the courage to write to his mother. He had his mother's address hidden in his coat pocket but was unsure whether to visit her. She had, after all, put both him and his brother into care.

*Would she want to see me now, after all this time? I don't even know if I would be allowed leave. What if . . . I couldn't go through that pain again?*

The letters were posted, and he waited patiently for a reply. But the hand of time intervened. Stephen's training was soon completed, and his regiment were ordered to France with strategic plans to engage in the battle of Vimy Ridge . . .

STEPHEN LAY IN silence, watching the distant light from the new moon in the starlit sky from the window of his training barracks. He had a sense of feeling lost and alone in a now unfamiliar country. He had returned for one reason only—to train to be a soldier . . . to fight. But he couldn't help but feel empty at the prospect of having to leave England and his unforgotten family, all over again. He was determined not to allow burning tears to fall from his eyes, so his vision remained blurred. But as he continued to fight the relentless resistance to sleep, a familiar dancing light appeared.

*I'm so tired, Annie. What's all this for? I don't understand. I'm so scared. What if my life will soon be over? What will I have achieved? What if I never see my family again? What if . . .*

*What if . . . what if . . . what if a bomb blows you up from limb to limb? What if the sky falls in and the stars disappear forever?*

*Can't you be serious just for once?*

*Why would I change now? Besides, I like being me.*

*I feel there's a long hard journey ahead. Are you coming with me, because if you are, I need you to stop playing games and help me?*

*Don't you know me by now? I can't promise anything. I will say one thing though—you need to practise your singing voice . . . so out of tune sometimes.*

*Why do I need to do that?*

*Oh, stop asking so many questions.*

*Why?*

*I've got a headache.*

*(Stephen's weary eyes drifted into a deep and peaceful sleep, as he felt Annie kiss him gently. The moonlight faded, and stars drifted silently across the closed window.)*

# 9
# Vimy Ridge

*"The song was wordless; The singing will never be done."*
— *Siegfried Sassoon*

THE STARLESS NIGHT choked within a cloud of dense black mist hovering its wings over the miles of the silent dead, where ghosts walked the treeless high ground of Vimy Ridge . . .

Stephen lay in a mud-sodden trench, in the sleepless darkness, waiting. The crossfire and embers of blood-soaked fighting rested in the early hours of the morning. His head ached as he stared at the multitude of rats tormenting his exhausted comrades. But it was the constant scratching from persistent lice that could be heard above their snuffled snores. He reached for his pen and note pad inside his top pocket and felt an immediate sense of deep inner peace as he wrote a letter, praying it would find some way of reaching Canada when this nightmare was all over. He started to scribble, and a blotted tear fell from his face onto the scrunched paper in his hand, as he suddenly remembered.

27th March 1917

Dear Ada,

It's hard to believe it's my eighteenth Birthday today, and there are so many miles between us. I still don't know if I made the right decision, but I feel a sense of duty to be here. Whatever happens now, I remember the love and kindness you have shown me, and I carry this in honour of you and Edgar, within my heart. I feel it somehow protects me from the enemy and keeps me safe. I've been sent over to France and my Battalion is undergoing training somewhere I'm not allowed to say. I've made some new friends, and feel part of something important, but I'm not sure what yet.

Hope all is well at the farm. Please don't worry about me. I've heard that war will soon be over. I pray that this is true. Please tell John I miss skating with him.

Thinking of you all,

Stephen

The pen fell from his fingers onto his chest as his breathing slowed down. His mind drifted into another dimension, until . . .

He took the deepest breath and ran through the blazing clouds of gunfire, as the spray of light almost blinded him. He choked from the black smoke, suffocating in the stifled air. Still he ran, over the corpses of horse and man, with the rats beside him, chasing the dead flesh, sucking on the open wounds, and feeding their fat bellies. The sound of shellfire blasted his ears as his boots sunk deeper into the stream of glistening red mud. His rifle fired into a sea of mist, surrounding him like an ocean drowning the rocks. He fell into the pool of blood and crawled through the human carnage. He lay with the mashed brains and organs, skin flying above the sunken breeze, splintered from broken duckboards and the persistent shellfire, crashing flashes of lightning across the black hollow sky.

Stephen's right eye ached as he stared at skeleton figures, rattling their shattered bones—men disfigured beyond recognition. Dreams broken in the shadowed dust of shrapnel-polluted darkness. Souls trapped inside the screaming shells of their silent voices. Beams of light blinding the way forward, and still they ran into the blast of the guns. Stephen crawled beside them. His fingers trembled as he fired his last bullet, gasped for breath, and sank deeper into the blood sodden mud. A clawed hand grabbed his arm and pulled him upright. He screamed . . .

'Steve! Steve.' A whispered voice echoed in the distance.

Stephen opened his eyes to a dusky violet sky, blinking through the doorway of the hut he had come to know as his resting place, with the sun barely touching the horizon. He looked into the eyes of a familiar face. Flickers of light reached him as he acclimatised to his surroundings.

'You were dreaming,' said Henry in a Welsh accent through crooked grey teeth as he clicked his fingers.

Stephen slowly left behind the terror of nightfall and breathed a deep sigh of relief, as reality returned to him.

'Yes, it was just a dream,' said Stephen as he picked up his pocket book and stared at the open blank page.

'When I was a lad, my dreams always left me with a smile on my face,' said Henry as he sighed deeply.

'Really?' Stephen asked.

'Come on, or we'll be late for training,' quipped Henry, smiling widely as an elongated scar was almost hidden in the dimple on his cheek.

Stephen rubbed his eyes as Henry helped him to his feet, and they both made their way towards the practice ground.

'There's no one here, they must be in the briefing hut,' said Stephen.

They ran towards the far right and ducked into a doorway to take their place in the crowded hut, with all eyes focused towards the front.

'At least we're at the back. I can't bear being in enclosed spaces,' whispered Stephen, trying to calm his breathing.

'Glad you could join us, privates.' Major General David Watson leaned slightly on a cane, with grey hair and a few lines of wrinkles under his small eyes.

'Yes, sir,' replied Henry, puckering his lips as if to kiss the air.

'Sorry, sir, I had a bad . . .' mumbled Stephen.

'Rat bite that got infected and needed immediate medical attention, sir,' exclaimed Henry, without pausing for breath.

A light murmur of supressed laughter echoed from the men sat side by side, desperately trying to pay attention to the map held up in front of them.

'Mm . . . listen carefully now lads, your life may depend on it. This map shows the tactical plan for Vimy Ridge. It is vital that we are all synchronised with the plan. All four Canadian divisions will assault after one week of continual bombing, following behind a creeping barrage. There will be four phase lines identified by code names: black, red, blue, and brown.'

'Can we choose our favourite colour, sir?' a voice quipped, near the front of the hut.

'Maybe you'd like to wear a ribbon in your hair to match your outfit, private?' Sergeant Major Harris asked, twitching his nose and raising his eyebrows.

Loud laughter echoed around the hut.

'Who asked that question?' Stephen whispered.

'It sounds like Rick, and did you hear an echo?' Henry rolled his eyes.

'Settle down now lads. We will attack and secure each line one by one, moving further into enemy territory. The fourth division's mission is to take Hill 145 or, as we know it, the pimple, the highest point on the ridge, including the Folie Farm, the Zwischen-Stellung trench, and the hamlet of Les Tilleuls. Any serious questions so far?'

Stephen raised his hand and cleared his throat.

'What's a creeping barrage, sir?' Stephen asked.

'Good question lad, private . . . ?'

'Duckhouse, sir.'

'A barrage of fire from 983 guns and mortars will move from one line to the next and provide a screen for our troops to hide behind. We will advance with perfectly timed and coordinated infantry assaults at a hundred-yard intervals every three minutes. The creeping barrage will allow us to take the enemy trenches before they have a chance to regroup. Over the next few days you will be involved in practising these tactics and timely assaults on the training field. We cannot rehearse this enough. Timing is crucial,' said Major General David Watson.

Stephen stared at the colourful map at the front of the hut, his eyes burnt, as if from the pain of falling inside it. He lifted himself up and followed everyone, moving out into the cool air where his body shivered without any sense of control. The buzz of chatter moved in different rhythms amongst groups of men gathered in circles outside the hut.

'There's Arthur,' said Stephen, moving closer through the crowd.

'Now the fun's about to begin, the battle's close, I have a nose for it. I can almost smell it,' said Arthur through cracked front teeth as he sniffed heavily.

'Are you sure that's not the smell coming up from the hole in your sock?' Henry laughed, his brown eyes twinkling with mischief.

'I've heard something's being planned for Easter Sunday,' said Stephen, rubbing his right eye.

'I would say, keep your ears to the ground, Steve,' said Arthur, scratching the top of his brown stubbly hair.

'With your nose in another direction,' said Henry, unable to resist.

They arrived at the training area where the battalion gathered, waiting for instruction.

'What's all that tape over the trenches?' Stephen asked.

'I guess we're about to find out,' said Henry with his arms folded.

'Gather 'round lads, no dawdling,' bellowed Sergeant Major Harris, twitching his nose.

'Do you think Twitchy stands to attention when he sleeps at night?' Henry whispered mischievously.

Stephen hid a smile and moved closer with Henry and Arthur at his side, determined to listen carefully and not miss any part of the instruction.

'Right, lads, I want lines of ten formations, each standing behind one another. March to it now, no time to waste, you're not out on a shopping trip,' Sergeant Major Harris continued.

'Where are Charlie and Hamish?' Stephen asked.

'There they are, with Billy, and the echo twins.' Henry smirked.

'D for Dynamite Company, over here,' said Charlie in his familiar soft Irish accent that reminded Stephen of Sundays at Kirkwall Church.

Stephen rushed towards them with Henry and Arthur trailing behind.

'Where were you at breakfast? You didn't miss much. What I'd give to be back at school reading *War and Peace* and looking forward to dinner time.' Hamish grinned widely as he stroked his ginger hair with his fingers.

'Now you're just taking me down memory lane,' said Stephen.

'It's what keeps us going . . . thinking of home.' Charlie's hazel eyes shone above the freckles on his nose.

'Have you heard from anyone . . . from church?' Stephen asked, trying to calm his breathing as thoughts of Flo filled his mind.

'My last letter from Ettie was last week. She says everyone's doing fine, but missing us,' said Hamish with his eyes downcast.

Henry moved closer to Billy, who stood panting slightly with his hands on his hips.

'Hey, Billy, this is your big chance to lose three stone and win the race,' he teased as he spat on his fingers to wet his silver side burns.

'I've lost some weight, it must be the bully beef,' said Billy in his defence as he carefully rubbed his belly, which hung over his trousers.

'Leave him alone. At least he's volunteered to fight in this bloody war,' said Rick, pointing his pencil at Henry, then putting it inside his tunic pocket.

' . . . to fight in this bloody war,' echoed Richie as he looked up at Rick with admiration glowing from his face.

'Oh, excuse me for living, full pint and half a pint. Have you both decided which colour hair ribbons you're wearing today, Rick, Richie, Richie, Rick?' Henry laughed and clicked his fingers.

'No, but I think I've captured Twitchy well enough,' said Rick as he showed them a sketch from his notebook.

' . . . captured Twitchy well enough,' echoed Richie, folding his arms.

They gathered round and giggled at the drawing of an exaggerated large pointed nose, withered moustache, large open mouth, and three tufts of hair.

'Hey, Henry, that could be you one day if you play your cards right.' Arthur sniffed loudly.

'That's enough wittering, lads! Now open your ears and keep your mouths shut. Cast your eyes on this model of the battlefield. The plan is for guns to open fire at zero-hour, fire for three minutes on enemy trenches at three rounds a minute, and then lift a hundred yards every three minutes, creating a space for you to enter without getting yourselves shot. Anyone of you air heads having trouble with the number three?' Sergeant Major Harris asked.

'What happens if we fall behind, sir, and don't get there quick enough?' Henry asked, sucking in his cheekbones.

'Falling behind will make you targets for the enemy mounted higher on the ridge but trying to get ahead of the artillery will put you at risk of being shot by our own guns. So, we don't want a merry dance now, do we, private? Am I making myself clear?'

'Yes, sir, clear as mud, I mean rats I mean . . . Yes, sir, very clear,' said Henry, as he pushed out his chest.

Stephen bit his bottom lip, determined not to move any part of his facial expression.

'Right. lads, D Company prepare to walk forward on my signal. Don't dilly-dally, you're not in a queue for theatre tickets,' said the Sergeant Major as he removed a pocket watch from his tunic.

'What about A, B, and C Company, sir? When are they practicing?' Henry asked, scratching his head.

'All in good time, private! Today is your turn. Aren't you the lucky ones?' Sergeant Major Harris bellowed.

To the sound of 'fire,' D Company practiced walking forward across the taped model battlefield as thunderous rain pelted the men from the relentless grey sky. Over two hundred men from D company listened attentively and acted on instruction. Stephen waited patiently for the signal to move forward.

'Damn bloody rain, does it ever stop in this God forsaken land?' Charlie whispered under his breath.

'Move it, D for Dur Company,' bellowed the Sergeant Major.

Stephen remained focused until Billy tripped over his bootlace, tried to grab Stephen's arm but fell head first onto the ground. The sound of loud laughter echoed around the practice field.

'On your feet, you sorry state of a private. You've just been blown to smithereens. Do we really need you to come back to life?' Sergeant Major Harris yelled.

Stephen and Hamish helped Billy stand up and wiped some of the mud from his eyes with the sleeves from their tunics.

'Stop prancing 'round him, we're not at an afternoon tea party at the Palace,' yelled the Sergeant Major.

'If only we were. Mm, tea and chocolate cake,' said Rick, licking the mud rain from his lips.

'Mm, tea and chocolate cake,' repeated Richie.

'Why is it, Richie, there's always an echo when you're around?' Henry teased.

Rick and Richie opened their mouths to speak, but the sound of the Sergeant Major's voice surrounded them.

'Let's speed things up now, ladies. It's time for some fun and games. You remember playing leap frog as girls, don't you?'

Silence returned beneath the dismal grey sky, as eyebrows knotted in a state of confusion.

'I can't hear you on this bright sunny day,' bellowed the Sergeant Major.

'Yes, sir,' echoed the sound of a single chant.

'This time, on my signal, each formation is to leap frog over the formation in front to maintain momentum as you advance forward. And no dilly-dallying, is that clear?'

'Yes, sir.' Low voices fell amongst the pellets of iced rain.

'Didn't quite hear that lads. It must be the rain blocking my ears. Is that crystal clear?'

'Yes, sir, crystal clear, sir,' came a wave of voices.

'Hey, Billy, be gentle now. Remember to leap frog over him and don't sit on his back for a rest.' Henry giggled.

Billy raised his left eyebrow but there was no time to respond as the signal to advance was imminent. Stephen leaped over the man in front, in perfect timing with his unit, but his right eye flickered as his mind flashed back to Albie, when they played leapfrog in the grounds of Peter Street Boys' Home, and the sound of distant laughter tore into his heart until he could hardly breathe. *I filled in the dots, Stevie.* The freshly cut grass and the smell of tiger lilies suddenly disintegrated into the charcoal mud of the taped battlefield, and Albie's face sunk deeper into the abyss of silence. Stephen trembled as he felt an ice-cold hand claw his left arm. *Albie . . .*

'Come on, Steve, three minutes are up, do you want to get yourself killed?' Charlie asked, not waiting for an answer.

'Look lively, lads, this is not a holiday camp,' yelled Sergeant Major Harris.

Rehearsals continued, in the wake of relentless repetitions, until the late afternoon found its way back to meet early evening darkness and the faded new moon.

'Right, lads, we'll call it a day. Only six more days of training and we'll have you ship shape and ready to go,' said Sergeant Major Harris.

'I bet I can guess what's for dinner,' said Billy, with his eyes focused on the trail back to the huts.

'Just close your eyes and imagine the smell of roast beef and potatoes,' said Henry, clicking his fingers.

Stephen's mind flashed back to Ada, the warmth of the kitchen, the sweet smell from her handkerchief lingering in the air, with waves of hot roast beef from the cooker. Ada moved closer, and he held out his hand . . .

'Bully beef, bully beef, bully beef, that's all I see,' said Charlie, staring into the distance.

The sound of loud laughter echoed, whilst their boots sank into the slosh of mud, until they reached the road ahead.

'There must be thousands of shells stacked so high along-side this road. More arrive every day. They must be expecting to use them all,' said Stephen.

'They're here for a reason, that's for sure,' said Hamish, his eyebrows knotted in the middle.

'Look over into the woods, they've erected horse standings. We must be expecting the cavalry,' said Charlie. His voice sounded like the melody of a song.

'I wonder when they're arriving? I'd like to go over and see if they need any help,' Stephen offered, remembering Del and Delwyn at Eurach Farm.

'Once a farmer, always a farmer.' Hamish smiled.

'It must be some time soon. Easter's only days away, and we go into battle,' said Billy, panting as he rubbed his chest.

'When do you think we'll be moved to the front?' Stephen asked.

'I reckon soon, when we've finished training. Then we'll be on night patrol and trench raids,' said Arthur, sniffing heavily.

'The next chapter of the 129th Wentworth Battalion begins. I hope you're writing this story in your pocket book, Steve. We need someone to remember us,' said Henry, with an unusual spark of sadness reflecting from his eyes.

The days of extensive training finally came to an end, but the freezing blizzards remained, drenching the faces of men determined to end the day, knowing the battle was moving closer, silent in its wake.


PELLETS OF RAIN rested behind dark clouds in the grey-blue sky, giving some relief from the days of persistent mud curdled showers . . .

'We've been ordered to another briefing. D company are expected before breakfast. I don't want to be late again,' said Stephen, putting his pocket book and pencil safely away inside his tunic.

'I just hope it's not more leap frogging, my legs are aching so bad,' said Billy, rubbing his thighs.

'It's not the only thing that'll ache if you get caught by a bunch of Jerries,' said Henry, spitting on his boot and wiping away some of the caked mud with a grey cloth.

They left the hut, leaving behind a sleepless night, and headed towards the command post. Major Shaw, standing with a baton under his arm and stroking his moustache diligently with his right index finger, waited at the front of the hut.

'Quiet now, lads, settle down,' said Sergeant Major Harris.

'Thank you, sergeant major. As you are all aware, the battle is set to take place at zero hour on Easter Sunday. The battalion will move to the front area from today. The Royal Engineers have been working day and night to create interconnected caves to enable you to move safely to the front of the enemy positions. Any Questions?'

Stephen watched Billy raise his hand, and as he did so, closed his eyes and held his breath.

'Are we to crawl through these caves, sir?' Billy asked.

'Scared you might get stuck,' whispered Henry.

A stifled murmur echoed through the hut, until the silence returned.

'Our engineers have learnt that the countryside between the British and German positions was originally full of underground caves from where chalk had been quarried during the Middle Ages. These holes have been around a long time and have now been linked to ensure a safe passage. All quarters are numbered, which you will be assigned before you enter. I think you'll find there will be no crawling, private, unless you're making your way to the latrine, of course.' Major Shaw's brown eyes squinted at the faces of the men before him as his lips hovered into a slanted smile.

The sound of relieved laughter rose from the surrounding murmur, and Stephen breathed freely again.

'What's up, Steve? You look quite pale,' Charlie observed.

'You know I can't stand enclosed spaces,' said Stephen.

'Don't worry, I've heard they've put a light railway inside, it can't be that enclosed,' said Hamish.

As D Company was dismissed, the battalion prepared to leave camp and the training area, to move forward into the caves, where a different world awaited them.


STEPHEN'S RIGHT EYE flickered as shadows moved between the shades of candle light on the enclosed walls.

'It's like an underground city,' said Stephen.

'Whoever thought of this must have been a genius,' said Charlie.

'Look, they've even built a hospital for the wounded,' said Hamish, pointing to the left.

'I've forgotten the number of our quarters already,' muttered Rick.

' . . . number of our quarters already,' muttered Richie.

'We're in number ten, there it is,' said Stephen, striding forward.

'Praise be to the Lord, it's opposite the canteen.' Billy raised his voice in appreciation.

'Let's dump our stuff and check out what delights are in store for us,' said Arthur, limping slightly from sore feet.

'If it's a treat like toffee delight, you can eat as many as you like, the state of your teeth,' quipped Henry.

'My teeth are in perfect working order, thank you,' said Arthur with a touch of indignation.

They entered their quarters and were met with a line of bunk beds and an unfamiliar figure, on his knees, clutching a small black book to his chest.

'Looks like we've got the Bishop in with us,' whispered Henry, raising his left eyebrow.

'That's just old Harold, he's recently back from chapel. If you need the latrine there's a choice of two buckets around the corner to the right,' came a croaky voice from behind them.

'No expense spared then,' said Henry as he turned around and noticed the others saluting a tall, slim figure.

'At ease, lads. If you need to ask anything, my quarters are next door. Not far to go.'

'You don't sound well, sir,' said Stephen.

'Had a touch of the flu, but I've been signed fit for duty.'

'If you're passing that on make sure it's the Jerry's and not us,' whispered Henry, as the officer walked away.

'That's Captain Alex Barrows. He's a canny officer,' said Harold.

'How do you know that, Bishop?' Henry asked.

'I fought beside him, at the Somme,' said Harold.

Henry's mouth dropped open, with a look of confusion on his face.

'So how come you had to enlist, Bishop? I would have thought a church service was more your cup of tea?' Henry jested.

'Have you not heard of the old saying, my son? Evil triumphs when good men do nothing,' said Harold.

Henry bowed his head, unsure what to say next, and started to click his fingers.

'Do you think I might make captain one day?' Arthur asked, touching his stubbly hair with his fingers as he watched the officer disappear into his quarters.

'You need to brush your cracked teeth and wash more often, before that day ever comes.' Henry grinned.

Stephen put his hand on Arthur's shoulder as he was about to retaliate. Arthur breathed heavily as he scowled silently in Henry's direction.

'Come on, let's go, or our dinner will be cold,' said Hamish.

'What, tinned bully beef?' Charlie laughed.

'Are you coming, Harold?' Stephen asked.

Harold placed his bible inside his sleeping bag and stood up. Stephen noticed something familiar about him but wasn't quite sure what it was. They shared a smile as Harold touched Stephen's arm, then they followed the others towards the vaulted kitchen area. They joined a queue, which led towards the stoves in the far corner, where cooks in shirtsleeves bustled around. Stephen coughed from the smoke circling the candles on each table, and the stoves, with tobacco and sweat masking the smell of food. The kitchen was busy, with men playing cards, eating, drinking, talking, listening, and waiting.

'It's that bloody maconchie meat stew again,' said Henry, spitting on the grey white slime on the ground.

'You mean man killer stew,' moaned Rick.

' . . . man killer stew,' moaned Richie.

'It's the turnips that don't agree with my stomach.' Billy sighed.

'Which is a nice way of saying you're going to fart your way down town, through the night, and keep us awake,' Henry teased.

'What's that dripping from the ceiling?' Stephen asked.

'It's the saturated ground above, leaking moisture through the roof,' said Harold.

The freezing water continued to drip from the ceiling, and they moved closer towards the stoves.

'We'll have the roast beef all round, from the a la carte menu, with a bottle of champagne in a bucket of ice. Oh, and I like my beef medium rare,' said Henry with a glint in his eyes.

'Enjoy your beef stew and toffee delight,' said the cook, raising his eyebrows and wiping the sweat from his forehead.

'Nice try, Henry,' said Charlie, smiling.

They gathered around a corner table with their rations and a flagon of rum.

'We must be going over the top soon enough if we're getting rum,' said Henry.

Stephen stared at the mahogany coloured liquid.

'Come on, lad, down in one,' said Arthur.

Stephen gulped the rum, feeling it burn the back of his throat.

'That's the spirit.' Henry laughed.

'Who's for a game of cards?' Rick asked.

' . . . game of cards?' Richie asked.

The waiting began in the faded candlelight. Waiting to sleep, to write letters to loved ones back home, for the next meal in the canteen, prayers in the chapel for some kind of absolution.

Stephen sunk his helmet into the reservoir and filled it with water. He poured it over his head and felt cool splashes tingle down his face. As the ripples of water disappeared he stared at his own refection, until it changed, and he could see Flo smiling back at him. *Come home soon, Steve.* Her soft voice slowly disappeared. Stephen touched the surface of water, desperate to bring her back, but his hand only sank into the depth of an empty space.

'Steve . . . Steve . . .'

Stephen turned around and saw Hamish calling him.

'Come over here, and see what I've done.' Hamish grinned.

Stephen walked over to the other side of the chalk wall and squinted to where Hamish was pointing. He removed his spectacles from his tunic pocket.

'It's a pig,' said Stephen.

'I carved it into the wall. It reminds me of the farm back in Ontario,' said Hamish proudly.

'Do you miss home?' Stephen asked.

'I'm going to write to Ettie and ask her to marry me. What do you think?'

'I think that's just great. I didn't know you felt that way about her. Congratulations, Hamish,' said Stephen.

'She hasn't said "yes" yet. But I know she's the girl for me,' said Hamish.

'I've got an idea, why don't we carve a mailbox into the wall? Then we've all got somewhere to put our letters and they might have a chance to reach the people we love,' said Stephen.

Hamish smiled widely, his green eyes reflecting sparkles of light in the grey darkness.

'Let's do it over here near the reservoir. Have you got your knife?' Hamish asked.

Stephen waved it in front of him, and they both designed and carved the mailbox they wanted into the chalk wall. When it was finished, they stood back, let their heads drop to the side, and stared at their creation.

'That should do it. It might even inspire everyone to write more letters,' said Stephen.

'Which reminds me, I have an important letter to write,' said Hamish.

They returned to their quarters to the sound of a rumbling thunder in the distance above ground.

'What was that?' Charlie asked.

'It's just a mine being blown. They've set up special listening spots underground where geophones are used to detect Jerry mines,' said Harold as he peered above the page of his bible.

'That's one less mine to worry about,' said Rick, clenching his fingers around his pen as his sketchbook dropped to the floor.

' . . . one less mine to worry about,' said Richie.

'Is it me, or is that bloody echo getting louder in the room?' Henry droned.

'Shh . . . listen,' said Arthur, running his fingers through his stubbly hair.

The sound of the mine echoed round the walls of the chalk caves, like rhythms of musical tones in the distance.

'We've got a mailbox now, where you can post your letters. It's at the side of the reservoir,' said Stephen.

Rick released his grip and let his pen go and smiled at Stephen. And the silence returned.

Later that evening, Stephen went to the chapel to pray quietly, as he had done for so many years on the farm. It had become a habit he was used to, that brought him comfort he could no longer be without. He knelt down in front of the wooden cross nailed to the chalk wall and opened the small bible Edgar had given him as a gift before he left Hamilton. Stephen immediately turned to proverb 3.6; but wasn't prepared for a voice from behind.

'In all thy ways acknowledge God and He will direct thy ways.'

'Harold, I didn't hear you come in. How did you know I was reading that proverb?' Stephen asked.

Harold smiled and gently touched Stephen's shoulder, before kneeling beside him.

'It's a favourite of mine,' said Harold, his bushy eyebrows almost touching the tips of his silver hair.

Stephen looked deeper into Harold's eyes. He could see arrows of light, like shooting stars filled with mystery, travelling to their final destination.

'Shall we pray together?' Harold asked.

Their voices came together with the Lord's Prayer.

'Our Father, who art in heaven, hallowed be thy name . . .'

They continued, moving towards quiet contemplation, waiting for their prayers to be heard, waiting for the next day and the next . . . so they could do it all over again. The minutes and hours and days passed through time.

Stephen lay on top of his bunk bed, staring at the chalk ceiling, listening to the sound of ink scribbling along paper, Henry clicking his fingers, and Billy breathing heavily, until the near silence changed to something quite different.

'Hey, Bishop! When I was a lad, I was told I had the voice of an angel. You got any songs we can sing?' Henry asked loudly.

'Which of the Lord's Hymns shall we sing, my son?' Harold asked quietly.

'I've got one,' said Arthur.

> If the sergeant drinks your rum, never mind.
> And your face may lose its smile, never mind.
> He's entitled to a tot but not the bleeding lot . . .

'You really need to take singing lessons, Arthur. You sound like a cat screeching for its mate.' Henry laughed.

'Come on, join in,' said Arthur, waving his arms in mid-air like a music conductor.

Stephen sat up, pens dropped to the floor and the sound of the song filled the stifled air.

> If the sergeant drinks your rum, never mind.
> When old Jerry shells your trench, never mind.
> Though the sandbags bust and fly you have only once to die,
> If old Jerry shells the trench, never mind . . .

Waves of laughter echoed around number 10 quarters as passing troops stopped at the entrance near the chalk pillar and joined in, holding their containers of rum close to their chests.

> If you get stuck on the wire, never mind.
> And your face may lose its smile, never mind,
> Though you're stuck there all the day, they count you dead and stop your pay . . .
> If you get stuck on the wire, never mind.

Stephen's chest ached with the pain of laughter as he sang along, unable to hear the sound of his own voice above the din.

> If the sergeant says you're mad, never mind
> P'raps you are a little bit, never mind . . .

A dancing light shimmered inside a yellow glow as it twisted into the face of Annie in the crowd. Stephen's right eye flickered as he watched her sing out loud, smiling mischievously and swaying from side to side, her blond curls transparent against the chalk enclosed walls.

> Just be calm don't answer back, cause the sergeant stands no slack
> So if he says you're mad, well—you are.

An echo of raucous hilarity vibrated off the chalk walls as the crowd dispersed and candlelight flickered amongst the shadows. Unseen, night arrived above the ground. Silence returned once more, above snuffled snores and heavy breathing. Stephen watched the yellow glow slowly spiral away in the distance. He turned over inside his woollen blanket to welcome sleep, but saw Annie beside him, cross-legged.

*I thought you'd left, Annie.*
*Why would I go when I'm having such a good time?*
*The good time is over, and I need to sleep.*
*How do you know it's bedtime? It could be daylight outside for all you know. You only know what they tell you, Stevie.*
*Well everyone else is asleep and I'm tired, so goodnight, Annie.*
*But I'm wide-awake and feel like singing again. How does the song go again? Though your face may lose its smile, never mind . . .*

Stephen crawled further underneath his blanket and cupped his ears with his hands as the echo of Annie's voice penetrated the space around him. Night slowly turned to day above the ground of this secret labyrinth.

During the early hours of the next morning, Stephen stretched out his arms and checked the room to make sure Annie had disappeared. He felt something different about today. It was a feeling he couldn't shake off. He quickly got dressed and headed towards the water reservoir.

'Steve, come over here,' called Hamish, sitting near the carved mailbox with tears in his eyes.

'What is it Hamish, are you well?' Stephen asked.

'I've never felt so good in my life. Look, it's a reply from Lettie. She says yes,' said Hamish.

'You mean, you're going to get married?'

'Yes, can you believe that, Steve?'

'Congratulations, Hamish, that's such great news,' said Stephen, shaking his hand.

'I wasn't sure she'd accept me, you know?'

'Why wouldn't she? You two have grown up together,' said Stephen.

'Let's head for breakfast. All this talk of marriage has suddenly made me feel hungry,' said Hamish, grinning widely.

Stephen put his arm around Hamish's shoulders, and they walked towards the canteen. They joined Henry, Billy, and Charlie at their usual table in the corner. Stephen sipped his beef tea slowly, trying to savour the taste.

'Sergeant major's just been in. It's time for inspection outside our quarters, straight after breakfast. This is it,' said Henry.

'I've heard zero hour's been changed to Monday,' said Billy.

'I guess we'll find out soon enough,' said Stephen.

Following inspection, Sergeant Major Harris cleared his throat, his voice echoing every syllable.

'Right, lads, order from high command. We go into battle at five-thirty am on Easter Monday, that's tomorrow morning, for those of you who don't know what day it is. Collect your weapons in an orderly way and be ready for stand to at five am. Is that clear?'

'Yes, sir,' came a multitude of voices.

Stephen spent the early evening of the night before the battle in quiet contemplation within the walls of the chapel before returning to his quarters.

'Come on, Steve, or you'll be late for dinner. We've waited for you. I've heard it's mutton broth and duff pudding,' said Hamish, grinning widely.

'Are you feeling tempted?' Charlie teased.

'I don't suppose Lettie will be serving such delights when you're married?' Stephen asked.

The sound of laughter rebounded off the enclosed chalk walls, with flashes of the farm and church life spinning inside Stephen's head. It felt so close he could reach out and touch the air around the distant town of Hamilton.

Early next morning all four Canadian divisions met to stand in symmetrical lines along the interconnected caves. Stephen's breathing raced ahead of the beat of his heart, and he could feel beads of sweat lingering at the side of his face. But he was determined to stay focused and listen to all four commanding officers. He had a strong sense that this was a moment in history that would never be repeated. Major General Watson, leader of the fourth division, stepped forward first. His eyes squinted, showing creases in the skin on his forehead, and his moustache almost covered his upper lip.

'As you know, this is the moment we've been waiting for. The training you have endured over the last few weeks has prepared you to go forward and fulfil the objectives laid out in the most strategic of battle plans. It is an honour to serve with you. May God go with each and every one of you.'

Major General Currie, leader of the first division, cleared his throat to speak. A tall figure, with long earlobes, full lips, a piecing stare, and wide upper body, stood proudly in military uniform.

'Under the orders of your devoted officers in the coming battle you will advance or fall where you stand facing the enemy. To those who will fall I say; you will not die, but step into immortality.'

A deep entrenched silence fell between the chalk walls of the enclosed caves. Stephen's right eye flickered as he tried to bring it into focus on the dancing light behind Major General Currie. Within seconds he saw Annie appear in his vision, waving at him. He gasped for breath as Annie pushed her way in between the two major generals and stood to attention saluting with her right hand. Stephen closed his eyes in the hope Annie would disappear and was only able to hear muffled sounds from Major Generals Burstall and Lipsett, from the second and third divisions, as their voices faded in the distance. But Stephen's hearing soon returned as Sergeant Major Harris bellowed the order to about turn and quick march to the far exit of the cave.

The sound of boots hitting the ground all at once rebounded off the chalk walls. Stephen's rifle slipped slightly through his hand. He quickly retrieved it as the steel bayonet fixed to the gun barrel reflected a spark of light from the distant candles he left behind.

The breaking of dawn brought silence over the deep mass of trenches. Stephen breathed in the freezing air and felt pellets of rain on his face. The stillness was broken with the blast of heavy machine guns and mortars bombing the German positions, sending clouds of charcoal smoke-filled shells into the sky. It was time. Stephen heard the command to go over the top. He could feel his legs trembling as he tried to force his right leg forward. His stomach churned until he felt like vomiting, and his right eye ached, wanting to close and go to sleep. He felt some relief from tension and more in control of his legs as he stepped forward, alongside the friends he had come to know.

In a well-rehearsed line of attack, the creeping barrage was put into action on the battlefield, and the face of reality left behind all training. Stephen walked towards clouds of mud spiralling into the air, with the chilled wind and iced twists of snow behind him. When needed, he held back in perfect timing alongside his division. He knew that his life now depended on everything he had learnt.

As they closed in on the first German trench, it was like looking into a reflection from a mirror, as ordinary men stared back at them.

'Drop your weapons, no one move,' ordered Captain Barrows.

'Oh, we do apologise, did we wake you?' Arthur asked.

'The Jerry's haven't even got their boots on.' Henry laughed.

'Wir geben auf,' came a combination of voices from within the trench.

German soldiers stood half naked with their arms in the air and their mouths wide open inside a space they believed was protected and safe from enemy invasion.

THE SECONDS OF the minutes fell into hours as German trenches were taken before the enemy had any time to react, forcing them to take cover whilst all four divisions of the Canadian Army advanced together, supported by the barrage of fire and the whirling, mass blizzard behind them.

Stephen's hand trembled as his finger hovered around the trigger of his rifle, ready to shoot into the space before him, as he continued to advance towards the right of Hill 145 with the fourth division. He felt reassured with Captain Barrows at his side. Prisoners were taken.

'Take these prisoners back to the light railway. They can help the stretcher-bearers evacuate the wounded,' said Captain Barrows.

'Yes, sir,' said two of the armed guards.

'Watch them closely so they don't escape or harm anyone, but remember, Canadian Brigade instructions are clear. German soldiers are to be treated in the same way as our own wounded,' said Captain Barrows.

The Guards saluted and headed back towards the tramways, ensuring the German prisoners moved in the opposite direction to the battlefield.

The element of surprise continued throughout the morning.

'Right, lads, we've secured the right of the pimple, it's time to advance towards the left,' said Captain Barrows, as he scratched his head, irritated by the lice feeding from his scalp.

Stephen's boots squelched through the trails of blood sodden mud as he followed his captain's lead. But he suddenly fell to his knees as he slipped on a broken duckboard, and the sound of heavy fire blasted from clouds of smoke on Hill 145, the highest point of the ridge.

'Take cover,' yelled Captain Barrows.

Stephen turned his head, almost in slow motion as he saw a vision of a torn body thrown into the air, twisting and spiralling out of control before reaching a pool of black purple blood.

'Hamish . . .' Stephen screamed.

Stephen crawled towards him under the relentless barrage of machine guns firing from the top of the hill. He turned Hamish's dismantled body over and wiped the mud from his eyes with his sleeve.

'Steve . . . my leg, I can't feel it,' choked Hamish.

Stephen reached into his bag of grenades and threw one a few yards ahead. The explosion created a hole big enough to take cover.

'Leave me, Steve, I'm finished, save yourself,' said Hamish.

Stephen's eyes reflected the terror that comes with fear of death, with a blend of peace and letting go.

'Listen to me, Hamish, you're not to give up, you have to fight,' said Stephen.

Stephen dragged Hamish's body towards the bombed crater. He unbuttoned his tunic. He used his knife to slice away his own cotton t-shirt from his body and covered the hanging charcoal flesh from the open gushing wound on Hamish's leg.

'Put your hand on top of this and press down,' said Stephen.

Stephen stretched out for the broken duckboard and cut into the wood to make a splint. He frantically dug his hands in the mud to find some wire to tie it with and grasped what looked like a severed, human arm. He choked as he bit his bottom lip and eventually found some hidden wire beneath the crater. He desperately cut away the sharp edges with his wire cutters and used the wire to tie the splint to Hamish's leg. Hamish screamed, as his eyes looked towards the black dust in the sky.

'Quick thinking, Steve, well done, you should have been an Army medic,' said Captain Barrows as he crawled into the crater.

Charlie and Henry appeared from a cloud of smoke behind them and fell into the safety of the hole in the ground. Charlie crawled towards Hamish.

'What have I told you about dancing in front of Bombardier Fritz,' said Charlie as he gently patted the side of Hamish's face.

'I'm not as nimble on my feet as I used to be. I bet the pigs can run faster than me now,' spluttered Hamish.

'He's lost a lot of blood, he needs hospital treatment,' said Henry.

'It's too dangerous to retreat,' said Stephen.

'I've heard first and second divisions have taken the red, blue, and brown lines. They're secured. The third division are creating a defensive line in the original trenches, to support us,' said Captain Barrows, his thick eyebrows knitted in the middle as he continued deep in thought.

Stephen grabbed another grenade from his bag and threw it ahead of them. It blew a mirroring crater in the ground.

'There's machine gunfire coming from a trench in the rear slope, sir,' said Stephen.

'Let's see if we can get closer to that machine gun. Try throwing more grenades at a further distance,' ordered Captain Barrows.

Blades of shrapnel whizzed through the air, escalating out of control. But as the smoke dispersed into the sinking mud, the machine gun continued to fire in all directions.

'It's no good, sir . . . we're too far away. We're short of about thirty metres,' said Charlie as he threw a grenade into the empty space ahead of them.

'We'll have to move from one shell hole to the next. Help Hamish and keep your heads down. I'll cover you, go,' said Captain Barrows.

Stephen and Charlie tried to drag Hamish, but he screamed out in pain.

'Help me lift him. I'll carry him on my shoulders,' said Stephen.

As Stephen ran forward with Charlie by his side, Henry stepped in front of him and fired continuously towards the top of the hill to provide a protective screen for Stephen and Hamish. In the cross fire, Stephen almost choked on the trickling blood from his bitten lip, as a human head dismembered from burning flesh rose into the falling sleet and disintegrated into the grey smoke-filled sky.

Stephen dived into the bombed shell hole before machine guns from the top of the hill blasted the edge and flew whirls of mud into the air, which became a camouflage to allow Captain Barrows and other troops from the fourth division crawl below ground for shelter.

'Right, men, start digging, we need this to be deeper. Use your knives, your hands, whatever you can get hold of, but dig fast. Form two lines, one covers whilst the others dig,' ordered the captain.

'Hey, I've found a souvenir,' said Rick, holding up a German helmet.

' . . . found a souvenir' said Richie, as he caught the same, with both hands.

But the sound of the helmet falling into the mud penetrated the dusty air, as Richie released it from his grasp.

'Bloody hell! A Jerry's head is attached to it,' said Henry.

Their eyes reflected the empty stare of death from the severed head.

'Come on now, lads, settle down, we need to focus,' said Captain Barrows.

The first line shot rounds of bullets towards German targets, whilst the second line continued to dig, some with their elbows when their hands got tired.

'Fire,' Captain Barrows repeated after every reload.

'If we had a shovel we could dig some funk holes to get more shelter,' said Stephen from the second line of defence.

'Did anyone think to bring one with them?' Henry quipped.

'It's no good, sir, the mud's turned to slush from the snow,' said Stephen.

Captain Barrows stared ahead of him, scratching his head at the back of his helmet as he sat knee deep in the river of mud. Stephen held a piece of snow that he'd grabbed from the side of the earth and watched it disintegrate in his hand, the rain falling heavily overhead. Until all he could see inside the iced fragments, was Albie smiling back at him, playing leapfrog.

*Watch me jump, Stevie . . . watch me . . . I bet I can jump higher than you . . .*

Stephen held his rifle tightly in both hands and climbed over the top of the crater. He jumped from shell hole to shell hole, until he reached thirty metres away from the German machine gun. Once in range, he threw a grenade, bombing the trench. He flinched before he rushed forward, his head spinning, looking for prisoners to take as he entered the wide dug out. Stephen stood at the top of the wooden steps, fixed to the side of the earth, that led down into the trench. He slowly descended into the dimmed lit space. But a remaining gunner aimed his rifle in his direction just three steps away from him. They stared into each other's eyes with a look of slight hesitation. Stephen lowered his firearm, but the German soldier fumbled with the trigger on his rifle. There was no time to think, only the words:

*It's him or me.*

Stephen forced his bayonet forward, thrusting it into the soldier's chest. He stared into the whites of the gunner's eyes as blood spurted from his mouth. Stephen's legs trembled into an empty sensation of numbness.

*He's just an ordinary man . . .*

Red curdled liquid dripped from the muzzle of Stephen's rifle onto the rigid body of the stranger before him. He collapsed to the ground on his knees and choked on his own vomit. But then heard a sound from the mangled limbs piled inside the trench.

'Who's there? Show yourself,' said Stephen, pointing his rifle in every direction around him.

'Nicht schießen!'

A German soldier crawled from beneath the torn flesh on the ground. But all Stephen could see was the Red Cross emblem around his left arm.

'Sie sind ein Sanitär?' Stephen asked.

'Ja . . . Sie sprechen Deutsch,' said the German medic, holding up his hands.

'Ja,' said Stephen.

Stephen relaxed his grip and lowered his rifle away from the unarmed medic, who yelled when he tried to free his foot from beneath a splintered duckboard. He rushed forward to help the medic free his leg and opened the medical bag at his side in search of something to stop the weeping blood. With precision, Stephen cleaned the wound and wrapped a bandage around the medic's ankle.

'Wie heißen Sie?' The medic asked.

'Ich heiße Stephen,' said Stephen.

'Hans . . .' the medic said as he held out his hand.

Stephen entwined his fingers around his, in a moment when all thought of war and killing disappeared, in a place where strangers met for the first time.

'Wo haben Sie Deutsch gelernt?' Hans asked.

Stephen closed his eyes and Ada smiled back at him from the remnants of his mind, with the light from her eyes shining deep within his, as he remembered the lessons she taught him. Stephen suddenly returned to the reality of his situation and found a water carrier near the machine gun, held it to Hans' mouth and helped him to drink.

'Danke,' said Hans as he slowly leant back against the wall in the far-left corner of the trench.

Stephen drank from the water carrier, relieving his dry mouth, removed his helmet and poured the rest over the top of his head. When his breathing became calmer, and he was sure that Hans was unable to move, he turned the machine gun to face the top of Hill 145 and continued to fire. His determination outranked any feeling, until he heard a sudden movement behind him.

'Hold your fire,' said Captain Barrows.

The captain climbed into the trench, followed by Charlie and Henry carrying Hamish with more troops behind them.

'Henry, take over the machine gun. That was a very brave thing you just did, Steve,' said Captain Barrows, laying his hand on Stephen's shoulder.

'Thank you, sir,' said Stephen as his bottom lip trembled slightly.

'Hey, Steve, look who followed us in,' said Charlie.

'Is there any food in here?' Billy asked, squinting round the trench.

'Can't believe you're thinking about your stomach at a time like this,' mumbled Arthur rolling his eyes.

'Stop squabbling you two and move the dead over to the far-right corner,' ordered Captain Barrows.

'There's a live one here, sir,' said Arthur.

'He's an Army medic,' said Stephen.

'Hold your fire, remember Hague Conventions,' said Captain Barrows.

Stephen slid his back down the wall, looked at familiar faces and smiled, feeling a sense of relief that he was no longer alone. He crawled over to Hamish, who had been placed inside a funk hole, carved into the side of the wall. Charlie tried to clean the deep gash in Hamish's leg, with water from a bottle he had removed from a dead gunner.

'How is he?' Stephen asked.

'I'm not sure he's going to make it,' whispered Charlie.

'He has to, he's got to pull through,' whispered Stephen.

'You think I can't hear you? You know, farmers have the reputation for the best hearing down town, even with their eyes closed,' croaked Hamish.

'Stay with us, Hamish, Lettie's waiting for you,' said Stephen.

'I'm counting on it,' choked Hamish.

'Können Sie ihm helfen?' Stephen asked Hans desperately.

Hans crawled closer to where Hamish lay and asked for his medical bag. He proceeded to remove the splint from Hamish's leg and stared at the open wound. Hamish's screams filled the space, and his eyes flickered to a close.

'Die Beine sind schlecht infiziert . . . es ist zu spät,' said Hans.

'What did he say, Steve?' Charlie asked.

'He's lost too much blood from his leg . . . it's too late,' Stephen whispered.

Hamish held out his hand to meet Stephen's, who knelt beside him.

'Lettie . . . tell her . . .' Hamish spluttered through the blood in his mouth.

His last breath rattled from the doorway of his throat to fall into a tapestry of silence, until . . .

'Hamish . . .' cried Charlie.

'Don't leave,' choked Stephen.

But their tears were lost with the pellets of iced rain falling from the relentless darkness.

The sound of machine gun fire continued to blast a surrounding echo and rebound off the protective sand bags, whilst Stephen stared into the smoke filled, red lit sky, changing the invisible landscape from day to night.

'Stephen, Henry, over here,' whispered Captain Barrows.

Arthur pulled Stephen's arm gently. 'You've got to let him go, Steve.'

'I can't, he's so cold,' croaked Stephen.

'He's gone home,' said Arthur as he covered Hamish's body with his ground sheet cape.

Stephen wiped his nose with the back of his hand. His dry lips slowly parted, as he noticed Henry click his fingers and point towards Captain Barrows.

'Yes, sir,' said Stephen as he crawled closer with Henry following.

'Message from high command. We're to be sent to the 87th Battalion for reinforcements. We need to move further forward. The Jerrys have got the advantage from the top of the pimple. Look over there to the west side of the hill. It's an enemy dug out. I'm going to crawl closer and see if there's a way I can get inside. Follow me but stay some distance behind. I'm going to enter alone. Wait for my signal. Oh and . . .'

Henry slapped some mud across Stephen's face.

'You don't want them Jerry's to see your pretty face, now do you, Steve?' Henry smirked.

' . . . black out your faces,' said the Captain.

Stephen spat out some of the slimy gritty mud that got stuck between his teeth and continued to paste the mud over his face, watching Henry closely.

'Whatever you do, Steve, don't smile,' said Henry as they climbed out of the crater, behind Captain Barrows, crawling on their stomachs through shell torn mud.

Stephen's elbows sank deeper into the charcoal ground as he continued to move closer to the target, his rifle starting to weigh heavy and slide through his wet hand. The captain stopped suddenly, turned, and put his fingers to his mouth. He then signalled for Stephen and Henry to hold their position.

Captain Barrows reached the edge of the dug-out and pointed his rifle and pistol towards German troops gathered around two machine guns.

'You're surrounded by the fourth division of the 87th battalion. Surrender your firearms and move away from the machine guns, or I will give the command for you to be shot,' said Captain Barrows.

'That's the captain's signal for us to move forward,' whispered Stephen, as Captain Barrows raised his left hand.

Stephen and Henry crawled towards the edge.

'Gentlemen, I give you the 87th Battalion, Canadian Grenadier Guards,' said Captain Barrows.

Stephen pointed his rifle towards the German troops in the dug-out with his finger hovering over the trigger. He relaxed his grip around the rifle when he realised the German soldiers had dropped their weapons, raised their hands, and slowly stepped back against the wall. Stephen followed Captain Barrows and Henry down some steep steps, deeper inside.

'Henry, count the prisoners and watch them closely. Steve, help me turn these machine guns around,' said Captain Barrows.

The German troops lowered their eyes to the ground; their uniforms caked in dry mud, their eyes sunk into the grey skin around their cheekbones.

'Thirty . . . eh thirty-one prisoners, sir,' said Henry as he picked up some stale bread coated in grey slime.

When the heavy guns were pointed in the direction of the top of Hill 145, Stephen fired bullets high into the chilled air by the side of Captain Barrows. As the blizzard continued, and the rats jumped through heavy fire beneath the invisible stars, the objectives from all four Canadian divisions were secured.

Later that day, Stephen marched to camp Camblain l'Abbe with his battalion, engulfed by a heavy snowstorm. He found the nearest hut, removed his equipment, and squeezed himself into an empty bunk bed amongst the crowds of troops sleeping or writing letters. As he turned on his side, he recognised a familiar face.

'Harold . . . it's good to see you,' said Stephen.

'Glad you made it, Steve. I've heard there's been over ten thousand dead or injured,' said Harold.

'We lost Hamish,' whispered Stephen, as his eyes gave way to a sleep he longed for.

But the darkest nightmare took hold, where he felt like part of him had been left behind to rot in the graves of victory where friends lay—the sweet relief of death holding their hands.

TWO DAYS OF rest passed, and the battalion returned to training. Orders were for working parties to repair the Lens-Arras road and the roads and tramlines between Bouchez and Givenchy, whilst reinforcements arrived. During early May, the battalion moved to Chateau de la Haie and took over Niagara camp, where training continued.

Stephen walked towards the bottom of the slope leading down from the Chateau, towards the bathhouse. He removed his uniform, stepped into the bath and closed his eyes.

*The water's not cold . . .*

Stephen sank deeper into the warm water with ripples of splashes dancing between his toes. And the soap slipped though Albert's fingers.

*Ah . . . can we go for a swim in the river tomorrow?*

'Steve, Steve . . .'

Stephen saw a blurred vision of Charlie standing at the side of the bath.

'You dropped the soap.'

'Oh . . . thanks, Charlie,' said Stephen.

'You need to report to Brigade Headquarters. Captain Barrows is asking for you,' said Charlie.

'Do you know what it's about?' Stephen asked.

'No, but I guess you'll soon find out,' said Charlie.

Stephen quickly got dressed and rushed out of the bathhouse, still buttoning up his tunic as he made his way towards the stone building in the grounds. He was shown into a square room with high ceilings and maps of the surrounding area hanging from the walls. Major Shaw remained seated behind a mahogany desk with his eyes focused on a writing pad. Captain Barrows was standing beside him.

'Have a seat,' said Major Shaw, as he continued to focus on his report.

'Thank you, sir,' said Stephen.

'It has been brought to my attention that you speak German,' said Major Shaw.

'Yes, sir,' said Stephen.

'As you are aware, we're preparing for an attack on Hill 70. We need someone to infiltrate enemy lines and determine any communication that might be useful to us. It's a great risk, but with your knowledge of the language, you have a chance of pulling it off. Any information you can gather, will greatly aid our offensive positions and give us an advantage,' said Major Shaw.

'I understand, sir,' said Stephen.

'The mission of course is top secret and highly dangerous with no guarantee of your safe return,' said Major Shaw.

'Count me in, sir,' said Stephen.

'Good man. Captain Barrows will brief you on further details. Good luck,' said Major Shaw as he held out his hand.

Stephen shook Major Shaw's hand and saluted. He was then led to a small side room, where he listened attentively. He heard the sound of his captain's voice, alongside the pounding of his own heart, but he felt numb inside, void of any feeling.

'The German Sixth Army Commander General der Infanterie Otto von Below is responsible for the area between Lille and Camrai. I will guide you as close to Lille as possible. You will be given a German uniform. Field Ambulances frequently travel from the dressing stations to where the Germans have set up camp. You will flag down one of them, faking injury. I plan to take the driver prisoner. Your main objective is to drive the van into the enemy camp and gain any information you can that might be helpful to our operation, and from there, you're on your own. Any questions?' Captain Barrows asked.

'How will I know which direction to drive, sir?' Stephen asked.

'You won't. We don't know exactly where German headquarters are based, it's guesswork. If the driver won't talk, then you will have to use your initiative,' said Captain Barrows.

'Yes, sir,' said Stephen.

Nightfall arrived, and Stephen changed into German uniform. He followed Captain Barrows across the outskirts of Lens and walked and crawled miles, until they came to an overgrown area shadowed by naked trees and burnt hedges near Lille.

'Now we wait,' said Captain Barrows.

The sound of an engine rumbled across the dirt track road and a field ambulance came into view in the distance behind a cloud of dust.

'Now's your chance, go,' said Captain Barrows.

Stephen rushed down the slope, with head and shoulders leaning towards the ground. He limped into the road, holding his leg, and waved to get the driver's attention. The ambulance came to a slow halt and the driver jumped out of the front seat.

'Können Sie mir helfen?' Stephen asked.

'Was passiert ist, um das Bein?' the driver asked, looking at Stephen's leg.

The sound of the trigger on Captain Barrows' rifle suddenly clicked in the driver's ear, and he raised both hands.

'Nicht schhießen,' cried the driver desperately.

Stephen questioned him, asking specific directions to the German camp. The driver spoke quickly, his lips trembling as he disclosed the information Stephen needed, and that his objective was to pick up medics to take them back to a nearby dressing station. Captain Barrows led the driver into the woods where they both became invisible from the road. Stephen jumped into the driver's seat, started the engine, and drove the field ambulance, hoping that he had been given the right directions and had not been tricked. After some distance, he came to a German roadblock ahead. He put his foot slowly on the brake and the ambulance came to a halt. A German guard checked over the van, and his suspicious eyes returned to the driver's seat where he noticed the Red Cross emblem around Stephen's left arm.

'Haben Sie eine Zigarette?' the German guard asked.

Stephen picked up a packet of cigarettes from the dashboard and offered it to the guard.

'Danke,' said the guard as he put one to his mouth and handed the packet back.

'Nehmen Sie das Paket, ich habe mehr,' said Stephen, determined to let the guard keep the cigarettes.

The guard smiled and gave the signal to lift the barrier. Stephen drove through steadily, desperately trying to hold his nerve. He found himself on the edge of the German camp, where the sound of pounding inside his heart echoed through his ears and vibrated around his chest. He scoured the area until he found the hospital and parked nearby, and with the silence of the engine, he regretted giving away a whole packet of cigarettes. He checked the glove box only to find a first aid tin. But then he felt inside his tunic pocket and discovered a squashed pack with one left, and a brass petrol lighter. He put the cigarette to his lips and inhaled the smoke and choked slightly.

Stephen waited a few minutes until his breathing calmed down, and then jumped out of the ambulance, holding his Red Cross Bag. He walked slowly through the camp, past accommodation huts, the bathhouse, stretcher-bearers heading towards the hospital, and troops smoking, talking, and playing cards. Stephen mingled in, almost unnoticed, or when he was, the Red Cross emblem around his left arm and the bag he carried seemed a sign of protection that no one questioned.

Until he heard the sound of a voice behind him . . .

'Mediziner! Was tun Sie hier?'

Stephen froze, his feet blocks of ice. He slowly turned to face a German officer who squinted with one eye and glared with the other, through his eyeglass.

'Ich . . . Ich habe einige Vorräte zu sammeln Geschickt, aus dem Krankenhaus, Kommandant,' said Stephen.

The German officer stepped towards Stephen and breathed heavily near his right cheekbone. Stephen could smell the aroma of pipe tobacco on his breath. His pouched stomach looked ready to burst out of his tunic, and his moustache twitched, touching the strands of hair inside his nostrils. Stephen remained still, his body rigid, convinced the officer could smell his English blood.

'Mm . . . worauf waren Sie?' the Commanding Officer yelled.

'Yawohl mein, Herr Kommandant,' said Stephen, saluting.

Stephen rushed forward, feeling his heart wanting to collapse and fall through his legs.

'Warten Sie ab!' the German Officer shouted.

Stephen's right foot stopped in mid-air as he could feel saliva at the back of his throat. He felt the ground beneath him as his leg trembled. Stephen turned slowly to face the commander.

'Sie gehen in der falschen Richtung, Sie Dummkopf,' the commander spat out into the cool air.

Stephen breathed with relief and ran in the direction of the hospital.

'Jawohl mein, Herr Kommandant,' said Stephen.

'Sie Dummkopf,' the commander muttered as he marched away.

Stephen tripped over his boot as he splashed through a trail of mud, determined to put himself as far as possible from the commander. He wiped his forehead with his sleeve to stop the beads of sweat falling into his eyes.

*How can I go back in that direction without being seen, now?*

A truck loaded with ammunition suddenly swerved to miss him, and Stephen jumped out of the way. But it was too late. Stephen was covered with slime mud. He spat out the repellent taste and shivered with cold as the wet sludge soaked his skin. He soon realised that he wouldn't be so easily recognised if he saw the same commander with his eye-glass again. Stephen slowly walked back, away from the direction of the hospital, with his head down, but his eyes alert. He eventually found the military headquarters at the far side of camp. He continued walking until a convoy of trucks passed by and the dust from the road acted as smoke screens for him to slip round the side of the building without being seen. He crouched down and found an open window. Stephen slowly crept towards it with the intention of climbing through, but he heard voices inside, so he sat very still in the long grass beneath it.

Stephen could hear every word that was spoken, clearly. He waited until he had the information he needed and crawled away from the side of the building. But as he stood up to turn the corner, he heard a voice call behind him from the open window. He slowly turned around with his hand ready to open his Red Cross bag and reach for his pistol, when he recognised the uniform of another German commander.

'Mediziner Ich nehme ein Bad. Warten Sie auf mich dort,' said the Commander.

'Jawohl,' said Stephen, and he watched the window close.

Stephen turned away and continued walking, holding in his relief in case it burst outside his chest. He passed the bathhouse without looking back and made his way towards the hospital where he had left the Field Ambulance. He started the engine, but it choked to silence. He turned the key again to hear it rumble. Stephen wiped beads of sweat from his forehead and put his trembling hands on the steering wheel. He reversed the Field Ambulance and slowly turned and headed towards the road that led him to the German barrier. The German guard recognised him and let him through without question. Stephen continued driving down the shattered dirt track with clouds of dust spiralling up behind the wheels, until he looked in his wing mirror and saw a convoy of German trucks heading towards him.

*It's over.*

Stephen knew he wouldn't be able to make it, even if he pushed the Field Ambulance to its highest speed. He slowly pulled over to the side of the road and reached for his pistol. He closed his eyes and tried desperately to steady his breathing. The convoy of trucks passed him by, some of the troops waving and smiling as they continued on their way. Stephen waited until they were out of sight, then jumped out of the Field Ambulance and vomited at the edge of the road.

When he returned and turned the key, the engine spluttered into nothing. He tried again, until he looked at the petrol gauge.

*Empty.*

Stephen grabbed his Red Cross bag, swigged from his water bottle, and walked away from the Field Ambulance towards the woods where he had left Captain Barrows hours before. He knew he had to get off the road as quickly as possible. After miles of walking, he found his Canadian uniform hidden in a hole behind some bushes, deep in the middle of the woods. He lay down and closed his eyes.

Stephen woke to the flicker of bats flying overhead across the burnt trees in the surrounding darkness. He quickly changed uniform and buried the German uniform in the hole where he had slept. He removed his compass from the Red Cross bag and drank the last of the water from his water carrier. His tired feet continued to walk in the direction of the Canadian camp.

The shadows from the enveloping trees reminded him of the tree lined path at Eurach Farm, and the smell of hay and fresh crops from the harvest filled his nostrils as his mind wandered back to a place where he felt safe and warm and loved, until he felt his mother's arms around him. As Stephen's imagination drifted back in time, his foot tripped over a fallen branch in the middle of a fern and he fell into overgrown woodland thickets.

'Ahh . . .' he cried as he reached for his left leg.

Stephen's right eye flickered as he noticed shades of light dancing between the dark leaves of the surrounding trees, and he heard a familiar voice singing.

*Keep the Home Fires Burning,*
*While your hearts are yearning . . .*
*Annie . . . Annie, is that you?*
*(The dancing light moved closer.)*
*Oh, Stevie, what a fine mess you've got yourself in. You're supposed to be on a secret mission and look at the state of you.*
*This is no time for teasing, Annie. Help me up.*
*I really don't think you're in a position to be giving me orders. Besides, your face is dirty. (Annie laughed.)*
*Stephen tried to untangle himself from the briar but the splinters from the fallen branch cut deeper into his leg.*
*(Annie continued singing.)*
*Though your lads are far away*
*They dream of home . . .*
*Annie! You're not helping. Please stop and go home.*
*I'll help you, Stevie, of course I will. On one condition . . . (Annie raised her forefinger.)*
*(Stephen looked at Annie with his left eyebrow raised.)*
*You sing along with me. What can be fairer than that?*
*This is no time for songs, Annie. (Stephen wiped his brow with his sleeve.)*
*Well, if you change your mind, I've got all the time in the world. (Annie danced behind the trunk of a nearby tree.)*
*Annie . . . Annie . . .*
*There's a silver lining*
*Through the dark clouds shining . . .*
*(Annie's voice drifted away in the distance.)*

*Okay, I give up. I'll sing with you, I promise.*

*(The dancing light returned.)*

*Stevie, haven't you learnt by now? I always get what I want in the end.*

*I'm waiting . . . (Stephen held out his hand.)*

*(Annie stepped in front of Stephen and put her palms in the aura around his head. He felt a warm energy tingle through his mind and body as he slowly raised himself up from the ground. The pain had disappeared from his leg.)*

*Well, about time! It took you long enough.*

*Don't forget your promise. (Annie smiled.)*

*(Stephen picked up his Red Cross Bag and put the strap over his shoulder. He continued to walk through the woods with Annie by his side.)*

*Turn the dark cloud inside out*

*Till the boys come home.*

*Keep the Home Fires Burning . . .*

*(They sang together. Until the echo of the song became lost in the towering burnt trees, and the sounds of the birds flying above, between the bowed branches and the velvet sky.)*

Eventually Stephen could see the accommodation huts in the grounds of Chateau de la Hai, in the distance. He passed a dugout with a patrol on look out. He knew his uniform would protect him from being fired at. Stephen continued to shuffle his feet towards his destination. He was at last close enough to the huts to hear the sounds of loud, breathless snoring like an out of rhythm orchestra that's lost its way. The smell of flatulence from men eating too much bully beef lingered in the air. Stephen smiled with relief. He felt safe in this place where familiarity greeted him. He looked up at the full moon shining down a cascade of light into the darkness. But just when he thought he felt calm again, his breathing became heavy as he felt his chest burn. He tried to climb the small steps leading to the battalion headquarters but collapsed with exhaustion.

Stephen heard Captain Barrows calling someone to help him. Then his eyes clouded over with a mist, where voices echoed and faces blurred into oblivion. Until he felt strong arms around him as he was lifted to his feet and almost carried into Major Shaw's office, where he was seated and given a glass of water.

'Thank you, sir,' choked Stephen.

'We'd nearly given up on you,' said Captain Barrows with his hand on Stephen's shoulder.

'When you're ready, private.' Major Shaw stared as he sat on the edge of his seat, leaning forward over his desk, sucking the end of his pipe.

'The German objective is to transfer local divisions to the Ypres Salient. They intend to use a new poisonous gas called a yellow cross shell containing some kind of sulphur mustard,' said Stephen.

'Well done, private, anything else to report?'

'German trenches have cut through the ruins of miner's brick homes, in the city of Lens, giving them shelter in dug outs. Their divisions have been ordered to defend their positions. There was no conversation about any impending attack,' said Stephen.

'You've done a good job, Private Duckhouse. A very courageous operation,' said Major Shaw, holding out his hand to shake Stephen's.

'Thank you, sir,' said Stephen.

'Lean on me,' said Captain Barrows as he helped Stephen to his feet.

They left battalion headquarters and headed towards the bathhouse.

'Get cleaned up. I'll send a medic over to look at your leg,' said Captain Barrows as he left.

'Thank you, sir,' croaked Stephen from a dry throat.

The water comforted him, and he closed his eyes until he heard the sound of Charlie's voice.

'Hey, Steve, you must have been in that bath for about three days.' Charlie laughed.

'Something like that,' said Stephen as the soap slipped through his fingers and made a splash.

Stephen was transported to the First Aid hut where he received medical attention, and his mind fell in and out of consciousness. The following day, his eyes flickered open as speckles of light filtered through the window, entwined with faded shadows. The velvet sky slowly drifted away.

# 10
# Hill 70

*"Oh Canada, we stand on guard for thee."*
— Canadian National Anthem

THE CANADIAN CORPS were ordered to the front-line Lens section in preparation for the attack on Hill 70. Artillery fire was on the increase from both Canadian and German trenches. Pellets of heavy rain fell from the black sky, mixing a cocktail of icy mud on the ground below. Following the usual inspections, attempts were made to improve the camp accommodation.

'How do they expect us to pitch these tents back into position? It's like being in the middle of a bloody mud bath. It's the beginning of August, did I miss the summer?' Henry grumbled.

'What are we doing in this Zouve Valley place anyway, no one seems to know?' Billy groaned, rubbing his stomach.

'It's not working,' said Charlie, wiping the rain from his eyes.

'The blankets are plastered with mud,' groaned Rick.

' . . . plastered with mud,' groaned Richie.

'Will you two give it a rest, you sound like bloody twins twittering the same language,' said Henry, scratching the scar on the side of his face.

'We need something to stop the rain flooding in,' said Stephen.

A young soldier suddenly appeared from behind them. His green eyes flashed as he grinned widely, with a pale complexion beneath his ginger hair.

Stephen's bottom lip trembled as he squinted to look closer.

'Hamish?' Stephen whispered.

'I've brought some wood from old discarded duckboards. I thought it might help,' said the young soldier.

Silence surrounded them as they stared at the figure before them.

'Blimey, it's the ghost of Hamish,' said Henry.

'If we make a floor from the wood, it will give some protection between the mud and the rain,' the young soldier continued.

'You're a welcome bright spark. Where did you come from?' Arthur smiled, showing his cracked front teeth.

'Wentworth County, Ontario. My Pa taught me to carve wood to make things that were useful,' said the young soldier.

'I lived in that area, on a farm in Hamilton,' said Stephen, suddenly unsure he wanted to share his experience of being a Home Boy with a stranger.

'Which farm?' the young soldier asked as he slipped in the slush and fell backwards.

Loud laughter echoed from Henry and Arthur, whilst Stephen and Harold helped him stand up. Curdled mud dripped from his tunic.

'Hey, Wood Head, stop playing in the mud, and bring them duckboards over here,' said Henry to the young soldier.

'Come on, lads, if we work together, we'll have this finished by tea time,' said Rick.

' . . . finished by tea time,' said Richie.

'Now there's a thought,' said Billy, licking his lips.

'Don't you ever think about anything else other than your fat belly?' Henry asked.

'I think about lots of things, when I get the chance,' said Billy, dropping his lower lip.

'I'm too tired to bother with this, I need a long soak in a bath,' said Charlie, stretching his arms up in the freezing air.

Captain Barrows emerged from behind the row of tents.

'The company's scheduled to be at the baths tomorrow morning,' he said.

They stood to attention as the relentless rain forced their eyes to squint, whilst their bodies froze in stillness like the solid wood around them.

'At ease, lads, come on. I'll give you a hand. When this rain eases off, we'll start work on building huts out of salvaged material. But this will have to do for now,' said Captain Barrows.

They worked together to fix the accommodation and bring shelter from the storm. Until the day moved through time to meet the night, and the black sky remained the same.

'Thank you, sir,' said Harold with an air of respect as Captain Barrows turned to move on.

'Try and get some sleep, lads, and let's hope this storm clears soon. We're set for a reorganisation of the platoons tomorrow afternoon,' said Captain Barrows as he disappeared.

Stephen tried to cover himself with a blanket full of dried mud.

'There's no way I'm stripping naked tonight, it's too bloody cold,' said Billy.

'You mean your Ma didn't pack your pyjamas, Billy boy? Besides, who wants to see your naked flesh in the middle of the night? That backside's shinier than the full moon.' Henry laughed.

'Plenty of girls would love to see me naked,' said Billy, smiling as if he was remembering a happy memory.

'In your bloody dreams!' Henry said, as he removed his boots.

'You seriously need to do something about your feet,' said Charlie as he retched.

'Such as?' Henry asked, indifferently.

'Like soaking them in carbolic soap and leaving them there until you die!' Arthur said as he put his hand over his mouth to stop himself choking from the smell.

Henry clicked his fingers. 'Hey, Wood Head, do you know any songs?' he asked, determined to change the subject.

The young soldier produced a harmonica from his tunic pocket and started to play a familiar tune. The words of the song filled the cold air as voices slowly raised from low to high tones inside the tent.

> If you were the only girl in the world,
> And I were the only boy,
> Nothing else would matter in the world today,
> We would go on loving in the same old way . . .

Stephen's mind flashed back to memories of Flo. The warmth from her eyes felt like it was burning inside him. He could hardly breathe as dry tears refused to fall from his glazed eyes. He reached out his hand . . .

> A garden of Eden, just made for two,
> With nothing to mar our joy,
> I would say such wonderful things to you,
> There would be such wonderful things to do.

Stephen trembled as he felt her soft touch. She slowly moved close enough until he could hear the beating of her heart.

> If you were the only girl in the world,
> And I were the only boy.

The sound of the harmonica fell into silence, and all eyes stared into an empty space under the roof of the tent, swaying in the direction of the blustering wind.

'You played a blinder there, Wood Head,' said Henry.

'What's your real name?' Stephen asked as he turned to the young soldier.

'Noah,' he said, quietly.

'That bloody figures! He's come to build us an ark.' Henry laughed.

'Leave the boy alone. He's done a good thing in helping us sort out shelter for the night,' said Harold.

'Hey, Wood Head, stay away from Bishop here, or you'll be on your knees bloody praying for the rest of the night, planning the next book of Genesis,' chuckled Henry.

'Shh . . . Twitchy is on the prowl. I just heard him clear his throat,' whispered Charlie as he covered himself with his blanket.

Stephen squinted with one eye, as he saw the shadow of Sergeant Major Harris through the canvas of the tent pass by outside. Loud and muffled snores echoed out of rhythm with each other and filled the sheltered space, until the pretence slowly changed to a welcome sleep.


STEPHEN FOLLOWED CROWDS of troops into a hut where headquarters was set up, at the edge of camp and entered the briefing room. Noah was close by, following Stephen like a shadow.

'Hey, Steve, come and sit here,' called Charlie from the back of the room.

'Hey, Wood Head, move up. Have you heard the latest?' Henry whispered as he squeezed next to them.

'You've washed your feet?' Charlie asked.

'That's funny you know, proper comedian you are. Listen to me, Byng's been replaced by some lieutenant-general, by the name of Currie. My reliable source, no names mentioned, tells me we're no longer attacking Lens but some high ground north of Lens,' said Henry as the words fell from the side of his mouth.

'I wonder why the orders have been changed?' Stephen asked.

'I guess we're about to find out,' said Charlie.

'Here comes Twitchy,' said Billy, leaning forward from behind them.

Sergeant Major Harris called for silence as he entered the front of the briefing room and twitched his nose as usual. He marched behind Major General Watson.

The room was full of men waiting and listening in anticipation. The sound of a dry cough filled the air, and someone with a bad bout of flatulence sent ripples of laughter round the room.

'Quiet!' Sergeant Major Harris yelled, his nose twitching three times faster than usual.

'Thank you, sergeant major,' said Major General Watson, leaning slightly on his cane.

'Sir!' Sergeant Major Harris stepped to the side.

'Settle down, men. We are preparing for an attack on high ground to the north, codenamed Hill 70, mainly because it's raised seventy metres above sea level,' said Major General Watson.

'I was right then,' whispered Henry, smirking.

'You mean your reliable source was,' muttered Billy.

'The plan is to take the high ground with a surprise assault and establish defensive positions. During training, we will be introducing a technique of predicted fire for the first time, which will greatly improve the accuracy of the artillery. Any questions?'

'What do you mean by predicted fire, sir,' Stephen asked.

'Good question, private. We will be using datum points and calibrated guns, which will improve the accuracy of the artillery. It will all become clear on the practice ground,' said Major General Watson.

'Is it me, or does anyone else have a clue what he's talking about?' Charlie whispered.

'You will be rotated through the reserve area and units will conduct training to prepare for the assault. Trench raids will be conducted south of Lens to mislead the enemy on where the attack will come,' Major General Watson continued.

'Will we be practicing a creeping barrage again, sir? Only Billy here is right good at leapfrog,' said Henry grinning.

Loud laughter echoed around the room. Billy lightly slapped the back of Henry's head, and a nervous silence returned.

'Yes, private, field howitzers will shell the enemy positions 440 yards in advance of the creeping barrage. During the early morning of 15th August, Royal Engineers will fire drums of burning oil into the suburb of Cite St. Elisabeth and other selected targets to build up a smoke screen for the creeping barrage.'

'I've heard the high ground has barbed wire up to about ten feet in height in front of the trenches, sir,' said Arthur, scratching his stubble brown hair.

'It's five feet, private. There are deep trenches and dug outs in the slopes, which makes for a perfect defensive position for the enemy. We believe there are many machine guns entrenched in the slopes, inside pillboxes of reinforced concrete. This is why the attack has to be rehearsed consistently until all troops know exactly what to do.'

'How do we protect ourselves against the German's flame-throwers and mustard gas, sir,' Harold asked, clutching his bible.

'Good question, private, and it will all become clear. We're working closely with the Air Force. Low flying aircraft have been ordered to spot areas of resistance and radio back the co-ordinates so the artillery can immediately respond with heavy shelling. We have been ordered to go over the top on the morning of 15$^{th}$ August. First Division will attack on the left, second division in the centre, and fourth division largely a diversionary attack on the right. Third division will be kept back in reserve. As fourth division, the diversionary attack will become clear to you all, during lectures later this morning. Any last questions?'

'I'm still not sure about the mustard gas, sir,' said Rick.

' . . . mustard gas,' said Richie.

'I'm now going to hand you over to the Divisional Gas Officer who will conduct a lecture on the use of gas and answer any further questions.'

A stranger entered the room, shuffled his heavy weight forward as he limped, showing an expression of discomfort on his taut pale face.

'Blimey, it's Billy's twin come back to life,' whispered Henry, smirking.


LIGHT DROPS OF rain from persistent showers fell from the sky, splashing against the canvas of a huge tent. Stephen congregated with his division for the morning religious service, to be followed by church parade. The chaplain, slightly stooped, led the service by announcing the first hymn. Stephen cleared his throat as a flash from Kirkwall Presbyterian Church enflamed his mind. Ada's eyes shone a distant light into his until his right eye flickered and he was somehow pulled back to the reality of his situation. Voices sang out, some high-spirited, some with tones of resentment, all mixed into an atmosphere of uncertainty.

> Onward Christian Soldiers!
> Marching as to war,
> With the cross of Jesus
> Going on before . . .

'Bloody chaplain's a joke. When was the last time he marched to war?' Henry grumbled.

> Christ, the royal Master,
> Leads against the foe;
> Forward into battle,
> See, His banners go!

'I know what I'd like to do with Twitchy and his banners,' wittered Arthur, as he frowned at Sergeant Major Harris bellowing out the lyrics.

As the rhythm of the song fell into a silent pause, the service continued with a chorus of dry coughing and muttering in the background, until the chaplain introduced the reading of Psalm 44.

'Hey, Steve, it's your turn. Speak up now, we want to hear every word,' said Harold.

Stephen made his way to the front of the tent and opened his Bible. His hand trembled slightly as he felt something dry fill the back of his throat. He opened his mouth, determined to let the words follow his nerves.

> . . . Through You will we push down our enemies:
> Through Your name we will trample those who rise up against us.

Henry gave Billy a friendly nudge on his arm as he noticed a tear falling down his cheek. Charlie held the side of his face in his hand to hide his emotion.

> For I will not trust in my bow,
> Nor shall my sword save me.

Rick and Richie sat with their mouths wide open. And Arthur bowed his head scratching his side burns.

> But you have saved us from our enemies,
> And put to shame those who have hated us . . .

Harold and Noah remained still in the silence of their own presence with eyes closed, listening, until the reading was complete. Stephen closed his Bible and returned to his seat.

'Well done, Steve, that was read perfectly,' whispered Harold.

'You did really well,' whispered Noah, gazing at Stephen in awe.

Stephen's breathing came back to a rhythm he recognised as a sense of relief filled his mind.

'Let's sing together our final hymn, Fight the Good Fight,' mumbled the chaplain.

> Every moment of your life time
> Every minute every day
> Fight the good fight every moment
> Make it worth the price we pay . . .

'You don't pay me enough, to sing this bloody song,' grumbled Henry.

The final hymn filled the atmosphere of the tent with great joy as the end of the service drew to a close.

The battalion made their way outside for the usual medical inspection. In the afternoon, work continued on the huts, using salvaged material to give more shelter.

'At least we won't have to sleep in those bloody tents tonight,' said Henry, splitting a piece of wood with his bare hands.

'Hey, have you heard, the commander's taken to his bed with some kind of sickness,' said Arthur.

'I don't feel so well myself. Do you think I can take to my bed?' Rick asked, rubbing his stomach.

' . . . take to my bed?' Richie asked.


THE NEXT DAY, Stephen woke to the sound of scratching.

'My bloody scalp itches,' said Henry, with his head in his hands.

'Your hair needs a good cut, it's getting longer than the Twitchy moustache. When you get to my age you might grow fine stubble hair like mine.' Arthur laughed.

'Hey, Steve, are you awake?' Charlie asked.

'I am now,' said Stephen.

'You used to cut John McPhail's hair. Why don't you get your scissors out and put Henry out of his misery?' asked Charlie.

'Whilst you're there, cut his bloody throat, then we all might get some peace,' said Arthur.

'Can you do that outside, I'm trying to read,' said Harold, peering up from his spectacles, as he was showing Noah a passage from his bible.

'We wouldn't want to interfere with Bishop's prayer meeting, would we,' grumbled Henry.

Stephen quickly got dressed and took his scissors from his backpack.

'It's stopped raining, and it looks like the grounds drying up. Let's go outside,' said Stephen.

'Are you sure you know what you're doing?' Henry asked, squinting.

'Trust me,' said Stephen.

Henry stepped outside the hut and sat down on a wooden chair near the entrance, feeling deflated.

'It looks like I've got no bloody choice, my scalp feels like it's on fire,' said Henry as he continued to scratch his head.

'Have you come to disturb the peace?' Rick asked, looking up from his sketchpad, as he sat on a wooden crate.

' . . . disturb the peace?' Richie asked as he watched Rick closely.

'Why don't you find something bloody interesting to draw?' Henry quipped.

'Richie, we'll finish later. This is just too much of an opportunity to miss,' said Rick as he turned and sketched Stephen cutting Henry's hair.

' . . . too much of an opportunity to miss,' said Richie, gazing at Stephen's scissors.

Henry scowled and fidgeted in his chair.

'You need to keep still, I don't want to snip your ear by mistake,' said Stephen as he continued to cut small pieces of brown and silver hair.

'Your bloody life won't be worth living if you do,' grumbled Henry.

'You do know your hair is full of lice,' said Stephen, taking a step back.

Billy suddenly appeared from the side of the hut, leaning his head to one side and whistling.

'Where've you been? Out for a morning stroll?' Henry asked.

'I've been to the bathhouse for a shave. You should try it,' said Billy, standing up for himself.

'I don't think that's a bad idea, and whilst you're there you need to wash your hair,' said Stephen.

Henry stood up, stretched out his arms, scowled at Billy, and walked towards the bathhouse, swinging his arms.

'Anyone ready for breakfast?' Charlie asked as he stepped outside the hut.

They walked over to the Division Canteen with their mess tins and joined the long queue inside the hut. Steam rose from big black pots in the far corner where the kitchen team served breakfast. Soldiers sat around tables, eating, drinking, smoking, laughing, or playing cards.

'We should have come earlier, it's too busy,' said Harold.

'What's for breakfast anyway? White splodge again?' Rick asked, rolling his eyes.

' . . . white splodge again?' asked Richie, sighing.

'They call it oatmeal porridge, it tastes more like bloody onion porridge to me,' said Arthur, scowling.

'Hey, Steve, it looks like the rum rations have arrived,' said Charlie, pointing to the brown jars stacked behind the steaming pots of porridge.

'We might have that later, served with dinner,' said Stephen.

'You mean with our pea soup flavoured with weeds and nettles?' Billy moaned.

'What does S.R.D. stand for?' Noah asked, squinting at the letters across the rum jars.

'I think it means supply reserve depot,' said Harold.

'Not likely, more like bloody service rum diluted,' said Henry as he pushed into the queue.

Sounds of grumbles from impatient troops behind him rose above the whirl of chatter in the canteen.

'Settle down, lads, they've been saving my place whilst I had a meeting at the bathhouse,' said Henry.

As soon as Stephen was served he looked down at his mess tin of porridge, mug of tea, and biscuit, and his mind closed down.

'Come on, Steve, there's an empty table over there,' said Charlie.

Stephen's eyes suddenly blinked back to the reality of his situation. They all huddled together around the wooden table. Stephen sat and drank his tea, a familiar comfort reminding him of the farm, but with a bittersweet taste. He remembered the smell of scrambled eggs, bacon, and coffee in the kitchen.

'This tea conceals the taste of water, and no bloody wonder, it's transported in petrol tins,' said Rick.

' . . . transported in petrol tins,' said Richie.

'Hey, don't forget to dunk that biscuit into your tea, Steve. You remember what happened to Arthur don't you?' Henry chuckled with a sparkle in his eye.

'You eat that biscuit like a man, Steve, and be as handsome as me.' Arthur grinned, showing his cracked front teeth.

'What are these biscuits made of, anyway?' Stephen asked.

'They tell us they're a mixture of salt, flour, and water, but they taste more like water and cement,' said Henry, scooping out the last mouthful of porridge from his mess tin.

'These biscuits are harder than the tin can the tea's served in,' moaned Billy, as he shuffled his overweight body to get comfortable.

'Come on now, Billy. Don't you think you could do with losing a few pounds?' Arthur teased.

'I've lost three stone already. A stone for every year I've fought in this war. If I lose anymore I'll look as slim as a duckboard,' Billy grumbled.

'I think the war might need to go on for a while longer before that happens,' said Rick, as he gulped down his tea.

' . . . for a while longer before that happens,' repeated Richie.

Stephen smiled kindly at Richie, at his attempt to hide the rush of nervous adrenaline clouding his mind. He knew how to calm him down, when Richie was feeling overly anxious, and his need to echo Rick got worse.

'I hear we're practicing throwing live bombs and rifle grenades this morning,' said Charlie, seriously.

'At least it's not bloody raining,' said Arthur.

'Hey, Billy, don't forget to throw from the right side, and not the Jerry's, just in case you get blown up.' Henry laughed.

Billy's head leaned to one side as he bit his lip. The Division Canteen emptied, and the smoke-filled space became quieter until all they could hear was the kitchen team clanging the pots as they cleared everything away.

'We better go, or Twitchy will be on the war path,' said Stephen.

They picked up their kits and rifles and rushed towards the training ground. Sergeant Major Harris bellowed out instructions as lines of troops practiced attack formation. Stephen ducked and made his way towards the back to join the last formation, whilst the others followed him one by one.

'Wait until Twitchy is looking the other way, then stand up together and blend in,' whispered Harold.

'How will we know when he's not looking, Bishop? I can't see a bloody thing,' whispered Henry.

'This isn't doing my back any good,' moaned Billy.

'We'll just have to take a chance. On three, one, two three,' whispered Stephen.

They stood up and moved forward with their formation.

'Where's Twitchy, I can't see him?' Arthur asked, wiping his brow with his sleeve.

'Where've you lot been? You're a disgrace to that uniform,' yelled Sergeant Major Harris from behind them.

'Yes, sir,' their voices sounded together as their bodies automatically stood to attention.

'I'm watching you lot. Don't you ever forget it. Now move it,' roared Sergeant Major Harris.

The practice ground lit up like firecrackers in the sky, with each formation moving forward to throw live ammunition into a space that was the rehearsal for the coming battle. Training continued over the next three days.


STEPHEN WATCHED THE clouds of smoke rise from Henry's tobacco and circle up to the roof of the hut as he lay beneath his blanket.

'Do you ever miss home?' Charlie asked from the bed beside him.

'It depends what you mean by home? There's not a day goes by when I don't miss someone,' said Stephen.

'Do you have a sweetheart back at Hamilton? I used to see you talk to Flo a lot when we were in church,' said Charlie.

Stephen's heart started to beat faster, and he could hardly breathe.

'Flo and I were just good friends,' said Stephen.

'You should write to her. I always thought she was keen on you,' said Charlie.

'Really? I don't know what gave you that idea,' said Stephen, blushing as Flo filled his mind.

'One thing I've learnt here, up to your knees in this mud pit, is that life is short. You never know what might happen. Why not take a risk? I bet you a shilling that Flo writes back,' said Charlie.

Stephen looked deeply into Charlie's eyes, wanting to believe him.

'How about you? Did you leave a sweetheart back there in Ontario?' Stephen asked, not able to stop thinking about Flo.

'No, there's no one for me. I really miss Hamish, though,' said Charlie, and his eyes became vacant, with a distant stare.

'He's here, watching us,' said Stephen.

Charlie fell into a deep sleep, and Stephen noticed a shadow in the darkest corner of the hut suddenly change to a sparkle, like the North Star in the black sky. The dancing light moved closer.

> *Annie, where've you been? You haven't been around for ages.*
>
> *I've been busy, Stevie, you know, doing a bit of this and that on the other side. Besides, I have a new friend.*
>
> *What friend? Who?*
>
> *(Annie stepped to one side, and a familiar figure smiled with warmth that filled Stephen's heart.)*
>
> *Hamish?*
>
> *I just wanted to say thank you, Steve. I know you did everything you could to save me. But I'm in a better place now.*
>
> *We miss you, Hamish.*
>
> *Just remember, where ever you and Charlie are, I'm right there beside you. I'll never leave you.*
>
> *You promise?*
>
> *(Hamish smiled as a faint shadow began to fall across his face. Annie linked his arm.)*
>
> *Come on now, I'm bored with this boy talk. We've got a battle to prepare for.*
>
> *(The dancing light faded in the distance, leaving a purple glow in the empty space they left behind.)*

STEPHEN'S BODY JUMPED awake as he heard a familiar voice in the distance. He looked towards the entrance of the hut.

'Wake up, lads, important briefing scheduled before breakfast. Orders have just come in. We're to relieve the 102$^{nd}$ Battalion Canadian Infantry tonight and take over the front line from Absalom Trench,' said Captain Barrows, his thick eyebrows knotted in the middle.

'Where's Absalom Trench, sir?' Stephen asked.

'If you want details it's to the east of the Cite du Bois de Lievin, but all you need to know is that it's on the right of Lens,' said Captain Barrows as he left the entrance to the hut.

There was a sense of urgency as Stephen rushed to get dressed, and in the midst of sudden chaos, Harold knelt down to pray.

'Who's moved my boots?' Billy asked as he hurried around the hut.

'Why would anyone want your size twenty-fives?' Arthur asked, struggling with the button on his tunic.

'Hey, Bishop, say a prayer for all of us. I've a feeling we're going to need it,' mumbled Henry, as the braces on his trousers snapped.

Stephen noticed Noah watching him with an intense, unspoken fear in his eyes as they both diligently wound their puttees around their legs. Stephen smiled, and Noah breathed with relief.

'Hey, Steve, I had a dream about Hamish last night,' said Charlie as he stared at his toe sticking out of his sock.

'Maybe it was because we were talking about him,' said Stephen, reaching for his cap.

'Yeah, but it was like he was right here with us,' said Charlie as he hastily looked through his kit bag.

'We're ready, we'll wait for you outside,' said Rick as he lit up two cigarettes, hanging from his bottom lip.

' . . . wait for you outside,' said Richie, as he held out his hand for one of the cigarettes.

Within seconds they were rushing towards the briefing hut.

'Hey, where's Bishop?' Henry asked.

'Still on his knees when I last saw him,' said Arthur.

'I'll go back for him,' said Stephen.

'I'll come with you,' said Noah.

Stephen turned to run in the opposite direction, but noticed Harold rushing towards them, clutching his bible close to his chest. They entered the crowded briefing hut breathless and stood at the back, which was the only space that was free.

'Good morning members of D company, we saved the back row purposely for late comers,' said Sergeant Major Harris, twitching his nose.

'I reckon Twitchy has got it in for us,' whispered Billy, his bottom lip drooped.

'He loves us really, in his own twitchy way.' Henry smirked.

'Officer present,' said Sergeant Major Harris, standing to attention, as Major General Watson entered the hut.

'At ease, gentlemen,' said Major General Watson, walking to the front of the hut, leaning on his cane.

An unnerved silence filled the air as lines of men waited in anticipation, and all eyes were watching Major General Watson.

'The Battalion has been ordered to move off from Zouave Valley tonight at nine pm, taking over the front line from Absalom Trench,' said Major General Watson; his voice was steady, and his eyes looked determined.

Sergeant Major Harris pulled down a map of the area, fixed to the front wall of the hut. He remained stiff, with his shoulders back. Only the occasional twitch of his nose contrasted with his stillness.

'As you can see, A company will be in right support in the new trenches, Cyclist and Cavalry. B company will take over the right front line from Absalom Trench to Crocodile. C company will be in left support in Crook Redoubt. Finally, D company will cover left front line, Cite St. Theodore. Any questions?' Major General Watson asked.

No one spoke or moved. A heavy silence like a dark cloud ready to break out in thunder hovered over the crowd in the hut. Minutes passed into an empty space.

'The battle of Vimy Ridge was one of the most momentous days in Canadian history. I have every faith in you all, that we can do the same with the capture of Hill 70. I wish you good luck, gentlemen, and may God go with you.' Major General Watson slowly walked towards the exit of the hut, with his cane in his right hand leading the way.

The silence turned into a rhythm of low-key chatter as the crowd made their way outside the hut into the warm, stifling air.


STEPHEN'S EARS BURNED from the artillery fire on both sides that had continued all day on the Front-Line Lens Section. He sat on an old wooden crate in an attempt to keep himself dry from the gushing mud below his feet. As night drew close, the consistent artillery fire changed to scattered shelling from the enemy.

'There you go, Steve, a nice cup of beef tea. That should keep you going,' said Harold.

Stephen wrapped his fingers around the tin cup and smiled at Harold, who then opened his kit bag. Whilst Stephen savoured the fantasy flavour of his tea, he stared at the black leather-bound Bible in Harold's hand. It reminded him of the days at Eurach farm with . . .

Edgar's evening bible readings near the light from the oil lamp. The warmth from the log burning oven stove. Ada's gentle, kind smile as she sewed meticulously. Catherine, asleep in the arm chair clutching her cane, and John, looking up at his father, listening attentively.

'Hey Bishop, read us something from that black book of yours,' said Henry.

Stephen shivered from the cool air. He sipped the brown liquid from his tin cup.

*This tea's cold.*

'Will you two stop playing cards for five minutes and have some respect for Bishop, he's about to speak,' said Arthur.

'Sorry,' mumbled Rick, looking up from the card deck and removing a cigarette from his mouth.

'Sorry,' mumbled Richie, as he did the same.

Charlie stopped checking his ammunition, whilst Billy woke up from a light snooze. Noah moved closer to Stephen.

A veil of silence fell over the dust-infested trench as Harold cleared his throat and read a passage from Deuteronomy 9:1-3.

> Hear, O Israel: Thou art to pass over Jordan this day, to go in to possess nations greater and mightier than thyself . . . Understand therefore this day, that the Lord thy God is he which goeth over before thee; as a consuming fire he shall destroy them.

Stephen's lips parted as his right eye flickered, and his heart thumped as if ready to tear outside his chest. Captain Barrows suddenly appeared, and Stephen sighed with relief. All men in close proximity of their captain stood to attention.

'At ease, lads, gather round. Orders from the Corps commander have just come through,' said Captain Barrows.

Stephen huddled closer and listened attentively.

'We are to move one platoon back to Crook Redoubt as left support. From there, I need a patrol to go out on a mission to cut wires in preparation for the operation scheduled for 15th August. Patrols have succeeded in gaining the enemy front line, but resistance from the enemy and the problem with the wire forced the two on the left out. I've selected you all. Are you with me?' Captain Barrows asked.

'Yes, sir,' came a rhythm of different tones.

'What's the plan for the 15th, sir?' Stephen asked.

'The main objectives of the assault are to inflict casualties and draw German troops away from the third Battle of Ypres. To achieve these objectives, we have been ordered to occupy Hill 70 quickly, to establish defensive positions. The enemy have three lines of defences, deep trenches strongly wired. Behind them are miners' houses and mine heads, which are being used to fire their machine guns. This is an important mission, not without its dangers, but vital to the attack on the fifteenth. We can do this. Any questions?' Captain Barrows spoke diligently, scratching his head, with his eyebrows arched under wavy black hair, and pale acne scarred skin.

Silence.

STEPHEN SAT DOWN on a broken duckboard and finished what was left of his rationed breakfast. But the bread made from dried potatoes, oats, barley, and pulverised straw was hard to swallow. He could only stare into the empty space before him, dreaming of another day, a different time. Until his eyes fell deep into the swirl of water beneath him, left over from the tumultuous lashes of rain the day before. He struggled to recognise the face looking back at him. His touch brought ripples to the surface where his mind only fell deeper into the slush of mud below.

He gasped for breath as he noticed his mother's face appear beside Ada, with the English and Canadian flags blurred behind them. He rubbed his eyes, but the image only became stronger, as they merged into one, reflecting his heart torn between two countries. He believed it was his duty to fight in the Canadian Army, but he could not forget the memories of his earlier life in England, and all that he had lost. He reached out to the freezing cold pool of water, but could only feel the warmth of a familiar hand holding his.

> *Annie . . .*
> *Well, who did you think it was, Stevie?*
> *Sometimes, Annie, I'm so afraid of death, and other times I don't feel afraid at all.*
> *There's no point in being afraid, Stevie. All you have to do is keep singing . . .*
> *But what if . . .*
> *What if a bomb drops on your head, what if the sky falls in, what if a unicorn flies over head, what if you see the stars for the first time, what if . . .*
> *Annie, can't you be serious for once?*
> *I've told you what to do.*
> *Which is?*
> *Keep singing.*

The murky water in the pool became calm again, and he felt the warmth leave him, and Charlie's voice bring him swiftly back to the reality of the moment.

'Hey, Steve! Give us a hand with fixing these duckboards.'

Stephen moved towards Charlie and spent the rest of the day repairing duckboards and filling sandbags, below ground, away from the snipers' gunfire.

'Hey, Rick, are you intending to do anything today, or are you just going to sit there, sketching us do all the work?' Henry asked, trying to remove a splinter from his thumb.

'Do you miss home, Steve?' Rick asked, looking up from his sketchpad from over his spectacles, and ignoring Henry.

' . . . miss home, Steve?' Richie asked.

'Home, that seems so far away,' said Stephen, his mind wandering between blurred memories of England and Canada.

'We'd be gathering hay now, back at the farm, ready for the winter,' said Charlie, scratching his head.

'I'd be cashing up the takings from the number of shoes sold, back in Toronto. I'd do anything for a nice pair of comfy shoes right now. These boots are killing me,' said Arthur, rubbing his swollen, wet feet beneath ripped grey socks.

'It's all this standing about in water-logged trenches. What I'd give to sit in my armchair next to a warm log fire, eating a tender beef stew,' said Billy, licking his lips.

'When you lot have stopped reminiscing, we need a volunteer to clean the latrines. I did it yesterday,' said Henry smirking.

Rick changed the subject, because he knew it was his turn.

'Do you ever get scared, I mean feel really scared about death?' he asked the empty space in front of him.

' . . . scared about death?' Richie asked, with his bottom lip quivering.

A silent moment cast its shadow, like an invisible veil across Crook Redoubt trench, and work stopped.

'We all have to die one day,' said Stephen, breaking the silence. 'For some of us that day will come sooner than for others. I just keep remembering what we're fighting for. Freedom! It has to be worth it.'

'Wise words, Steve, wise words indeed,' said Harold. 'The Lord God be with us.'

'Amen to that!' Billy said, chewing on his last bit of stale bread he'd saved from breakfast.

The quiet ambience soon changed when Henry did what he always did when the atmosphere became dark. He cleared his throat, took a deep breath, and began singing his favourite song, in a husky voice, and out of tune.

> The Bells of Hell go ting-a-ling-a-ling
> For you but not for me:
> For me the angels sing-a-ling-a-ling,

'Come on lads, join in.' Henry laughed.

> They've got the goods for me.
> Oh! Death, where is thy sting-a-ling-a-ling
> Oh! Grave, thy victory?
> The Bells of Hell go ting-a-ling-a-ling
> For you but not for me . . .

The song continued with some men finding their way around harmonising, and some not so much. Stephen remembered Annie's words and sang out loud, until the sound of the song turned to raucous laughter.

Later that day, the troops gathered for dinner and the usual maconochie stew. Stephen stirred his cold chunks of fatty meat and vegetables in the thin gravy, and tried to imagine he was eating Ada's delicious hot beef stew that was served in the warm candle-lit kitchen, with the log burning stove crackling beside him. But the bitter chill taste of reality stuck in his throat like cubes of ice unable to melt. Not even the ration of rum could remove the cold, frosty shivers that tingled down his spine.

Stephen remained quiet in the gathered circle of men, with an air of anticipation wavering over their heads. The last of the sunlight disappeared beneath the clouded, dusty horizon, and time called back to them . . . a time they had waited for, patiently throughout the day. Until their captain's voice rose above the silence.

'Right, men, are we ready? We just need to stick together. The attack on Hill 70 begins at dawn. The sooner we get out there and complete the mission, the sooner we return. Put these pliers inside your tunics and cut as much barbed wire as you can. Good luck!' Captain Barrows said.

They crawled above the trench and entered the area to the left, where dogged resistance from the enemy continued. The darkness from the coal black sky stretched like a blanket over hidden stars, locked away from sight.

'Stay low, lads,' whispered the captain.

They followed his lead, completely trusting in his judgement. They moved like vipers through the mud beneath them. Until they crossed enemy lines and started to cut the first of the barbed wire. Sweat dripped from Stephen's wrist as the pliers slipped into the mud beneath him. He felt around in the wet slush, until a hand appeared in front of him with the black steel pliers on its palm.

Stephen looked up with relief and lifted his thumb to Harold as a sign of gratitude. The task continued, until Captain Barrows signalled to head for the second line of defence. Stephen crawled alongside Harold, with Noah close behind.

A beam of light flashed out from the obscure dimness, moving steadily across Hill 70. Stephen ducked his head so close to the mud he could almost taste it. His breath raced faster than his heartbeat, until his mind wandered towards . . .

. . . the sweet smell of maple leaves falling into the tree-lined path that led to the farm. He could see the orange-violet sunset shimmer over the long stretch of cornfields, beckoning him to reach for his journal in its secret place and write. His breathing became calmer, and he smiled at the freedom his pen gave him.

The sunlight slowly faded as he felt a cold, wet touch on his shoulder. He breathed with relief as he saw Rick beside him, signalling to continue through the swirling darkness. More wires were cut, until it was time to crawl towards the third and final line of defence.

Suddenly, Richie opened his mouth wide in preparation to sneeze from the layers of dust settled on the landscape. Rick was there, just in time to put his hand over his mouth and squeeze it away into silence. Stephen remained still beside men who had become friends, who he had shared so much of his life with, in such a short period of time. He waited until it was safe to continue. But his lip trembled as a joyful sound fused through the thin, sticky air.

*Someone's whistling.*

Murmured voices, with vibrations of light laughter, sent tingling shivers through his spine. He lay in the freezing slush, listening to his own heartbeat bursting through his chest, above a language he had come to know as the enemy.

Stephen blinked at the blue-black sky glistening like a broken mirror, reflecting the darkness below. Lost moments of time fell away into a cloud of . . . sweet maple biscuits, milky coffee and the sunlight dancing over the cornfields . . .

Until a pungent smell of damp tobacco, from circles of smoke rising above, stuck in his nostrils, bringing him back to an unknown reality. And still he waited.

The silence returned. With an air of relief grasping their lungs, they proceeded with cautious determination. The snip-snap of the wire cutting was bringing them closer to a return to Crook Redoubt trench, where safety awaited them, at least until sunlight.

They were seconds from completing the mission, when Stephen heard Arthur grunt in pain. It felt like an empty echo, as the realisation that he had cut the tip of his index finger, instead of the tangled barbed wire, shot through his mud riddled body. It was like shock waves, sending a message that the silence had been disturbed. All movement came to a sudden halt. Stephen reached for his handkerchief that Ada had sewn for him before he left and always kept in his pocket. Now grey and worn, but still able to cover the blood dripping from hanging flesh. Henry grabbed the end of a splintered, broken duckboard and shoved it between Arthur's teeth. Specs of rosy pink blood mingled into the flow of marshmallow mud, until the sound of half joyful whistling fell into a listening silence, beneath the unfamiliar trench of the enemy, and the potential face of death. Stephen waited with the echo of silence from his comrades.

Minutes of the hour passed in the thrill, cold, damp night, until Stephen breathed deeply as he heard muffled voices. The return of the unknown whistling song rose from the abyss, to blend with the streams of crystal mist. With his heartbeat in tune with the caress of relief rippling through his body, he waved to Captain Barrows that it was safe. The snip- snap of steel pliers meeting tangled barbed wire, falling into the sludge beneath them, continued.

Eventually, they had followed their orders through to the end. It was time to return to the safety of Crook Redoubt trench, which they called home. Stephen and Charlie helped Arthur turn and crawl back to where they had come from. They dragged their dense boots behind them, losing sight of the way back. There was no end to the black hole that surrounded them.

'It's this way,' whispered Rick, biting his lip.

' . . . this way,' whispered Richie, whose dirty, blond curly hair stuck to the pearls of sweat that lined his anxious face.

'You two couldn't find your way out of your own bloody back yard,' quipped Henry, whose humour could still find a spark in his eyes, even in the confused uncertainty.

'Come on, lads. Let's stick together, or we'll end up getting caught,' said Captain Barrows, who remained calm in the intensifying panic.

But as Stephen stared into his glazed eyes, he saw a truth that could not be denied—and knew he had lost his way. Stephen trusted his captain's intuition and command, even in the whirlwind of confusion, lost inside his head.

*How could anyone find their way out of this?*

Even the rats seemed disorientated as they scurried in all directions, twitching, sniffing, and spreading their invisible layers of disease. Stephen noticed Billy flinch as he scratched his head. His weight made him slower than the others, but there was always someone looking out for him. His bottom lip quivered and his huge belly almost burst out of his tunic as he continued to crawl through the pool of marinated slush. He slowly followed Harold, who he trusted would guide him to salvation.

'Wait! I've lost my bible,' whispered Harold, as he frantically searched through the sea of ice-cold mud.

'Found it,' whispered Noah as he retrieved it with trembling hands.

'Bless you, my son,' said Harold, as he put it inside the ground sheet cape in his kit bag.

They continued to advance in the lost darkness, until . . .

The night suddenly lit up like a multitude of firecrackers in the black haunted sky. They were fired on from all directions. Stephen froze as he felt his heart beat against his chest so fast he could hardly breathe. His hands trembled, unable to reach for the trigger on his rifle.

They were surrounded. Stephen blinked as he noticed multiples of German uniforms, but their faces remained blurred from his hazy vision. Until he realised they were standing with rifles pointing at the heads of his comrades. There was an unnerved motionless stillness, stuck somewhere in the shocked realisation that their path back to safety was blocked.

Captain Barrows held his right hand in the air, blood dripping from his sleeve. 'We surrender.'

German soldiers moved closer towards the ten men who had fought with courage and fortitude. Stephen lifted himself up to standing, by leaning on his artillery gun. He was relieved that in the crossfire of bullets, he remained unharmed. The darkness of the sodden mud shrouded him completely, blacking out his face, but the light from his eyes continued to shine.

'Wir nehmen keine Gefangenen,' snarled one of the German soldiers.

'Aber wir sind in Uniform. Was ist mit den Haager Konventionen?' Stephen asked.

The sound of fire continued in all directions, but it was the bullet that was fired into Stephen's groin that made him scream in agony.

'Das wird Ihnen beibringen, nicht zu deinen Vorgestzten zu antworten.' The German soldiers laughed as they continued to taunt their captives.

Stephen held his groin as he fell back into a river of mud. Harold tore his tattered t-shirt and held it down in an attempt to stop the bleeding. The bristles from his unshaven face were turning grey, but it was the shadow of darkness across his eyes that Stephen noticed.

'I think it's over,' whispered Stephen, as his body writhed in pain.

'Don't give up, Steve. Trust in God our saviour,' Harold said, in a hoarse voice.

'I can't feel my leg,' said Stephen.

'Steve, tell them we're in uniform. Mention Hague Conventions,' said Captain Barrows.

'I just did, sir,' said Stephen.

'We stand as one, Steve, or we don't stand at all,' said Harold.

'I can't move,' said Stephen.

'Come on, Steve, grip my arm,' whispered Henry.

Stephen was close enough to almost touch the elongated scar across the side of his face, and his jaw slightly tilted from a street fight in a distant memory.

'When I was a lad, and I was shot in the groin . . .' said Henry.

'This wouldn't be one of your stories, would it?' Stephen asked.

Henry smiled wryly, whilst he and Charlie helped pull Stephen to his feet.

'Fangen Die an zu graben und wir zeigen Ihnen wie ein Gefangener aussieht!' a German soldier yelled from a dark shadow that embraced his face, until his features seemed invisible.

They were each given a shovel and forced to dig deeper and deeper into the dying ground. Ghost riddled bodies awaited the foreseen outcome. Until Harold's voice was heard above the scrape of the shovel meeting the earth, murmuring the words from Psalm 23:4.

> Even though I walk through the valley of the shadow of death, I will fear no evil, for you are with me; your rod and your staff, they comfort me . . .'

The ten men from the 87th Canadian Battalion, fourth Division, "D" Company, continued to dig in a rhythm of comradeship that spurred them on, closer to the silence of the grave.

'It's been good knowing you, Steve. Do you think Hamish is looking down on us?' Charlie asked.

'Sure, he is. Whatever happens from here, they can never kill our spirit,' said Stephen.

'But they can't kill us, surely? That's murder,' said Rick, biting his bottom lip.

' . . . murder,' said Richie.

'It's been an honour and a privilege to serve with you,' said Captain Barrows.

The men who served under him raised their hands to mirror his salute. But the silence between them lasted seconds, before the German soldiers threw mud at them, and they were forced to continue digging.

'Do you think now might be a good time for a song, Henry?' Rick asked, touching the pocket of his tunic, where his sketchpad was hidden.

' . . . a good time for a song, Henry?' Richie asked, from the ditch below.

Henry cleared his throat as he dug deeper into the ground, with a determination that refused to give up.

> Oh Canada!
> Our home and native land!
> True patriot love in all thy sons command.

'Come on, lads, sing your hearts out,' said Captain Barrows, wiping beads of sweat from his brow.

Arthur sang out through his cracked teeth, and Charlie's Irish voice, born from the church choir harmonised softly, with Richie naturally following Rick's lead behind them. Billy pushed his stomach in to try and hide the sound of hunger pains, and Harold grasped his bible to his chest, but they sang along anyway. Noah moved closer to Stephen's side as he tried to stop his fingers from trembling. Each member of the Battalion found the words to join in, until the rhythm of the song synchronised with the shovels scraping through the greasy mud.

> With glowing hearts we see thee rise,
> The truth North strong and free! From far and wide,
> O Canada, we stand on guard for thee.

Stephen felt the touch of Annie's hand, as he gazed towards the velvet sky reflecting through her eyes. The words that touched his lips, vibrated from the warm breath that left his ice-cold body.

> God keep our land glorious and free!
> O Canada, we stand on guard for thee,
> O Canada, we stand on guard for thee . . .

The blade of the knife ripped open the first in line . . .

He could only watch, reflecting the agonised terror of knowing the sharp-edged blade was getting closer. His heart sank into a void of surrender, where there was no escape, no mercy, no freedom . . . until . . .

A dancing light shone from a glistening shadow in the darkness as Stephen looked up from the pool of blood mingled with clustered mud, past the dust and smoke of gunfire. He blinked and with his right eye could see the velvet sky stretched out above—waiting for him. He choked on the last, rattled breath leaving his defeated body, and whispered . . .


O Canada . . .
    we stand . . .
        on guard . . .
            for thee . . .

# Coda
## *Seedling*

*"You never really understand a person until you consider things from his point of view . . . Until you climb inside of his skin and walk around in it."*
— *Harper Lee*

THE QUEST TO find Stephen's secret journal continues . . .

During my research journey, I was led to one of the most significant connections to Stephen—the great granddaughter of Stephen's foster parents, in Canada. Margaret Bonham McPhail was researching her own family tree when she felt compelled to find Stephen's relatives in England. With the blessing of a bond formed beyond the bloodline, forever connected from the spirit of Stephen, the foundations of friendship grew stronger with time—much like the branches of a maple tree reaching towards the leaves and creating a new home.

The union between England and Canada remains in a different time and generation, and strangers have become close as family. And it appeared that Margaret was as intrigued with the idea of Stephen's missing journal as I was. However, there was a need for more specific information for the door to open, and research evidence to shine its true light and show itself.

Whilst a thousand words can bring a painting to life, seeing the original of Eurach farm for the first time, preserved for over five generations, stirred deep emotions that became lost in my own silence.

With Margaret's spiritual openness and understanding, I was able to move forward in a way I could not have done, without her love for family stories and history. The painting of Eurach farm became far more than a memory of a time echoed from the past. It was an artefact representing the many lives that had walked the path, in the shadow of leaves from the protective maple trees, to reach the warm glow of a sunset dancing its way over the rooftops.

I became hypnotised by sketches of the barn, from emails that left Canada, and arrived in England—showing a ground and first floor view (called second floor view in Canada). I began to realise just how extensive the inside space was. I knew there would be many challenges ahead, and maybe more than a million different, secret hiding places, but this was a journey that had my total focus and commitment. The more I looked deeper into the sketches of the barn, I had a sense of Stephen's spirit inside the space, which mirrored back to me. I could feel his deep emotions, with reflections of him playing, hiding, working, and writing.

From the moment we connected, I felt Margaret by my side, sharing this journey, in the same way as Stephen walked alongside her great grandparents, over a hundred years ago.

I continued to be inspired with an unwavering passion to listen to Stephen's voice, guiding me along an unknown path to fulfill an incomplete destiny. And I have known, from the first moment I heard his name, that I would take more than a million steps, even those that fulfill a lifetime, to discover his most precious, secret writing.

I was aware of going through a process of change, perhaps reflected in a mirror image to Stephen. I continued to strive to open a closed door where there were challenges to face, in a world where I imagined he internalised his truth and hid the secrets of his closed heart. Much like a robin that might make its nest in a maple tree to enjoy the sweetness of its protective bark, and waits for the winter season, to sing its song.

Faced with the quest to find Stephen's journal, I knew I needed the freedom with my own writing to change direction at any given time. I felt an invisible cord pulling me forward into the unknown, a journey that needed to remain fluid, because it could take me anywhere. I had to be ready to follow in Stephen's footsteps, to *climb inside of his skin and walk around in it,* to somehow get inside his head and find a way to come closer to lost experiences.

# *Sapling*

*"We can speak without voice to the trees and the clouds and the waves of the sea.
Without words they respond through the rustling of leaves and the moving of
clouds and the murmuring of the sea."* — *Paul Tillich*

THE SAPLING PERSISTS with its rise to meet the sweet maple leaf.

I felt I had to discover more about Stephen's admission to Barnardo's. But I found myself unable to receive any form of contact from Barnardo's because I was not Stephen's next of kin. I asked my mother, who, in her seventies, remembers Stephen's name being spoken when she was a little girl growing up in the early 1940s. My mother, as one of Stephen's eldest descendants, requested the information on my behalf.

The admission history arrived in the form of archive documents, letters, and photographs. I was able to look into Stephen's eyes, from a time captured in the stillness of a primitive camera. And through the twisted curve of my own emotion, I could only wish against all hope that he had been the son I have never had.

The photographs of Stephen and Albert fell into the shadow of my own silence. Both were just how I had imagined them to be. In comparison to Stephen and Albert, my nephews Ben and Jack have very similar features, the same light and dark shades of hair colour, and were the same age when the photographs arrived in my hand. I imagine they had very comparable personalities. My nephews live within a circle of love and security with a family that nurtures them and aims always to keep them safe. Ben has won poetry competitions for his creative writing, and remains focused, and Jack has swimming and diving medals for his achievements in water. Both always ask questions, share a love for football, and are sensitive in their own way. They have modelled my fictional creation of Stephen and Albert's characters with an ease I would not have had access to, if it hadn't been for their existence. I cannot imagine my life without them.

It was just one hundred years ago that poverty could not allow the same light to shine on Stephen and Albert. Their lives were to be very different and take a complete change of direction. On the 10th March 1910, just two months following Ellen Duckhouse's signature that sealed the fate of Stephen and Albert, they embarked on the ship that took them to a new world—SS Tunisian. I have no understanding as to how Stephen and Albert survived the boat journey, but they arrived in St John (New Brunswick) Canada, nine days later, on the 19th March 1910. From here, they were taken to one of Canada's receiving houses.

More than one hundred years later, in 2013, I made the same journey to Canada and arrived in just seven hours by flight, travelling the identical 3,823 miles, with my mother, aunt, and cousin, to meet the descendants of Stephen's foster parents. During the first few days of my field trip, we visited Hazelbrae Barnardo Home Child Memorial in Peterborough. I found myself standing in front of my own reflection with a camcorder in my hand, in the presence of thousands of Home Children, captured in history, and never forgotten through the light of their names. I turned to notice the air breathe through the rustling leaves from the strength of the twisted branches nearby, as they swayed towards me, as if speaking their own language of silent memory, from the roots to the bark.

I froze for a moment in time, whilst I noticed my mother and aunt sat on a bench nearby, in silence. I could feel their sadness, entwined within each other's hearts, as family history stared back at them. The ghosts of two young boys returned to tell their story, spilled out from the bloodline with their memory. And as I continued to sense Stephen and Albert, *speak without voice to the trees and the clouds and the waves of the sea,* my mother's hand reached up to touch the empty air.

# *Pole*

*"We are aware only of the empty space in the forest,*
*which only yesterday was filled with trees."*
*— Anna Freud*

THE CHILDREN OF the English landscape are transported to Canada, whilst a sapling continues to evolve into a pole, and a young tree persists with its rise to meet the sweet maple leaf.

I stayed at the farm where Stephen was sent as a Home Boy in 1910. Whilst Stephen would have travelled to Eurach Farm in horse and cart, we arrived by car, along a tree lined path.

I felt Stephen with me, as I took the deepest breath in awe of this serene and tranquil place. I remembered the first time I made a connection with Margaret, whose car we now followed down the same path Stephen had travelled, just over a hundred years before this most precious moment. There was a mixture of uncertainty and magical synchronicity, as we at last arrived at our destination. I felt Stephen's energy intensify, as all transport stopped, and the engines became silent. And I could feel ghosts from the past come forward to greet me, in the same way they would have held out their hand to welcome Stephen . . .

Margaret introduced us to her parents. Ivan and Ruth McPhail, both in their eighties, were standing on the steps of their home just behind the stone farmhouse. It felt like being held in the arms of family. It was Ivan's mischievous eyes that I noticed the most, to the sound of laughter and agreement from both Margaret and Ruth. I could see the familiarity of his father's face, Margaret's grandfather—the young boy who played with Stephen in a different generation and time, but memories never lost through the continuity of the bloodline.

Through meeting Ivan's only son, John, and the current farmer of Eurach Farm, I witnessed fun and laughter that echoed around the space he absorbed with his light-hearted energy. And I imagined his grandfather with the same name and personality, calling out to Stephen . . .

We were welcomed into the hearts and home of strangers, who I felt I had known all my life. We unpacked our luggage, in the same way I imagined Stephen would have done on his first day of arrival, with his Barnardo's trunk that still remains at Eurach Farm. The trunk is made of wood and covered in imitation alligator skin with four tiny wheels inside the corners of the base. It is heavy. I can't imagine young children carrying it full of clothes and boots, travelling across the ocean in a boat, in the hope of a new life. Inside the trunk, Stephen has written his name with a blue crayon, with the number seven above. In the far-right hand corner the blue crayon continues: *Steve gave me his trunk when he enlisted for war. John McPhail.*

I had at last arrived at Eurach Farm and felt Stephen's overwhelming energy pushing me towards the barn, the place where he used to play with John, and I believed he hid his most precious writing. I was excited and fearful that I might not discover his journal, but I could hardly wait to look with my own eyes, in the hope that Stephen would guide me to his secret hiding place.

I had a sense of small stone steps leading to the front door of the farmhouse, a door that was hardly used. I imagined the family using the doors at the side and the back of the house for easy access to the barn, with a well-tended flowerbed at the side of the house. As I took one step after another around the working farm and barn, I felt Stephen with me, guiding me forward to unseen sights that had lived previously in my imagination. But I noticed there was a mowed lawn where I imagined the flowerbeds . . .

It was the next day at Eurach farm that my strong connection with Margaret proved right when she told me she knew where I wanted to be. At last I was inside the barn with Margaret and my cousin Jane. But I hadn't expected the two floors to be so expansive. I began to doubt my ability to discover Stephen's journal that I felt was calling out to be found. It seemed that so much was at stake, I could hardly breathe with the weight of responsibility. I continued to climb up into the eaves of the straw mow, on the stacked hay. I moved beneath the beams and looked and touched the walls. I stared out at the yellow cornfield that met the horizon, from the granary where the air was cooler.

It was in the barn where Stephen used to play and work, that I could feel his strong sense of purpose, secret sadness, and determination, leading me on to find unspoken and lost memories. And the barn became a special place, drawing me to want to return every moment of the day.

*Stephen, help me. Where did you hide it?*

I sensed him with me. But I wanted to find his writing so much I had overpowering feelings that seemed to shut down my intuition and immobilise my whole body, with not knowing which direction to take.

I returned to the barn later that evening with Margaret and a torch in hand with renewed energy and determination to continue the search. The dust from the smell of sweet, dry hay tinged the air and formed patterns of lines and dots on my jeans as my eyes remained wide open in search of Stephen's journal.

The third day at Eurach Farm arrived, and I again visited the barn with Margaret and my family. We watched the cattle arrive in the milking rows, with Margaret's brother, John, in full control of guiding them to enter their pen. John's confidence with animals seemed to be shadowed by generations that had gone before him. I felt them still watching. But it was John's voice that dominated the space in this time, a velvety concoction of strength and calm that echoed around the barn. Then Margaret showed me the exact spot where Stephen and John had a vision of a horse. My eyes lingered at the empty space on the wall, in the area where the stables had long disappeared and been replaced with new milking rows. And just for a moment, I thought I saw a shadow of a horse pass me by, watching me with a ghostly stare from the distant past.

I continued to sense Stephen's disappointment as I desperately tried to listen to his guidance. But I could feel myself becoming more frustrated with the empty search leading to an undiscovered trail. I had a desperate need to hear Stephen guide me to where I needed to be during those precious moments in the barn, but I *was aware only of the empty space in the forest* . . .

# Snag

*"A thing may happen and be a total lie; another thing may happen and be truer than the truth."*
— Tim O'Brien

I WOULD HAVE been happy spending all my time in the barn searching for Stephen's journal, but during the three days we stayed at Eurach Farm, there were other commitments that I also enjoyed being involved with. A small local newspaper wanted to interview both the Duckhouse and McPhail families. It was a time when both families gathered for a Sunday Church Service, a newspaper interview, and a beautifully organised dinner around the table in Ivan and Ruth's dining room. I felt blessed to know the McPhail family and have the opportunity to spend these precious moments with them—moments that have become unforgettable memories.

When we attended the service at Kirkwall Presbyterian Church, we received a warm and kind welcome from strangers in the community, who remembered Stephen's name. We sat in the same church that Stephen attended with Margaret's great grandparents, in a different generation and time. We were close to a plaque on the wall with Stephen's name as a casualty of war. The maple leaf is etched into the carving above the names of those who lost their lives in the First World War.

We also explored Strabane United Church, Ontario. It was here that we found a memorial erected by the patriotic citizens of Strabane to perpetuate the memory of their five sons killed in action. But it was one specific name that reflected through my eyes as I found myself staring into the concrete stone . . .

Stephen's age was incorrect, but this was the first time I discovered his 'murder' acknowledged—a significant moment, which I wouldn't have had, if not for this particular experience. The imprint on the stone speaks from the mind of someone or maybe many, who made the decision that these names would continue to live on, to be watched over by other generations.

I felt a stream of emotion as I found myself standing there, repeating the word in my head . . . *murdered* . . . I shivered in the warm morning sun light. The silence lingered with only the whisper from nearby maple leaves, until the click of the camera took over, and memories were captured in time.

During my last evening at Eurach Farm, I sat in the farmhouse kitchen with Margaret at the same table that remains from a hundred years before. I touched the oak wood with both hands and felt electrical currents shoot through my body, and I knew this was the exact spot where Stephen used to sit. We talked about Stephen's undiscovered journal, his separation from his brother, and his very different experience from Albert. We both agreed—Albert needed to be found . . .

The final morning arrived, and I felt a mixture of sadness and laughter fill my heart until it over spilled with the weight of memories spreading their light from a spiritual place out of reach. I had a sense of Edgar and Ada preparing the wagon and horses to go to market, with vegetables and eggs to sell. Stephen putting his journal in his pocket and walking towards the barn with John following like a shadow behind him. And the horses running across the fields in no particular direction, maybe because it was too hot and they didn't feel like ploughing the fields that day.

Then I became drawn to a space behind the barn, from a bedroom window, where my eyes lingered on a mature maple tree in the distance, without knowing why. I felt that the tree had some significance for Stephen and John when they played together. I imagined them building a tree house that became their secret place where they used to hide things.

When my field trip to Eurach Farm came to an end, and my quest to find Stephen's journal had not transpired in the way I had hoped, I left with a deep sense of loss in my heart. But I was determined that I would not give up and vowed to return, to continue the search. It was the connections with the McPhail family that were the most heartfelt during my visit. I didn't want to leave them. Although my mind raced with ideas that I felt compelled to transform into my writing, I felt the deepest sadness when it was time to say goodbye. The car continued to move away with the sound of the engine purring through the protective gaze of the towering maple trees, side by side, whilst wings of shadowed leaves fluttered in the gravel below. And I knew, as my aching arm would not give up the wave until the McPhail family were shades in the distance behind the green leaves we left behind, that something had changed within me. I wasn't aware of just how deep the change was at the time. But I know now. Some people have a way of touching our hearts and staying forever.

As my journey continued, in the search for truth, I learnt that *a thing may happen and be a total lie; another thing may happen and be truer than the truth*, between the stars beneath the velvet sky.

# Tree Spirits

*"The dead are more real than the living because they are complete."*
— *Siegfried Sassoon*

WHEN I LOOK at the photograph of Kirkwall Presbyterian Church, Ontario, the memory of our visit returns. It is the faces of strangers that I will always remember, with Stephen's energy beside me, like a warm glow and a voice spurring me on, telling me to continue to search and write.

I know from family stories Margaret has shared with me, that Stephen used to play with John. So, I imagine that he wasn't always alone in his head with his writing and missing his family. He seemed to have fun and companionship.

I appreciated more than ever the contact with Margaret Bonham McPhail, when we were both busy with our own lives in different parts of the world, and yet still able to send emails across a vast and deep enigma of ocean. I continued to research Stephen's life, but the more I sat down to write the more I felt the ink on the page take on a rhythmic dance of its own—a movement back and forth through time.

I searched and delved and felt Stephen with me, guiding me closer to his life experiences. I continued to listen in the hope of hearing his voice, leaving me a trail of clues to find a lost story. And when I sense him beside me and look into his eyes from his framed photograph on my desk, I believe he is close, and I am not alone. I have the strongest feeling that it was Stephen's imagination that helped him survive as long as he did. Maybe that's why I perceive him telling Albert stories and reading to him during those quiet moments whilst they were still together.

As I drift into the essence of Stephen's strength and guidance with me on this journey, I have the deepest feeling that I am transported back to that time a hundred years ago, almost as if I am there beside him. I have a strong sense that Stephen communicated with spirit from a very young age, which is why the development of his relationship with Annie is presented from the beginning of the story. The character Annie was created from an inner consciousness, that Stephen had a sister who was stillborn. With Stephen facing so much loss in his life, I wanted someone who would stand by him from the beginning to the end of his life, someone with whom only he could communicate.

The character John, from a place in the spirit world, represents the loneliness and aloneness Stephen feels being torn away from his family and acts as a slight distraction to the responsibility I feel he would have felt for his younger brother. Stephen's spiritual experiences echo their voice through the fiction because this is all an act of storytelling—from family history, research, and my own personal intuition.

Whilst wondering if Ada had help with domestic household chores, such as cooking, I discovered from Margaret Bonham McPhail, that Edgar's mother, Catherine McPhail lived with them at Eurach Farm. Catherine's character has been inspired from the information Margaret shared with me, as intuitively I felt that there was another female at Eurach Farm at this time. During my second field trip to Canada, I was told Catherine had a fall in her home and went to live with Edgar and Ada at Eurach Farm. She had a bedroom on the ground floor, which is now the front living room used by the current generation. As her back curved more, they used to shorten her cane. Catherine died at Eurach Farm. The 1911 Census provides evidence of the members of the household and their employment, and includes: Edgar McPhail, Farmer, Ada, John, Catherine, and Stephen Duckhouse, Domestic.

I can only imagine the emotional heartache that both Stephen and Albert felt during the process of separation, and what they were left with. They only had each other, but even the last link with their bloodline was taken from them. It felt important to show how Stephen may have survived such trauma, and so I imagined him withdrawing into a spirit world, where *the dead are more real than the living.*

## *Splitting*

*"A people without the knowledge of their past history,*
*origin and culture is like a tree without roots."*
— *Marcus Garvey*

SINCE THE SEPARATION of Stephen and Albert at Peter Street Boys Home, Toronto, Albert had become an enigma. It was Stephen's deep and heartfelt connection with his younger brother that continued to draw me back to a determination to find the truth and discover Albert's unknown destiny.

Email contact with Albert's grandson, Chuck Norris, who has extended family in the USA, has brought truth and unseen knowledge into the open, from beyond the bloodline. There were times when I believed Albert might not have survived the possible hardship he experienced at the Thompson Farm. But research showed me a different path and a new discovery.

Chuck Norris was unaware of his grandfather's early life. He knew nothing of Albert's experiences in the care of Barnardo's, and as a Home Child at the Thompson Farm in Canada. It has become clear that Albert never disclosed the truth about his early life, reinforcing my intuition that he had a difficult experience by not talking about it. When he was of age to leave the farm, he travelled across the border at Niagara Falls to Buffalo, New York, and changed his name to Albert J. Edwards, which is why it was so difficult to trace him.

The missing phalanges on Albert's left hand reflect a time passed when a young boy sat in front of the lens of a camera with his brother Stephen.

But Stephen's arms had long disappeared from sight, into the battlefield beneath the velvet sky.

The news of discovering Albert had survived and went on to live a life of his choice was something of great emotional relief. I can only hope that he found a way to leave behind the pain of separation, and heal that part of him, from some form of absolution.

The glare comes from the photograph being stuck to the glass of the frame. But it survived, in the way Albert did . . .

Albert was left standing and lived to old age. He died in 1982 and is buried at Byron Cemetery, Byron, Genesee County, New York, USA.

In September 2017, I returned to Canada for a second field trip with my mother and cousin Jane. It was here when we crossed the border at a Thousand Islands Bridge with Margaret Bonham McPhail and her husband Glyn into Batavia, New York, that we met Albert's grandchildren for the first time—Chuck with his wife Lisa, Susan and Deanna. Their sister, Valerie lives in Las Vegas which was too far for her to travel, but she was in our thoughts.

From a planned itinerary from Chuck Norris, we drove to Byron Cemetery where we saw Albert's gravestone. It was a surreal moment as my mind moved through time from a young boy born Albert Edward Duckhouse, to the changed name on the cold gravestone before me. A convoy of cars where two families were reunited continued on a journey that led us to the Hagen Farm where Albert and his wife Rosemarie lived and worked, and brought up their three children. From here we then arrived at a house in Leroy where Albert and Rosemarie lived in older age, and the factory where Albert worked until he retired.

The convoy of cars continued to its final destination—a family lunch, where a table was booked in a section of a restaurant called the Library. It was here we shared a mixed cocktail of family stories, childhood memories, sadness, laughter, and photographs. It felt like reaching for books from an old dusty shelf, blowing away the cobwebs, and learning about family history. And the splitting of the tree where there had been a hollow emptiness for generations, came together to find its roots, *with past history, origin and culture.*

# *Mature Tree*

*"And this, our life, exempt from public haunt, finds tongue in trees books in the*
*running brooks, sermons in stone, and good in everything."*
*— William Shakespeare*

A YEAR BEFORE my second field trip to Canada in 2017, Margaret visited England to celebrate her sixtieth Birthday. She arrived with a special gift. I listened attentively to her story. Ivan and Ruth McPhail had water flood the cellar of their home—an anomaly. Whilst they cleared away old boxes covered in dust from years gone by, they found something that the current generation had no idea was there. Margaret handed me a small package wrapped in gold paper. I opened it gently. It was a small blue book with orange flowers and yellow, brown, and green leaves on the sleeve. *Duchess Renee—An Episode In The History Of The Reformation by Sarson C.J. Ingham.* I opened the book carefully and my bottom lip trembled as I read the handwriting inside . . .

> With Love, From Miss Ratcliff, To Stephen Duckhouse, leaving
> England for Canada March 10th1910. In all thy ways acknowledge
> God and He will direct thy ways. Prov-3.6. God Bless You.

I removed my spectacles, and tears filled my eyes with an emotion that wouldn't allow them to fall from my face. I suddenly noticed Margaret looking at the book. It was the first time she had seen it, as her mother, Ruth McPhail, had wrapped and posted it to her home address to bring with her to England. Margaret continued her story. Ruth wanted me to have the book, but she had made sure she read it before it left the farm. I was told it was a heavy read. It felt so light in my hands, sending a warm energy glowing through me. I felt Stephen in the room with us, watching close by. As I held the book near my heart, I sensed that Miss Ratcliff had watched over Stephen, even for a short time, and he had been loved.

During my second field trip to Canada, we stayed in Montreal Hall for two nights before meeting Margaret at the Upper Canada Village where we visited Aultsville Train Station—now a museum with a British Home Child Exhibition.

I listened attentively to a volunteer from the Ontario East British Home Child Family Group (OEBHCF), who are descendants of British Home Children. I learned that Aultsville is one of Ontario's lost villages, which were flooded for the St. Lawrence Seaway in 1958. Here we saw artefacts, documents, and books, all in memory of the Home Child. But it was the memorial quilt, hanging on the wall, crowded with photographs of Home Children, that drew my attention. Their faces stared back at me from a different time and generation. As I looked into their unfamiliar eyes, I was told that the sunflower was chosen to represent the British Home Child because they represent hope. Sunflowers have always been my favourite flowers, because when I gaze at their circle of light, I feel they do inspire hope.

We stayed with Margaret and her husband Glyn one night before driving to Ottawa. Here we were shown the city's prominent buildings—Parliament, Rockcliffe, the home of diplomats, the British High Commission, the American Embassy, the French Embassy, the War Memorial . . . *what a beautiful city.* But it was inside the Canadian War Museum that touched my heart and left me frozen in silence as I stepped back in time, walking through the space of the exhibition *Vimy—Beyond the Battle.* I found myself standing before a display of artwork, with hundreds of different coloured ribbons pinned to the frame. As I moved closer, I noticed names on each ribbon, of those who had given their life, in battle. I reached out and chose a red ribbon and wrote Stephen's name across it. Then I attached it to the display. In those few moments, I felt part of something—like I was breathing life back into Stephen, keeping his memory alive.

During the last few days of my field trip, we stayed at Eurach Farm, at the home of Ruth McPhail, on our return from Batavia, New York. Again, it was like being in the arms of family. Ruth McPhail is a very special lady—kind, generous, with many stories to tell. But this time there was someone missing. Ivan McPhail died in March 2017, whilst doing what he loved, driving his tractor on the farm. He was a farmer to the end of his life. Although it felt different somehow without him, I could still sense his mischievous smile in the quieter moments.

With the arrival of Saturday morning, Margaret had arranged to drive me to meet her Aunt Hazel, Ivan's sister, who remembers Edgar and Ada when she was a little girl. She welcomed me into her beautiful home. And with a reputation within the family as being a generous hostess, we were offered coffee and cake. Aunt Hazel had kindly typed out her early memories of life with her grandparents, most precious moments that have been included in Stephen's story. I felt so privileged to have met her, to have listened to her stories, and spent this special time with her. It has been one of the most significant milestones of my research, alongside the family stories that Margaret has shared with me, through this journey.

On our way back to the farm, Margaret drove past Valens School where Stephen and John attended, now converted to a house. We continued to Guelf Market where Edgar and Ada used to travel in their horse and wagon to sell vegetables, honey, bread, and eggs, over one hundred years before. The same building in a different time. And as the car continued down the tree lined path we passed the mowed lawn at the side of the farm house, and Margaret told me that Ada had always kept flowerbeds there.

With searching the barn, watching the leaves of maple trees surf the breeze, listening to family history, heeding the words from the sermons at Kirkwall Presbyterian Church, reading books—all with a sense of Stephen by my side—I know that where there is love, there is *good in everything*. I have found love, here.

## Old Tree

*"What is the good of your stars and trees, your sunrise and the wind, if they do not enter into our daily lives?"*
— *E.M. Forster*

I WASTED NO time in approaching Margaret's brother, John, to request his help in my search for Stephen's journal. John kindly agreed to let me have access to the barn and supported me with trying to discover something that I still believed was hidden in this special place. I felt confident in John as I watched him climb a ladder to the top of stacked round hay bales, with torch in hand. I looked up and saw his silhouette in the shadows between the beams, and I heard him say *come up*. I declined. But he insisted, reassuring me he would hold the ladder. I slowly climbed up into the eaves of the barn, holding my breath. At last I reached the top and felt my head spin. But it was when John started to playfully shake the ladder with Margaret half way up, that I felt myself wanting to faint. *Breathe . . . just breathe.*

The search began four years after the original quest. I was now convinced that Stephen had hidden the journal above, to the right-hand side of the barn. *Above right . . . above right.* The torch shone its bright light between layers of dust settled on the beams, as the sweet dry hay tinged my nostrils. I cried out as I saw something resting on a beam attached to the wall near the entrance. John moved closer . . . it was a piece of wood. I became mesmerised by a pile of hay on top of beams slightly to the right of the middle of the roof, near the entrance to the barn. But it was too far away to reach from either side. I asked about the hay. It had lain dormant for generations and was most likely there when Edgar was alive. John planned to move it, but he told me it had to be done carefully, to protect him from potential illness, as anything could be inside that hay, including mice, as they had lazy cats. *Anything could be inside that hay . . .*

I was disappointed as I climbed down the ladder but determined to continue the search. Then Glyn appeared with an even bigger torch and headed towards the straw mow. I followed him but kept looking back at the entrance to the barn. *You're going the wrong way.* But I felt help was at hand, and I appreciated the time and support I was given with the quest to find Stephen's journal. At the end of the day as we closed the door of the barn, I heard Glyn say, *you need more focus.*

I believed Glyn was right. When I was alone that evening, I sat with my journal and sketched the entrance of the barn. I put the tip of the pen on the paper, in the middle of the huge wooden slide door, and asked Stephen for guidance. *Left, or right?* My hand slowly moved towards the left-hand side. I realised *above right* meant when I was standing inside the barn and looking outwards. *We've been searching the wrong side.*

During our second day at the farm we found ourselves back at Kirkwall Presbyterian Church for the Sunday service. We again sat near the plaque with Stephen's name, as a casualty of war. There was a female Reverend who led the service and filled the church with her natural warmth and light. I felt blessed to be in this special place again. At the end of the service, something made me want to explore the left side of the church. I found a plaque on the wall, half way down. *In memory of the McPhail family.* Margaret told me that it was where Edgar and Ada used to sit, with Catherine, John and Stephen. I sat in the pew. I felt my body tingle with warmth, as a sense of peace filled my head. *Why haven't I discovered this before?* I had assumed all this time that Edgar and Ada had sat to the right of the church, just because Stephen's name was on a plaque on the wall on that side. Just as I had assumed *above right* meant as I entered the barn looking inside. I realised how much depends on where I stand in life, and how left and right can mean opposites, depending on which direction I look.

I returned to the barn after lunch with Margaret and Jane. I stood inside the barn and looked outwards. The orange glow of the resting sun cast shadows in darkened spaces to meet the late afternoon. I rubbed my right eye and felt the warmth of a velvet aura, as my mind became focused. *Above right.* I was again mesmerised by the pile of hay on top of wooden beams slightly to the right of the entrance to the barn. I realised I didn't need to do this alone. I asked Jane to stand in front of the barn, to close her eyes and think about Stephen, allowing her intuition to take her hand to the left or right. Within seconds her arm went in the direction of the left. When Margaret did the same, my eyes again lingered on the pile of hay, as I now felt sure that above right meant looking outwards from inside the barn. *If only I could reach that pile of hay . . .*

During the afternoon I sat with Margaret and John on the terrace of the farm house, enjoying the warm glow of the sunshine. It was here they shared family stories of life during their great grandparents' time. Two log burning cooking stoves in the kitchen, they heated and lived in one room in winter, pipe from the log burning stove through the wall of Stephen's bedroom, well in the outside white shed, cisterns underneath the summer room and kitchen to catch and store rain water, outside privy, orchard at the back of the farm, pond between Eurach Farm and the Fletcher Farm where Stephen and John used to skate, the sleigh they used in snow, Edgar's first car, a Grey-Dort . . . and the stories continued.

Later the same day, we returned to Kirkwall Presbyterian Church and enjoyed a concert in support of *The Canadian Food Grains Bank,* with a free-will offering to be given in memory of Ivan McPhail. I felt the church overflow with love and cherished memories of an elder whose presence was so sadly missed. During the evening, we were invited to dinner in the farm house where the current generation of the McPhail family gathered.

It was during our last morning that I asked John if he had time to help me have one final look in the barn. He climbed the ladder positioned on the right side of the barn, opposite to where we had previously looked. He moved the ladder all around *above right.* John used the torch from Margaret's mobile phone, but its light only shone into empty darkness. I was again mesmerised by the pile of hay *above right.* I believed that if Stephen's journal was still inside the barn, it had to be there. It was the only place we had not searched. John promised to let me know if he found anything when he planned to move it. We slid back the heavy wooden door of the barn. But just before it closed I thought I saw a dancing light in the shadows of the enclosed darkness. I walked away with a heavy heart and looked back. *I'm so sorry, Stephen. I tried. I really tried.*

When I returned to England, Margaret sent photographs of inside the barn, during our search to find Stephen's journal. I can see orbs around the untouched pile of hay, in the surrounding darkness. Was Stephen trying to tell me something? Or was it just shimmers of light reflecting through the open spaces of the barn? I only know that when I look closer, I imagine Stephen, calling out from the velvet sky.

As we prepared to leave Eurach Farm, I climbed into the car and sat next to Jane, with my mother settled on the back seat. I turned to wave to a family who I knew, in the deepest corner of my heart, I loved. Jane started the engine and drove sturdily down the long, maple tree lined pathway. The car turned left at the end of the lane, and I looked back at Ruth, Margaret, Glyn, and John. They were still waving, but became smaller in the distance between us, like dots on the Tiger Lily flower. And I began to see the world through different eyes . . . *the stars and trees . . . sunrise and the wind . . .* because where there is great love there are always miracles.

# *Over mature*

*"What passing-bells for these who die as cattle?*
*— Only the monstrous anger of the guns."*
*— Wilfred Owen*

THROUGH THE DISCOVERY of documents, emails, and photographs, I began to map Stephen's journey from the moment he signed his attestation paper. My connection with the McPhail family left me feeling privileged and thankful to know them. I discovered a kindness that I felt had travelled through the generations from over a hundred years before. And when Margaret gave me a copy of a photograph from the Edgar McPhail and Ada Alde McPhail collection, I was moved to silence . . .

I stared at the photograph in my hand
Until . . .
my eyes lingered on the light above
Stephen's head . . .

I could sense the young boy looking back at me from a mature face with the same eyes, but different emotion. Following one of the biggest decisions of his life, Stephen was left with self-doubt about enlisting with the Canadian Army at such a young age. This has been retrieved from a family story that has travelled through the generations.

Stephen found himself returning to England on the 30 August 1916, aboard the SS Olympic, a sister ship of the Titanic. From finding inspiration from the many regimental documents and war diaries preserved through the doors and corridors of archives, I was able to trace Stephen's movements with his regiment from England to France, discovering that he was originally with the 129th Wentworth Battalion, transferred to the 123rd, and later sent to the 87th Battalion when the 129th was broken up at the front for reinforcements. Researching deeper into the realms of the past, I learnt that whilst Stephen was involved in extensive training and preparation for the Battle of Vimy Ridge, the final victory came at a high cost. That cost was 10,602 casualties from the four Canadian Divisions involved. There were 3,598 killed and 7,004 wounded, with around 4,000 prisoners of war from the German Sixth Army. Men became numbers. Stephen survived. Until, he was involved in the preparations for the Battle of Hill 70, leaving behind *the monstrous anger of the guns*.

# Log / debris

*"As was the custom in such cases, the pear tree was charged with murder and sentenced to be uprooted and burned."*
— *Robert Graves*

ON THE 14TH August 1917, the day before the Battle of Hill 70 commenced, ten men from the 87th Battalion (Canadian Grenadier Guards) were out on patrol and lost their way behind enemy lines . . .

Almost three months later, news reached the Toronto Star, and the war crime was in print.

### Ten Bodies Found on Lens Front, Captured by Germans at Hill 70, Throats Cut

*Toronto Star*
*Saturday, November 10, 1917*
*Transcribed by: M. I. Pirie*

This may have been an unconfirmed wartime rumour. All of the men were in fact originally with the 129th Wentworth Battalion, and were subsequently sent to the 87th Battalion when the 129th was broken up at the front for reinforcements. Additionally, all are reported killed or missing at Hill 70 between August 14-16th, 1917. Seven of the ten men are remembered on the Vimy Memorial, the other three have marked graves. All of the men named are listed on the Vimy Memorial, except for Capt. Alexander Solomon.

### CUT CANADIAN'S THROATS: Word Reaches Hamilton of Ten Men Found on Lens Front Captured by Germans.

*Hamilton, Nov. 10*—Word has been received here that the bodies of the following ten men, who enlisted with the 129th County of Wentworth Battalion, had been found on the Lens front with throats cut:

Capt. Alex Solomon [Lt. 87th Battalion, died Aug. 15, 1917, buried Lieven]

Pte. Arthur A. Bland, 633 Spadina Avenue, Toronto [Pt. 87th Battalion, died Aug. 14, 1917, Vimy Memorial]

Harold Crowe, Alberton[2] [Pt. 87th Battalion, died Aug. 14, 1917, Vimy Memorial]

Pte. Stephen Duckhouse, Puslinch[3] [Pt. 87th Battalion, died Aug. 14, 1917, Vimy Memorial]

Richard Fenning, Waterdown[4] [Pt. 87th Battalion, died Aug. 14th, 1917, Vimy Memorial]]

Richard Jones, 1132 Barton street east[5][Pt. 87th Battalion, died Aug. 14, 1917, Vimy Memorial]

Harry (Henry) Jones, 132 Belmont avenue[6] [Pt. 87th Battalion, died Aug. 16th, 1917, buried Cabaret-Rouge]]

W.H. Jones, 333 Emerald street north[7] [Pt. 87th Battalion, died Aug. 15th, 1917, buried Loos British Cemetery]]

N.L. Krick, Glanford Station[8] [Pt. 87th Battalion, died Aug. 14th, 1917, Vimy Memorial]

Charles F. Kirby, Bartonville[9] [Pt. 87th Battalion, died Aug. 15, 1917, Vimy Memorial]]

They were captured by the Germans, and when the Canadians made a drive they found the bodies.

[1]Reported missing. Native of Napanee, Ontario. Shoe store clerk in Toronto. [2]Alberton, Ontario. Crowe was born in Liverpool, England. Farm hand. Enlisted in Ancaster, Ontario. [3]Puslinch, Ontario. Duckhouse was born in Birmingham, England. [4]Waterdown, Ontario. Fenning was a native of Country Antrim, Ireland. [5]Hamilton, Ontario. R. Jones was born at Stockton-on-Tees, England. [6]Hamilton, Ontario. Henry Jones was born in Rhyl, Wales. [7]Hamilton, Ontario. William Henry Jones was born in Peterborough, England. [8]Glanford Station, Ontario. Krick was born in Binbrook Township, Wentworth County, Ontario. Farmer. [9]Bartonville, Ontario. Kirby was born in Mitcham, Surrey, England.

It is clear from Stephen's last will and testament that his thoughts were with his mother when he signed his name on a document that spoke his truth. Whilst reading the surviving will, I could feel Stephen's memories of the hardship and heartache of those early years, torn away from his family, but a mother's love never forgotten.

Time travelling inside my imagination and researching archives continued, whilst always returning to the current generation. But it was my field trips to Canada that allowed me to feel closer to Stephen's truth. Whether Stephen's journal will ever be discovered, now begins to fade into the distance of time, entwined with the narratives I have tried to create from the realms of imagination. The quest has been the motivation and inspiration behind writing Stephen's story. It has been the drive that has helped me to continue writing and researching, on a journey that has now come to an end. Where ever Stephen's journal might be, or even if it exists, it has given me an energy filled with determination and a sense of duty to create stories from a lost time and bring memory back to life. If I have come even close to the writer I imagine Stephen was, then the time I have given has been worth every moment I have lived inside my head.

My thoughts now begin to drift into an empty space. Stephen has no marked grave, no peaceful place where loved ones can go to remember him, to pray, to feel close to him. Like thousands of others like him, he is commemorated at the Vimy Memorial in France. Through the decades of post war, the memorial site has grown and developed in a way that those who lost their lives were unable to.

It was the year of 1936 when King Edward VIII unveiled the Canadian National Vimy Memorial. I was drawn to a statue of a female figure known as Mother Canada who stands with her head bowed and represents the nation of Canada mourning the thousands of lost lives. The view of the Lens-Douvai plain stretches out before her.

Stephen's name is on a list at the Vimy Memorial, watched over by Mother Canada, torn away from his own mother, he left his foster mother to do his duty. And even if *the pear tree was charged with murder and sentenced to be uprooted and burned,* through the search for a secret journal, my personal quest has been to bring an injustice into the light. Stephen's spirit lives on. His voice will never die.

Stephen is amongst the whispers of the maple leaves,
the sunlight dancing with the shadows,
and between the stars beneath . . .
. . . the velvet sky.

# Notes

## Chapter 1
**p. 7** 'This is a war Budget...': from "The National Archives Learning Curve Britain 1906-18. Achievements of Liberal Welfare Reforms: Gallery 2" www.nationalarchives.gov.uk/education/britain1906to1918/g2/gallery2.htm

## Chapter 2
**p. 37** 'St Martin was a soldier . . .': from "St Martin in the Bullring >> Heritage" www.bullring.org/heritage/

**p. 39** 'In 1805, during the Battle of Trafalgar, Nelson...': from Admiral Horatio Lord Nelson (1758-1805)
www.bbc.co.uk/history/historic_figures/nelson_admiral_horatio_lord.shtml

## Chapter 5
**p. 114-115** Ambrose, Robert S, and Carey, Phoebe. *One Sweetly Solemn Thought.* From: Timeless Truths, Free Online Library library.timelesstruths.org/music/One_Sweetly_Solemn_Thought.

**p.112** 'She observed the branches of the trees . . .': from Sarson C.J. Ingham, *Duchess Renee An Episode In The History Of The Reformation,* Wesleyan Methodist Sunday School Union, London E.C.

## Chapter 6
**p. 153** 'Great Britain declares war on Germany . . .': from The Long, Long Trail – The British Army in the Great War of 1914-1918
www.longlong trail.co.uk/battles/the-kings-message-to the army/

## Chapter 7
**p. 167-168** 'April 26, 1915. Ypres, Belgium . . .': in *Chronicle of Canada,* Elizabeth Abbott (ed.), Chronicle Publications Montreal, Quebec, 1990 p.564

**p. 212.** 'Under the orders of your devoted officers in the coming battle . . .': from Buchan, John and Newbolt, Henry, *Days to Remember: The British Empire in the Great War (illustrated),* Echo Library 2015.

**p. 241, 249** '...pea soup flavoured with weeds and nettles . . .' From: 'The Food That Fuelled The Front'. Imperial War Museums.
www.iwm.org.uk/history/the-food-that-fuelled-the-front

**Coda**

**P. 240** Photograph—permission to print from Margaret Bonham McPhail, great granddaughter of Edgar and Ada Alde McPhail. From the Edgar and Ada Alde McPhail Collection.

**p. 280-281** 'Ten bodies found on Lens Front . . .': from Pirie, M.I. "Ten Bodies Found On Lens Front Captured By Germans." *Toronto Star* 10 November 1917.

Cherie Battista is a Cognitive Behavioural Psychotherapist. She graduated in 1986 with a BA in Physical Education and Drama, and completed her MEd in Educational Psychology at the University of Manchester, whilst teaching full time. In 1994, she changed career and qualified as a professional Counsellor. Since qualifying, she has completed a Postgraduate Diploma in Psychoanalytic Observational Studies, and Postgraduate Diploma in Cognitive Behavioural Psychotherapy. She has worked as a professional Counsellor in Education, Occupational Health, and NHS. She currently works as a Cognitive Behavioural Psychotherapist.

Her interest and passion for writing began in childhood, creating short stories and poetry based on autobiography. In 2011 she commenced an MA in Creative Writing: Innovation and Experiment at the University of Salford, and achieved a lifelong ambition when she graduated in 2013, with a Distinction in her final Creative Project. Her first book *Secrecy and Synchronicity* was rewritten whilst studying her MA.

In 2015, she was asked to read a short extract from *Secrecy and Synchronicity*, during the University of Salford's "LGBT History Month: An Evening With Jackie Kay"—appointed as the University's Chancellor and Writer in Residence.

Her PhD research was a practice- based investigation into the experiences of Home Children and the First World War. The aim of the thesis was to create a biography of her ancestor based on archive and field research, family history and fiction, which developed into her second book *The Velvet Sky*.